Your Family Will Love It!

Your Family Will Love It!

Quick and Healthy Weekday Meals for the Hard-to-Please

Rodale Press, Inc.
Emmaus, Pennsylvania

EDITED BY JEAN ROGERS, *PREVENTION* MAGAZINE HEALTH BOOKS

Copyright © 1995 by Rodale Press, Inc.

Illustrations copyright © 1995 by Melanie Marder Parks
Front cover photograph copyright © 1995 by Alan Richardson
Back cover photograph copyright © 1995 by Kurt Wilson/Rodale Stock Images

Front cover recipe: Basil Marinara Chicken with Vermicelli (page 117)
Front cover photographer: Alan Richardson
Back cover photographer: Kurt Wilson
Food stylist: Anne Disrude
Prop stylist: Betty Alfenito

Library of Congress Cataloging-in-Publication Data

Your family will love it! : quick and healthy weekday meals for the hard-to-please/
    from the food editors of Prevention Magazine Health Books.
        p.   cm.
    Includes Index
    ISBN 0–87596–256–4 hardcover
    1. Quick and easy cookery   2. Nutrition   I. Prevention Magazine Health Books
    TX833.5.Y68   1995   94–23899
    641.5'55—dc20

Distributed in the book trade by St. Martin's Press

4 6 8 10 9 7 5 3 hardcover

— OUR MISSION —

We publish books that empower people's lives.

RODALE BOOKS

Your Family Will Love It!
EDITORIAL STAFF

Managing Food Editor: Jean Rogers
Editor: Mary Jo Plutt
Contributing Writer: John D. Forester, Jr.
Book and Cover Designer: Joel Avirom
Design Assistant: Jason Snyder
Illustrator: Melanie Marder Parks
Senior Book Designer: Elizabeth Otwell
Associate Art Director: Faith Hague
Studio Manager: Joe Golden
Recipe Development: Nancy Baggett, Susan Belsinger, Ruth Glick
Nutrition Consultant: Linda Yoakam, M.S., R.D.
Copy Editor: Kathy Diehl
Production Manager: Helen Clogston
Manufacturing Coordinators: Eileen F. Bauder, Patrick T. Smith

Prevention MAGAZINE HEALTH BOOKS

Vice-President and Editorial Director: Debora T. Yost
Art Director: Jane Colby Knutila
Research Manager: Ann Gossy Yermish
Copy Manager: Lisa D. Andruscavage
Senior Vice-President and Editor-in-Chief, Rodale Books: Bill Gottlieb

Contents

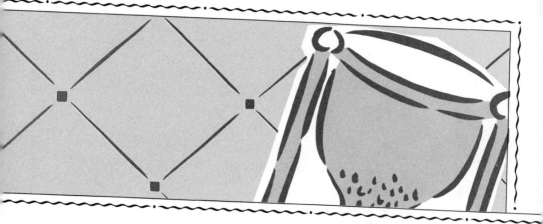

Putting Your Family First

*I*s your dinner table a battlefield—a backdrop for the nightly tug-of-war that pits your concerns about nutrition against your family's insistence on eating only the foods they like, regardless of whether the meals are good for them? If so, it's a situation that's likely complicated by your need to get dinner on the table quickly five nights a week.

Good nutrition *is* a major concern for many homemakers. Like them, you're no doubt aware of the dangers of a diet that's high in fat, cholesterol and sodium. According to the 1994 *Prevention* Index, 52 percent of the adults surveyed are trying to reduce the amount of fat in their diets. In addition, 61 percent make an effort to consume enough fiber, and 50 percent are taking steps to cut back on sodium.

Despite these efforts, many of us still have diets that fall short of recommended guidelines. Our fat intake averages 37 percent of total daily calories— a level higher than the 30 percent most doctors and health agencies advise. Fiber intakes fall short, coming in at about half of what's needed for optimum health. And sodium consumption soars above the suggested 2,400 milligrams.

Compounding the problem of balancing health and eating satisfaction is the fact that both adults and children tend to get less than their fair share of servings from the vegetable, fruit, bread and milk groups. And both are consuming too many fats and sweets.

Although many people do try to modify their diets for the better, they still often fall short of their goals. So you needn't feel guilty that you have trouble getting your family to eat right.

Nor should you think you're the only one facing this dietary challenge. What you should do is take comfort in the fact that it is possible to make seemingly small—but nutritionally significant—changes that will allow both you and your loved ones to win the mealtime war.

In this chapter, we look at some of the biggest eating challenges that most families face and offer solutions for dealing with breakfast-skippers, packing nutritious brown-bag lunches, satisfying finicky eaters and fitting from-scratch cooking into a busy schedule. In the rest of the book, we provide over 300 homey, tasty, healthy recipes that your family *will* love—guaranteed.

Wake Up to Your Nutrition Needs

There's no question that the number-one meal of the day is the first meal of the day. Studies have shown that eating breakfast is associated with a more balanced diet, improved performance in school and at work, consumption of fewer daily calories and lower cholesterol levels. That's more than you'd expect from a meal that so many people are inclined to skip.

A study of ten-year-olds as part of the Bogalusa Heart Study in Louisiana found that 16 percent of the children went without breakfast and that they didn't make up the missed calories and nutrients—including vitamins A and B_6 and calcium—at other meals. Further, the Iowa Breakfast Studies showed that children who ate breakfast had more energy and greater scholastic achievement than breakfast-skippers.

But kids aren't the only ones who need to eat a good breakfast. The morning meal helps rev up your metabolism. People who don't eat breakfast have metabolic rates 4 to 5 percent below normal, according to studies done at George Washington University in Washington, D.C. That might not sound like much, but this metabolic slump could lead you to gain one pound in seven weeks—not what the doctor ordered if you're watching your weight.

Both adult and school-age breakfast-skippers are more likely to have higher blood cholesterol levels than those who eat a morning meal. In one study, the lowest cholesterol levels were among those who regularly ate high-fiber cereal each morning—although eating *anything* was better than holding out until lunch.

It doesn't take much effort to start mornings off with a healthy bang. If you or your family members are not eating breakfast, try to figure out the reason why.

If "no time" is the excuse, set the alarm for 15 minutes earlier. You'll at least have time for a bowl of cold cereal, juice and a piece of fruit.

Also, keep healthy breakfast-type foods on hand so there are plenty of choices. Fresh and dried fruits, reduced-fat and fat-free yogurts, cold cereals,

The Mix-and-Match Lunch Box

Bored with your usual bag lunch? Worse, are your kids tired of their usual lunch fare? Add a bit of excitement to noon meals with these mix-and-match ideas. There's an endless number of variations. And by eating a varied diet, you're more apt to get all the nutrients you need for optimum health.

THE MAIN EVENT

- Lunch meat, chicken salad, tuna salad or other sandwich filling stuffed into pita bread or spread on bagels, tortillas, English muffins, Boston bread, hamburger rolls, rice cakes or party breads
- Waffle sandwiches made with reduced-fat peanut butter mixed with mashed bananas
- Cold baked chicken with the skin removed
- Main-dish pasta salad
- Low-fat cottage cheese mixed with dried or drained canned fruit
- Leftover stew, soup, chowder, chili, macaroni and cheese or spaghetti with sauce
- Baked beans with cubes of low-sodium, low-fat ham
- Turkey ham wrapped around melon balls
- Baked potatoes with low-fat toppings (If desired, reheat the potatoes or cook them from scratch in the microwave.)
- Mini kabobs made with cubes of cooked turkey breast and reduced-fat cheese
- Cooked and peeled shrimp with cocktail sauce
- Whole-grain crackers spread with reduced-fat herb cheese or peanut butter

FRUIT AND VEGETABLE MUNCHIES

- Whole oranges, bananas or peaches, small bunches of grapes or little containers of berries
- Apples stuffed with a mixture of reduced-fat peanut butter and finely chopped dried fruits
- Raisins and other dried fruits
- Mini fruit kabobs
- Applesauce
- Fruit snack packs in light syrup
- Raw or lightly cooked baby carrots, asparagus spears and cauliflower and broccoli florets with fat-free salad dressing for dipping
- Celery sticks stuffed with light cream cheese or reduced-fat peanut butter
- Kosher dill pickles
- Vegetables marinated in reduced-fat Italian salad dressing

PORTABLE SNACKS

- Plain popcorn
- Low-fat potato chips
- Hard or soft pretzels

- Reduced-fat or fat-free yogurt
- Baked tortilla chips
- Low-fat dry cereal
- Fat-free plain or pizza-flavored mozzarella string cheese sticks
- Cinnamon graham snacks
- Apple or banana chips
- Fat-free mini popcorn cakes (caramel, cheese or lightly salted)

BEVERAGES

- Fruit juice
- Skim milk
- Chocolate milk made with low-fat or skim milk
- Instant sugar-free cocoa mix
- Herb tea or flavored iced tea
- Lemonade
- Sodium-free seltzers and sparkling beverages
- Reduced-sodium vegetable juice cocktail or tomato juice

HEALTHY DESSERTS

- Muffins
- Reduced-fat plain and fruit-filled cookies
- Animal crackers
- Fortune cookies
- Ginger snaps
- Reduced-fat cake
- Canned reduced-fat snack pudding
- Low-fat granola bars
- Angel food cake

low-fat breakfast bars, bagels, homemade low-fat muffins or quick breads and frozen pancakes or waffles are all convenient to eat. You can even take many of these foods with you for a grab-and-go breakfast when you're running late.

Of course, nothing says you must eat traditional breakfast fare in the early hours. If leftover pizza, meat loaf, lasagna or roast chicken, for instance, speaks to your appetite more than oatmeal does, go for it. Add a glass of low-fat milk to round out the meal. Other savory ideas include tortillas spread with light cream cheese and sprinkled with chopped fresh vegetables or mini sandwiches of low-fat lunch meats.

For many, not being hungry first thing in the morning is the reason for skipping out on breakfast. If your lack of appetite is from late-night snacking, curtail the evening munchfests. Try to drink a glass of juice before leaving the house and pack a nutritious snack for later in the morning. The muffins and quick breads offered in this book are quite portable and are good cold or reheated in the office microwave.

Finally, don't forget that parents are role models. If you make a healthy breakfast an important part of your day, your kids are more apt to pick up the habit.

The Brown-Bag Rebellion

The secret is out of the bag—bag lunches can be tasty, fun and, yes, nutritious. More people than ever before are eating meals away from home. Although that includes dinners and breakfasts, most of the meals are lunches. Unfortunately, bag lunches have a bad reputation. Kids trade for what they want and throw out the rest. Adults resort to fast-food establishments, vending machines or skipping lunch altogether rather than carrying food from home. You can prevent these occurrences by making bag lunches appealing.

One way is to enlist your kids' participation in their lunch preparation. It's an immutable law that food kids make themselves rarely goes uneaten. Younger children can select food items from an appealing (to them), prescreened (by you) list. They can wash and wipe produce, spread the fillings on bread to make sandwiches and pack items into small containers or plastic bags. They can even help to clean up afterward. Older children can take a more active role in planning their menus, shopping and even preparing simple recipes.

Participating in food decisions will make your children feel important. Encourage them to look through cookbooks for ideas. Remind them that many dinner leftovers are good cold or can be kept hot until noon in a Thermos. On page 4 is a mix-and-match lunch box of ideas to help guide you and your children in making wise food decisions.

Another way to encourage healthy lunch habits is to make lunchtime fun time. Everyone loves special surprises and games. The following easy ideas can put smiles on the faces of your loved ones and make lunch worth looking forward to.

- Tuck in a small note, greeting card, funny riddle or cartoon.
- Add your own fortunes to store-bought fortune cookies.
- Cut sandwiches or cereal bars with large-size cookie cutters.
- Draw a funny face on the shell of a hard-cooked egg using nontoxic markers.
- Use colorful stickers to seal plastic bags closed.
- Celebrate the holidays with decorated napkins and paper plates.
- Turn snacks into presents by closing plastic bags with curly ribbon or adding a bow to a juice box.
- Have children select their own lunch boxes or decorate paper bags with crayons or colored markers.

- Line lunch boxes with colored tissue paper.
- Gift wrap an extra treat for lunch, such as an individual box of raisins.
- Include a small homemade jigsaw puzzle—glue a photo to a piece of cardboard and cut it into puzzle pieces.
- Thread ring-shaped cold cereal pieces onto a piece of shoestring licorice and tie the ends together for a snack bracelet. (Include an extra for a friend.) Licorice is a low-fat candy and, as such, is preferable to a chocolate bar, for instance.
- Package a handful of dry alphabet pasta for a quick, after-lunch scrabble game.

Packing a safe lunch is as important as packing a nutritious one. To guard against food-borne illnesses, follow these three basic rules.

Keep food clean. Special care begins in the kitchen. Always follow safe food handling practices when shopping, storing and preparing lunch items. Use clean paper and plastic bags that are free from grease and food crumbs. Wash out all containers—even lunch boxes—with hot, soapy water before packing them with food.

Keep hot food hot. Ensure that hot items stay quite hot (above 140°, at which point the food is still too hot to touch). Pack the food in a vacuum bottle that you've preheated by filling it with hot water and letting the water stand in the bottle for two minutes.

Keep cold food cold. This includes leftovers and other items that are going to be reheated in a microwave at work. Pack food that is refrigerator-cold in a vacuum bottle that you've chilled—open—in the fridge. Milk, yogurt, pudding that isn't in a shelf-stable container and one-dish meals containing meat or cheese should always go in a Thermos. Insulated bags, ice packs and freezer gel packs can also help keep foods cold. You may even want to freeze items like juice boxes or sandwiches before packing them in a lunch box. The frozen food will keep the rest of the lunch cool and be thawed enough by noon to eat.

Dealing with Finicky Eaters

"I don't want that." Those words have precipitated more mealtime skirmishes than probably any others. How do you handle a kid who will eat only sugar-coated cereal for breakfast, greasy chicken nuggets and fries for lunch and mashed potatoes and dessert for dinner? What do you do with a teenage daughter who's on a fad diet?

First off, don't panic. There are some simple things you can do to head off food fights (that is, fights over food). Start by making mealtime a kid-pleasing experience. Then incorporate some of our tricks for sneaking extra nutrients into the food that they will eat (see the opposite page).

Throughout childhood, a youngster's rate of growth fluctuates, and so does her appetite. Many parents worry that their children don't eat enough, but children will eat as much as they need to when they are hungry. In addition, little children have little stomachs. They simply cannot eat large portions of food at one sitting. Instead of trying to feed them three big meals a day, think in terms of three smaller meals and at least two snacks. Space these mini meals about 1½ to 2 hours apart so your child has time to digest the food before the next round appears.

A big heaping plateful can be overwhelming in the tiny eyes of a child. A kid-size portion on a small plate is much more inviting. As a rule of thumb, one tablespoon of food for each year of the child's life can be considered one serving. If a child is two years old, for example, two tablespoons would equal one serving. (You can always dish up seconds.) Child-scale utensils make eating more manageable. And finger foods are like a magnet to kids. Children also eat more slowly than adults and get easily distracted. So practice patience and try to limit the amount of excitement and activities before and during mealtime.

Serve foods that are attractive in color and shape, easy to eat and innately appealing to children. If cooked carrots meet with resistance, try whole raw carrots—young children often like raw or lightly cooked vegetables rather than fully cooked ones. They also prefer foods that they can easily identify and that are mild in flavor.

Finally, make mealtime a happy time. "Parents should establish expectations and reinforce them throughout the meal," says Corinne Montandon, Dr.P.H., R.D., a nutritionist with the U.S. Department of Agriculture Children's Nutrition Research Center and assistant professor of pediatrics at Baylor College of Medicine in Houston.

So take a deep breath and calm down. Do not beg or order your child to eat at dinner. If a child refuses to eat, simply tell him he is expected to sit at the dinner table with the family because mealtimes are also for socializing. Continue to offer small portions of each food. And don't use foods as a reward or punishment. Kids go through food stages . . . so hang in there.

Healthy Snacks for Hungry Kids

Like it or not, snacks are a prime source of calories in your child's diet. Capitalize on that by having foods on hand that are low in fat and high in carbohydrates, vitamins and minerals. Remember that to appeal to young children, the foods should be convenient, easy to hold and, most of all, fun. Here some sure kid-pleasers.

- Reduced-fat peanut butter on celery sticks, apple slices, bananas or reduced-fat crackers
- Fat-free and reduced-fat crackers, such as saltines, animal crackers and graham crackers
- Ginger snaps or reduced-fat cookies sandwiched together with frozen fat-free yogurt
- Potato nachos (microwaved potato slices topped with salsa and shredded reduced-fat Cheddar cheese)
- Mini bagels with light cream cheese
- Party-size breads with low-fat lunch meats or reduced-fat cheeses
- Raisin bread spread with apple butter
- Toasted oat ring–shaped cereal mixed with dried cherries, cranberries and blueberries
- Bite-size crisp wheat, rice and corn cereal squares
- Dried fruit mixtures using cherries, cranberries, blueberries, apricots, apples and raisins
- Juice boxes
- Frozen juice, ice-milk or pudding bars
- Frozen seedless grapes and strawberries or cubes of watermelon and cantaloupe
- Fresh peach or banana slices served with fat-free vanilla yogurt for dipping
- Frozen fat-free yogurt
- Sugar-free flavored gelatin prepared with fruit
- Reduced-fat mini muffins
- Melon balls

In the meantime, here are some ways to sneak nutrition into the foods your young ones will eat.

- Make soup with milk instead of broth or water.
- Replace one-quarter of the ground beef in casseroles or burgers with cooked brown rice, bulgur or couscous or with cooked, chopped dried beans.
- When preparing vegetables, cook them using a small amount of water. Microwaving and steaming are especially fast ways to cook

vegetables. Quick-cooking in a minimal amount of water preserves more of the vitamins, such as vitamin C and the B vitamins.

- Add shredded vegetables and fruits—carrots, zucchini and apples—to meat loaves, burgers, sandwich fillings and pancake and muffin batters for added fiber. In general, don't remove edible peels from fruits and vegetables.
- Growing bones need plenty of calcium. Get it by serving calcium-fortified orange juice (a cup has as much calcium as an equal amount of milk), calcium-enriched bread and lime-processed tortillas. Crumble or puree tofu made with calcium sulfate into dishes where it won't show, such as chunky spaghetti sauce or meat loaf. Use low-fat cheese sauces on vegetables.
- Add nonfat dry milk powder to sauces, soups and ground meat mixtures.
- Serve pudding and tapioca made with low-fat or skim milk. Make low-fat milk shakes with skim milk, frozen fat-free yogurt and fresh fruit.
- Replace half of the fat in baked products with baby-food prunes or applesauce. (Use 3 to 4 tablespoons prunes or ½ cup applesauce for each ½ cup of fat that's replaced.)
- Thicken cream soups with pureed cooked vegetables, such as potatoes, carrots and squash, instead of heavy cream.
- Replace ½ cup of the flour in cookies, muffins and biscuits with wheat germ for a boost in fiber. Sprinkle wheat germ on top of cold cereal, salads, casseroles and frozen fat-free yogurt.
- Mix ¼ cup sodium-free seltzer with ¾ cup juice for a healthy, homemade cooler.

Too Busy to Cook?

For many, the weekday dinner hour has become the dinner rush hour. We dash home from work, cook, eat, clean up and run out the door to meetings, ball games and a host of other family activities.

Time has become one of today's most valued commodities. There just isn't enough of it to do everything, including cooking nutritious dinners for the family. The key to streamlining mealtime chores is planning. Spend a little time each week preparing menus and a shopping list, and you'll be able to make healthful meals in minutes—without wearing yourself to a frazzle. Below are some ways you can fit healthy cooking into your busy schedule.

- Keep a shopping list posted on the refrigerator. As you run low on pantry, refrigerator and freezer staples, add them to the list so you don't run out.
- Arrange your grocery list according to your supermarket's store plan to eliminate unnecessary backtracking.
- Plan dinners around one-dish meals or combination dishes, such as casseroles, stir-fries, soups, stews and sandwiches. Team the entrée with an easy-to-fix vegetable, salad or bread. Opt for a wholesome fruit dessert.
- Save your written menus and use them again next month.
- Spend 15 minutes in the evening doing prep work for the next day's dinner. You could wash and dry salad greens, chop onions and other vegetables, cut meat into strips or measure dry ingredients, for instance. You could even prepare a portion of a recipe, such as the sauce or marinade.

- Stock up on homemade freezer meals for those evenings when you have only a few minutes to pop something into the microwave. Freeze family-size batches of soup, spaghetti sauce with meatballs and other one-dish meals. Or freeze individual portions for when family members are on different schedules.
- Make your own convenience items: Boil enough potatoes, rice, beans or pasta for a week. Brown a batch of ground meat and freeze it in small portions for future casseroles, soups and sauces. Form ground meat into patties to freeze for quick burgers. Chop onions, peppers and celery and spread them separately on baking sheets lined with plastic wrap; freeze until hard, then break the pieces apart and transfer them to plastic bags.

When shopping, stock up on convenience items that are good for you. They may cost a little more than ones you make from scratch, but they'll save you valuable kitchen time, meet your good-nutrition criteria and please your most finicky family member. Here are a few to start with.

- Frozen, unseasoned single vegetables or medleys in bags
- Tropical fruit salad canned in juice or light syrup
- Three-bean salad in jars
- Frozen strawberries and melon balls in bags
- Six-ounce cans of low-sodium vegetable or tomato juice or fruit juice
- Shredded and sliced reduced-fat and fat-free cheeses
- Reduced-sodium canned broth and reduced-fat soups
- Turkey breast and roast beef from the deli counter
- Skinless, boneless chicken breasts
- Canned, boneless, skinless pink salmon
- Canned water-packed tuna
- Shredded cabbage and carrots in bags
- Broccoli and cauliflower florets in bags
- Fresh salad mixtures in bags
- Reduced-fat spaghetti sauces
- Salad bar produce—chopped onions, sliced carrots and mushrooms, spinach leaves, broccoli and cauliflower florets
- Fajita and stir-fry kits from the meat and produce departments
- Quick-cooking rice and couscous
- Canned beans

Other ways to take the hassle out of mealtimes include:

- Getting added mileage from your meals by cooking once and eating twice. That can go beyond simply reheating leftovers. Cook a double portion of meat or poultry and use the extras in a casserole, main-dish salad, sandwiches, pasta sauce or soup.
- Recruiting family members as helpers. They can set the table, make the salad and microwave the vegetable while you're preparing the entrée.
- Dovetailing your preparation steps. While the water is coming to a boil for the pasta, begin browning the meat for the sauce or slice the bread for the meal.

- Making use of timesaving gadgets. Use a food processor for chopping and shredding, a microwave to speed up one or two steps of a recipe, no-stick cookware to ensure easy cleanup, a Crock-Pot for slow-simmered meals that are ready when you get home or a pressure cooker for making dried beans or other long-cooking foods in a hurry.
- Choosing recipes that use quick-cooking methods, such as microwaving, stir-frying, broiling, grilling or sautéing.
- Using wide saucepans and skillets to speed heating liquids, sautéing vegetables, browning meats and so forth.

Fun-Loving Snacks

Black Bean Salsa

$\mathcal{H}$ere's a tasty way to perk up commercial salsa that gives it added fiber. To keep your snack low in fat, serve this dip with no-oil tortilla chips or with crisp, raw vegetables.

MAKES 2½ CUPS

- 1 can (15 ounces) black beans, rinsed and drained
- ¾ cup reduced-sodium salsa
- 1½ tablespoons finely chopped chives or scallion tops
- 1 teaspoon chili powder
- ½ teaspoon sugar
- ½ teaspoon ground cumin
- ¼ teaspoon dry mustard
- ⅛ teaspoon salt (optional)

In a medium bowl, stir together the beans, salsa and chives or scallions. Mix in the chili powder, sugar, cumin, mustard and salt (if using).

Cover and chill in the refrigerator for at least 30 minutes to blend the flavors.

THINK AHEAD: This dip keeps well, so you can store it for up to 3 days in the refrigerator.

Per 2 tablespoons: 22 calories, 0.4 g. total fat (14% of calories), 0 g. saturated fat, 0 mg. cholesterol, 101 mg. sodium

---

Tortilla Pinwheels

Reduced-fat Cheddar and fat-free cream cheese add to the rich taste of this Southwestern-style snack. When buying tortillas, check the package label for the fat content, since brands vary greatly. The ones we used here have less than 2 grams of fat each.

Makes 32

- 1 medium onion, chopped
- ½ cup fat-free cream cheese, softened
- ½ cup (2 ounces) finely shredded reduced-fat Cheddar cheese
- ¼ cup salsa
- 2 tablespoons chopped scallion tops
- ½ teaspoon chili powder
- 4 flour tortillas (8″ diameter)

Place the onions in a 1-cup glass measure. Cover with a piece of wax paper and microwave on high power for 1 to 1½ minutes, or until the onions are softened.

In a medium bowl, combine the cream cheese and Cheddar until they are well-blended. Stir in the salsa, scallions, chili powder and onions.

Spread the mixture evenly on the tortillas. Roll up each tortilla and cut into 8 slices. Discard the curved ends of each roll.

THINK AHEAD: Pinwheels may be made ahead and kept in the refrigerator for 3 to 4 days.

Per 2 pinwheels: 26 calories, 0.7 g. total fat (25% of calories), 0.4 g. saturated fat, 2 mg. cholesterol, 68 mg. sodium

---

Mexican Cheese Dip
with Tortilla Chips

*Y*ou don't have to give up chips with dip to eat healthfully. We greatly reduced the fat of this favorite snack just by using lower-fat cheese in the dip and serving it with store-bought, no-oil tortilla chips. Look for the chips in the snack section of your supermarket or at a health food store. For a different treat, serve this creamy dip with raw cauliflower or broccoli florets or with cubes of French bread.

MAKES 9 SERVINGS

- 1 tablespoon cornstarch
- 1 teaspoon chili powder
- ¼ teaspoon dry mustard
- ⅛ teaspoon ground black pepper
- 1 cup 1% low-fat milk
- 1¼ cups (5 ounces) finely shredded reduced-fat sharp Cheddar cheese
- ½ cup (2 ounces) shredded fat-free sharp Cheddar cheese
- ½ cup mild or medium picante sauce
- 6 cups no-oil tortilla chips

In a small saucepan, stir together the cornstarch, chili powder, mustard and pepper. Using a wire whisk, stir in the milk until well-combined. Cook and stir over medium heat until the mixture begins to thicken and just comes to a boil.

Slowly stir in the reduced-fat and fat-free cheeses. Continue cooking and stirring just until the reduced-fat cheese has melted. (The fat-free cheese will not completely melt.)

Transfer the mixture to a food processor or blender. Process until completely smooth. Place in a microwave-safe bowl and stir in the picante sauce. If the dip has cooled, microwave it on high power for about 30 seconds.

Serve warm with the chips.

THINK AHEAD: You can make this dip ahead and store it, tightly covered, in the refrigerator for up to 2 days. To heat it, make sure it's in a microwave-safe bowl and cover the bowl with a piece of wax paper. Microwave on high for 1½ to 2 minutes, stirring well after 1 minute, until heated through.

This recipe makes a generous amount of dip, so you can also reheat the leftovers in the microwave. Start with 30 seconds, then stir the mixture well. Continue microwaving in 10-second intervals until the dip is warm.

Per serving: 148 calories, 4.3 g. total fat (25% of calories), 1.9 g. saturated fat, 13 mg. cholesterol, 362 mg. sodium

---

It's So Easy... It's Kid Stuff

TOASTED TORTILLAS

*T*here's an easy alternative to fatty potato and tortilla chips for after-school snacking. Damian Grismer, formerly chef and general manager at Kramer Books and Afterwords Cafe, a unique bookstore containing a restaurant in Washington, D.C., favored this idea.

Just toast some plain flour tortillas in the oven until they're golden brown. They are very cheap, easy to make and low in fat and salt. They're just the thing for a youngster's imagination. And the toasted tortillas keep well, so you can make them ahead for kids to embellish when they get home from school.

One interesting topping combination that adults and adventuresome kids will like is low-fat sour cream, smoked salmon, capers and a sprinkle of chopped scallions or red onions. Kids should have no trouble coming up with their own favorite toppings.

Open-Faced Cinnamon and Fruit Bagels

*A*lthough these make terrific after-school snacks, they're also good as quick breakfast fare. In fact, you can carry them along to work if you put 2 bagel halves together to form a sandwich.

MAKES 8 SERVINGS

- 1 container (8 ounces) soft-style fat-free cream cheese
- ⅛ teaspoon ground cinnamon
- ½ cup raisins
- ½ cup pitted, chopped dates
- 4 plain or raisin bagels, split

In a small bowl, stir together the cream cheese and cinnamon until well-combined. Stir in the raisins and dates.

If desired, heat or toast the bagels. Spread the fruit mixture on the bagel halves.

THINK AHEAD: You can make the fruit mixture ahead and store it, tightly covered, in the refrigerator for up to 4 days. Spread it on bagels just before serving.

Per serving: 190 calories, 0.7 g. total fat (3% of calories), 0.1 g. saturated fat, 3 mg. cholesterol, 394 mg. sodium

---

Peppy Cheese Quesadillas

When you need a quick pickup, here's an easy snack. These quesadillas are also good as a light lunch and are especially popular with kids. If they—or you—don't like spicy foods, leave out the jalapeños and replace them with additional sweet red or green peppers. When tomatoes are in season, thinly slice or dice a ripe one and add it along with the onions and peppers.

MAKES 4 SERVINGS

- 8 corn or flour tortillas (6″ diameter)
- ¾ cup (3 ounces) finely grated or shredded Monterey Jack or Cheddar cheese
- 1 small red onion, thinly sliced
- ½ cup thin sweet red or green pepper strips
- 2 fresh or canned jalapeño peppers, seeded and finely chopped (wear disposable gloves when handling)
- ¼ cup chopped and loosely packed fresh cilantro
  Reduced-fat sour cream, fat-free plain yogurt or salsa

Warm a griddle or medium skillet over medium heat. Add 1 tortilla and heat each side for 15 to 20 seconds. Remove and cover to keep warm.

Place a second tortilla in the pan and heat for 15 to 20 seconds. Turn it over, then sprinkle 3 tablespoons of the cheese on top. Sprinkle with a quarter of the onions, a quarter of the sweet peppers, a quarter of the jalapeño peppers and 1 tablespoon of the cilantro. Top with the prewarmed tortilla.

By this time, the bottom of the quesadilla will be lightly browned. Press down on it with a spatula to help the layers hold together. Carefully turn the quesadilla over. Cook for another 30 to 60 seconds, or until the cheese has melted and the bottom is lightly browned. Serve immediately or keep warm by transferring the quesadilla to a baking sheet and placing it in a warm oven.

Repeat with the remaining ingredients to make 3 more quesadillas.

To serve, use a pizza cutter to cut each quesadilla into 6 wedges. Serve topped with sour cream, yogurt or salsa.

Per serving: 211 calories, 7.7 g. total fat (33% of calories), 4.2 g. saturated fat, 19 mg. cholesterol, 403 mg. sodium

Pepper Pita Rounds

These snacks are so easy to make that older children can prepare them after school. For fancier versions, use roasted pimentos from a jar, water-packed artichoke hearts or reconstituted sun-dried tomatoes in place of or in addition to the other toppings. If you'd like the pita to be crisp and the cheese to turn golden, use a toaster oven. Assemble the rounds and bake at 425° for about 10 minutes.

MAKES 4 SERVINGS

- 4 whole-wheat pita breads (6″ diameter)
- 1 cup reduced-sodium tomato sauce
- 4 mushrooms, thinly sliced
- 8 tablespoons diced sweet red peppers
- 4 tablespoons sliced scallions
- 1 cup (4 ounces) shredded reduced-fat mozzarella cheese

Place 1 pita, curved side up, on a microwave-safe plate. Using a spoon, spread ¼ cup of the tomato sauce over the top. Arrange a quarter of the mushrooms on the sauce. Sprinkle with 2 tablespoons of the peppers, 1 tablespoon of the scallions and ¼ cup of the cheese.

Microwave on high power for 1 minute. Check to see if the cheese has melted and the pita is thoroughly hot. If necessary, microwave for 20 seconds more. Cut into slices and serve hot.

Make 3 more pita rounds using the remaining ingredients.

Per serving: 278 calories, 6.3 g. total fat (20% of calories), 3.1 g. saturated fat, 16 mg. cholesterol, 489 mg. sodium

---

Garden Pita Pockets

*T*his wholesome snack can double as a light lunch. If you like, you can remove the seeds from the cucumber and tomato before chopping them. To seed the cucumber, halve it lengthwise and scoop out the seeds with a spoon. To seed the tomato, cut it in half crosswise and gently squeeze each half to pop out the seeds.

MAKES 8 SERVINGS

- 1 medium cucumber, peeled and chopped
- 1 ripe medium tomato, chopped
- 1 cup shredded spinach or lettuce leaves
- 6 scallions, sliced
- ½ sweet red or green pepper, chopped
- ½ cup (2 ounces) crumbled feta cheese
  Pinch of salt
  Pinch of ground black pepper
- ¼ cup fat-free or reduced-fat plain yogurt
- 2 tablespoons chopped sweet pickles
- 1 tablespoon ketchup
- 1 small clove garlic, minced
- 1–2 teaspoons lemon juice
- 4 pita breads (6″ diameter), halved

In a medium bowl, combine the cucumbers, tomatoes, spinach or lettuce, scallions, peppers, cheese, salt and pepper. Mix well.

In a small bowl, stir together the yogurt, pickles, ketchup, garlic and lemon juice.

If desired, heat the pitas in a toaster or toaster oven. Take about half of the yogurt mixture and spoon some into the pocket of each pita. Then add the vegetables and top with the remaining yogurt mixture. Serve immediately.

THINK AHEAD: Kids can assemble these sandwiches for themselves if you prepare the vegetable mixture and the yogurt sauce ahead. Store them separately.

Per serving: 127 calories, 2.5 g. total fat (17% of calories), 1.2 g. saturated fat, 6 mg. cholesterol, 318 mg. sodium

---

Tex-Mex English Muffins

*T*his recipe gives a Tex-Mex twist to those perennial favorites, English-muffin pizzas. To make bite-size versions for your next party, use mini bagels or small English muffins and sliced cherry tomatoes.

MAKES 2 SERVINGS

1 sourdough or plain English muffin, split

½ cup (2 ounces) finely shredded reduced-fat sharp Cheddar cheese

2–4 teaspoons mild or medium picante sauce

2 large tomato slices

Shredded iceberg lettuce, chopped scallions or minced fresh cilantro (optional)

Lightly toast the muffin halves in a toaster or toaster oven.

Place the muffins, cut side up, on a microwave-safe plate. Sprinkle the cheese on top. Microwave on medium power (50%) for 35 to 45 seconds, or just until the cheese begins to melt. (Alternatively, heat in the toaster oven until the cheese melts.)

Transfer to small serving plates. Spread each half with 1 to 2 teaspoons of the picante sauce and top each with a tomato slice. Garnish with the lettuce, scallions or cilantro (if using). Serve immediately.

Per serving: 143 calories, 4.7 g. total fat (30% of calories), 2.1 g. saturated fat, 15 mg. cholesterol, 555 mg. sodium

---

Spicy Mini Olive Pizzas

*U*sing the microwave lets you create a homemade pizza sauce in minutes.

- 1 small onion, finely chopped
- ½ cup chopped green peppers
- 1 small clove garlic, minced
- 1 can (8 ounces) tomato sauce
- 3 tablespoons sliced black olives
- 1 teaspoon dried basil
- ½ teaspoon dried oregano
- ⅛ teaspoon crushed red-pepper flakes
- 6 English muffins, split
- ¾ cup (3 ounces) reduced-fat mozzarella cheese
- 3 tablespoons grated Parmesan cheese

In a medium microwave-safe bowl, stir together the onions, green peppers and garlic. Cover with a piece of wax paper. Microwave on high power for 1 to 2 minutes, or until the onions are tender. Stir in the tomato sauce, olives, basil, oregano and pepper flakes.

Place the muffin halves, cut side up, on a baking sheet. Broil 2″ from the heat for 1 to 1½ minutes, or until lightly toasted.

Spread a generous tablespoon of the sauce on each muffin half, leaving a small rim around each edge. Then sprinkle each half with 1 tablespoon of the mozzarella and ¾ teaspoon of the Parmesan.

Broil 2″ from the heat for 1½ to 2 minutes, or until the mozzarella is melted and the muffin edges begin to brown. Serve immediately.

THINK AHEAD: This sauce keeps for 3 to 4 days. Store it, tightly covered, in the refrigerator. To make an individual serving, use a toaster oven. Broil 1 or 2 muffin halves, add the toppings and broil until the cheese melts.

Per serving: 210 calories, 4.4 g. total fat (19% of calories), 2.1 g. saturated fat,
2 mg. cholesterol, 725 mg. sodium

Chili-Cheese Popcorn

*T*he trick to making this savory snack is to add the Parmesan seasoning mixture while the popcorn is still hot so that the cheese will slightly melt and stick to the popcorn. Use homemade air-popped corn because it has no added fat. In a pinch, you could use commercial reduced-fat microwave popcorn.

MAKES 14 CUPS

14	cups hot air-popped popcorn
1½–2	tablespoons grated Parmesan cheese
½–1	teaspoon chili powder
¼	teaspoon dried oregano or marjoram

While the popcorn is popping, in a custard cup, stir together the cheese, chili powder and oregano or marjoram.

Transfer the hot popcorn to a large bowl and quickly toss it with the cheese mixture. Serve immediately.

THINK AHEAD: While you're popping corn for this snack, make enough extra plain popcorn to munch on tomorrow night.

Per cup: 29 calories, 0.2 g. total fat (7% of calories), 0.1 g. saturated fat,
0 mg. cholesterol, 13 mg. sodium

≫ Tips from the Family Chef ≪

HERBED POPCORN

*T*o warm up her guests on brisk New England days, innkeeper Barbara Lauterbach keeps mulled cider piping hot on the woodstove in the parlor of her Watch Hill Bed and Breakfast on the shores of Lake Winnipesaukee in Center Harbor, New Hampshire.

"We are also big on dried fruits," she says. "So I like to keep slices of dried apples, pears and other fruits out for the guests to nibble on."

But her favorite treat is popcorn. Not just any popcorn, but herbed popcorn, flavored according to her mood and the contents of her cupboard. "You take all the herbs in your cabinet and go to town," she says.

Barbara sprays her freshly popped plain popcorn with a little no-stick vegetable spray or olive oil so the herbs will stick to it. Then she tosses the popcorn with dried tarragon, oregano, thyme, basil, rosemary or any combination of them.

"You do whatever strikes your fancy," she says. "I put out a big bowl of that and in an hour it's empty."

Once when she was low on herbs, she tried tossing the popcorn with a prepared Cajun spice mix, and the result was a delightful surprise.

"It's tasty, and it's low in fat and high in fiber," Barbara says. It's such a popular snack that she keeps it on hand to quell the gnawing appetites of the students in the cooking classes that she conducts at her inn.

Caramel Popcorn Balls

*T*his is a project for a snowy afternoon. It's a healthier version of caramel popcorn, which is often surprisingly high in fat. Be sure to remove any unpopped kernels from the popcorn before making the balls, because those little nuggets are really hard on the teeth if you bite into them. For variety, you could eat the caramel popcorn without forming it into balls.

MAKES 15

- 10 **cups air-popped popcorn**
- ½ **cup light corn syrup**
- ½ **cup light molasses**
- ½ **teaspoon cider vinegar**
- 2 **teaspoons reduced-calorie tub-style margarine or butter**

Place the popcorn in a very large glass or metal bowl. Set aside.

In a large heavy saucepan, stir together the corn syrup, molasses and vinegar. Attach a candy thermometer to the side of the saucepan, making sure the bulb is not touching the bottom.

Cook over medium heat, stirring occasionally, until the mixture comes to a boil and thickens. Continue cooking, stirring occasionally, until the thermometer registers 252°. Then cook and stir constantly for 12 to 15 minutes or until the thermometer registers 255°.

Remove the saucepan from the heat. Remove the candy thermometer. Stir in the margarine or butter. Be aware that the syrup is very hot; be careful not to get any on your hands.

Carefully pour some of the syrup over the popcorn. Then use a large wooden spoon to stir it in and coat the popcorn. Repeat several more times until all the syrup has been used and the popcorn is well-coated. Set aside until the popcorn is cool enough to handle without burning yourself.

Lightly oil your hands. Gently shape the mixture into 15 (2″) balls. Place the balls on a piece of wax paper and cool completely before eating.

Per ball: 79 calories, 0.4 g. total fat (5% of calories), 0 g. saturated fat,
0 mg. cholesterol, 15 mg. sodium

Caramel Apple Bites

*H*ere's a nutritious, super-easy snack that older children can make after school. Just be sure that they know how to use the microwave safely and can handle a sharp knife.

MAKES 1 SERVING

3 caramels, cut into small pieces
1 tablespoon dark corn syrup
1 teaspoon water
1 large apple, cored and cubed

In a medium microwave-safe bowl, stir together the caramels, corn syrup and water.

Microwave on high power for 30 seconds. Stir, then microwave for 15 seconds, or until the caramels are completely melted.

Stir well and mix in the apples until all the pieces are coated. Eat with a fork.

Per serving: 238 calories, 5.2 g. total fat (19% of calories), 3.1 g. saturated fat, 5 mg. cholesterol, 52 mg. sodium

---

Honey-Cinnamon Baked Apple

*W*hat could be easier as an afternoon snack than an apple that bakes in minutes in a microwave oven? It can also double as a nutritious dessert.

MAKES 1 SERVING

1 large cooking apple (such as Granny Smith, Rome Beauty or Winesap), cored
2–3 teaspoons honey
⅛ teaspoon ground cinnamon
¼ cup frozen fat-free vanilla yogurt (optional)

Place the apple in a 2-cup glass measure or a small, deep, microwave-safe dish.

Drizzle the honey in the center and over the top of the apple. Sprinkle with the cinnamon.

Loosely cover with wax paper. Microwave on high power for 2 to 3 minutes, or until the apple is tender when tested with a fork. Let stand for 5 minutes, or until slightly cool.

To serve, transfer the apple and juices to a serving dish. Top with the frozen yogurt (if using).

Per serving: 125 calories, 0.5 g. total fat (3% of calories), 0 g. saturated fat, 0 mg. cholesterol, 2 mg. sodium

---

Chocolate Frozen Yogurt Pops

*T*his is a healthy, inexpensive version of the frozen yogurt pops you find in the supermarket. For fruit pops, use strawberry or raspberry syrup instead of the chocolate.

Makes 8

- 1 **cup fat-free or reduced-fat plain yogurt**
- 3 **tablespoons light corn syrup**
- 2 **tablespoons chocolate syrup**
- ½ **teaspoon vanilla**
- ⅔ **cup 2% low-fat milk**

In a small bowl, use a fork to stir together the yogurt and corn syrup. Stir in the chocolate syrup and vanilla until well-combined. Add the milk and mix well.

Pour the mixture into 8 (6-ounce) ice-pop molds or paper cups, filling each about three-quarters full. Cover the molds with their lids or the paper cups with foil. Insert the sticks (use wooden ice-pop sticks if using paper cups). Freeze until solid. To serve, remove the pops from the mold according to the directions that came with it or peel the paper from the cups.

Per pop: 60 calories, 0.5 g. total fat (7% of calories), 0.3 g. saturated fat,
2 mg. cholesterol, 40 mg. sodium

MAKE HEALTHY SNACKING EASY

*C*hef Elizabeth Terry believes that children, given their choice, will eat what is good for them. The trick is to offer them a variety of healthy treats and let them create their own snacks.

"I still have children at home, and we do a great deal of snacking," says Elizabeth, whose Savannah restaurant, Elizabeth at Thirty-Seventh, is on the ground floor of the home she shares with her husband and two daughters, Celeste and Alexis, a college student.

So Elizabeth makes certain that there are fresh fruits and vegetables cut up in the refrigerator for her daughters to work with. And she's found that her girls can be very creative.

"One of Celeste's favorite snacks is a layered dip," she says, explaining that the 14-year-old makes layers of chopped scallions, yogurt, salsa, avocado and cheese. "She serves it with green pepper strips, carrot strips and taco chips. And all her friends love it."

Elizabeth says that children actually seem to prefer healthy foods—if parents make those things available. "I don't know of a child who doesn't like fresh strawberries," she says. "And they love grapes. But taste the grapes first to make sure they aren't sour."

She also suggests pineapple spears, cucumbers and carrots cut into various shapes. "I always cut the carrot bottoms into rounds and the tips into strips. The different shapes add variety."

For healthy drinks, she suggests allowing kids to experiment with shakes made with yogurt, honey and fresh fruit.

Easy Twin-Berry Yogurt Shake

When you want something cool and refreshing on hot, sticky summer days, this shake will hit the spot. Best of all, it's good for you!

MAKES 1 SERVING

- ⅔ **cup frozen unsweetened whole strawberries**
- ⅔ **cup frozen fat-free vanilla yogurt**
- ¾–1 **cup cranberry juice cocktail**

Place the strawberries in a blender or food processor. Process until coarsely chopped.

Add the frozen yogurt and ¾ cup of the cranberry juice. Process the mixture for 1 minute, or until smooth. (If the mixture is too stiff to easily blend, add enough of the remaining ¼ cup cranberry juice to slightly thin it.)

To serve, spoon the mixture into a tall glass.

Per serving: 190 calories, 0.3 g. total fat (1% of calories), 0 g. saturated fat,
0 mg. cholesterol, 543 mg. sodium

Chocolate-Chip Granola Bars

Here's a two-for-one snack. The bars taste just like chocolate-chip cookies but have the good nutrition of low-fat granola.

MAKES 15

- ⅓ cup honey
- 2 tablespoons light corn syrup
- 1 tablespoon brown sugar
- 2 cups rolled oats
- 3 tablespoons finely chopped pecans
- ½ cup raisins
- ¼ cup mini chocolate chips

Preheat the oven to 250°. Line the bottom and sides of a 15″ × 10″ jelly-roll pan with foil. Coat the foil with no-stick spray. Set aside.

In a medium microwave-safe bowl, stir together the honey, corn syrup and brown sugar until well-combined. Microwave on high power for 40 to 50 seconds, or until the mixture is almost boiling. Stir in the oats and pecans.

Transfer the mixture to the prepared pan, spreading it out evenly. Bake for 30 minutes. Remove the pan from the oven and stir in the raisins. Let the mixture cool slightly.

Using the back of a spoon and the edges of the foil, press the mixture into an evenly thick 12″ × 6″ rectangle. Then place a piece of wax paper on top and firmly press down on the mixture until it is very compact. Remove the wax paper.

Coat the blade of a large sharp knife with no-stick spray. Using the knife, cut the rectangle lengthwise into thirds, then cut it crosswise into fifths to make 15 bars; try not to cut through the foil.

Sprinkle the chocolate chips on top. Return the pan to the oven and bake for 30 minutes. Turn off the oven. Let the bars dry and cool in the oven for 1 hour.

Gently separate the bars, using the knife to retrace the cuts if necessary. Cool completely.

Per bar: 117 calories, 2.7 g. total fat (20% of calories), 0.2 g. saturated fat,
0 mg. cholesterol, 4 mg. sodium

Banana-Chocolate Shake

*Y*ou're guaranteed to think this is as good as an ice cream–parlor shake. For variety, try other flavors, such as strawberry, chocolate chip or French vanilla.

MAKES 1 SERVING

- 1 small ripe banana
- ½ cup frozen fat-free chocolate or chocolate ripple yogurt
- ¼ teaspoon vanilla
- ⅔–¾ cup skim milk

Slice the banana and place the pieces in a small plastic bag. Close the bag and freeze for at least 1 hour, or until the pieces are frozen.

Transfer the pieces to a food processor. Add the frozen yogurt, vanilla and ⅔ cup of the milk. Process with on/off turns until the mixture is well-blended and the bananas are finely chopped. (If the mixture is too thick to process easily, gradually add enough of the remaining milk to slightly thin it.)

Scrape down the sides of the container. Continue processing until the mixture is completely smooth and creamy. To serve, spoon the mixture into a tall glass.

THINK AHEAD: When you have extra bananas on hand, slice and freeze them so that you can make this shake at a moment's notice.

Per serving: 246 calories, 1.3 g. total fat (4% of calories), 0.4 g. saturated fat,
3 mg. cholesterol, 155 mg. sodium

Classic
Heartwarming Soups

Southwestern Asparagus Cream Soup

*T*he jalapeño chili pepper adds a zesty Southwestern note to this low-fat cream soup. If your family doesn't care for spicy foods, leave the pepper out.

MAKES 4 SERVINGS

- 1 teaspoon nondiet tub-style margarine or butter
- 1 teaspoon olive oil
- 2–3 large cloves garlic, minced
- 1 jalapeño pepper, seeded and finely chopped (wear disposable gloves when handling)
- 1 pound asparagus, trimmed and cut into 1″ pieces
- 2 cups vegetable or defatted chicken broth
- 1 cup 1% low-fat milk
- 2 slices whole-wheat bread, torn into crumbs
- ½ cup water
- ½ teaspoon salt (optional)
- ¼ teaspoon ground black pepper

Melt the margarine or butter in a large saucepan. Add the oil, garlic and jalapeño peppers. Cook, stirring, over medium-low heat for 2 minutes.

Add the asparagus. Cook and stir for 1 minute. Add the broth. Bring to a boil, then reduce the heat. Cover and gently simmer for 5 to 7 minutes, or until the asparagus is tender.

In a small bowl, mix the milk and bread crumbs. Let stand for 5 minutes.

Using a slotted spoon, remove the asparagus from the broth. Separate the tips and set them aside. Transfer the spears to a blender or food processor. Add the milk-bread mixture. Process until smooth. Return the blended mixture to the saucepan. Stir in the water, salt (if using) and black pepper. Cover and cook over medium-high heat for 5 minutes, or until heated through.

To serve, ladle the soup into bowls. Top with the asparagus tips.

Per serving: 115 calories, 4 g. total fat (29% of calories), 1.4 g. saturated fat, 3 mg. cholesterol, 230 mg. sodium

---

Vegetable Harvest Soup

*T*his soup is perfect for using end-of-the-season corn, tomatoes and just-dug potatoes. Canned tomatoes and frozen corn will work just as well.

MAKES 6 SERVINGS

12	ounces potatoes, cubed
1	cup water
1	tablespoon nondiet tub-style margarine or butter
1	tablespoon olive oil
1	medium onion, chopped
1½	stalks celery, chopped
4	cups vegetable or defatted chicken broth
2	cups fresh or frozen whole kernel corn
1	large tomato, chopped
4	cloves garlic, minced
1	teaspoon dried thyme
1	cup 1% low-fat milk
3	dashes angostura bitters (optional)
½	teaspoon salt (optional)
¼	teaspoon ground black pepper

Place the potatoes and water in a 1-quart microwave-safe casserole. Cover and microwave on high power for a total of 6 minutes; stir after 3 minutes. Let stand, covered, until needed.

Melt the margarine or butter in a large saucepan. Add the oil, onions and celery. Cook, stirring, for 4 minutes.

Drain the potatoes and add to the pan. Stir in the broth, corn, tomatoes, garlic and thyme. Bring to a boil. Reduce the heat, cover and simmer for 10 minutes.

If desired, transfer the mixture, in small batches, to a blender or food processor and puree. Return the mixture to the pan.

Stir in the milk, bitters (if using), salt (if using) and pepper. Cook, stirring occasionally, for 5 minutes, or until heated through.

Per serving: 179 calories, 5.6 g. total fat (26% of calories), 1.8 g. saturated fat, 2 mg. cholesterol, 281 mg. sodium

---

Curried Broccoli and Potato Soup

Curry powder gives this vegetable soup an Indian twist. Because curry powders can vary in flavor from one manufacturer to another, you should taste the soup as it cooks and adjust the seasoning to your liking. If you're using a mild curry powder and would like a more spicy soup, add a pinch of ground red pepper. For variety, replace all or part of the broccoli with cauliflower.

MAKES 6 SERVINGS

- 1 tablespoon canola oil
- 1 medium red onion, chopped
- 2–3 potatoes (12 ounces), diced
- 6 cups vegetable or defatted chicken broth
- 1½ pounds broccoli, cut into bite-size pieces
- 3 large cloves garlic, minced
- 2 teaspoons curry powder
- ¼ cup golden raisins, chopped
- ¾ teaspoon salt (optional)
- ¼ teaspoon ground black pepper
- ½ cup fat-free plain yogurt (optional)

Warm the oil in a large saucepan over medium heat. Add the onions. Cook, stirring, for 3 minutes, or until tender. Add the potatoes. Cook, stirring, for 3 minutes more.

Add the broth. Stir until well-combined. Bring to a boil, then reduce the heat. Add the broccoli, cover and gently simmer for 10 minutes.

Stir in the garlic and curry powder. Cover and gently simmer for 5 minutes, or until the vegetables are tender.

Working in batches, transfer half of the mixture to a blender or food processor. Process until pureed; stir into the rest of the soup. Add the raisins. Season with the salt (if using) and pepper.

Cook for 5 minutes, or until the soup is heated through and the flavors are well-blended. Remove from the heat. Stir in the yogurt (if using).

THINK AHEAD: If you won't be serving the whole amount of soup at one time, ladle individual portions into soup bowls and stir a spoonful of yogurt into each. The soup will reheat better and won't curdle if the yogurt is not mixed in.

Per serving: 156 calories, 4.1 g. total fat (20% of calories), 0.3 g. saturated fat, 0 mg. cholesterol, 370 mg. sodium

---

≫ Tips from the Family Chef ≪

STOCKS AND SAUCES

*S*auces are a quick way to flavor low-fat entrées like poached fish or chicken breasts. The trick is to make them without resorting to cream and butter. And you can do that simply by adding some flavorful pureed vegetables, according to Scott Howell, the chef/proprietor at Nana's in Durham, North Carolina.

Pureed roasted garlic is especially flavorful and adds an extra dimension to sauces. "It's great if you want to add a nutty flavor to whatever you're cooking," Scott says. But you can also use other vegetables, such as carrots and onions, which give a more subtle result.

Scott also relies on stocks to add flavor to poached foods. One of his favorites is celery stock, which he uses to poach fish. "It adds a very clean and fresh flavor to the fish," he says. Fennel, which has a strong anise flavor, also makes an interesting stock.

Another stock he relies on is mushroom, made by simmering mushrooms in water for two hours. He strains it and then reduces it down to concentrate the flavor even more.

"One thing I've learned when making vegetable stocks is to keep the lid on the pot for the whole time," Scott says. "It helps hold the flavor in the stock."

Butternut Squash Soup

*I*f you don't have butternut squash or prefer another variety of winter squash, you may substitute acorn, hubbard, delicata or even pumpkin.

MAKES 6 SERVINGS

1	large butternut squash (2–2½ pounds)
1	cup water
1½	tablespoons olive oil
1	cup chopped onions
1	stalk celery, chopped
1–2	tablespoons grated fresh ginger
3	cloves garlic, minced
3	cups vegetable or defatted chicken broth
2	teaspoons curry powder
1	teaspoon sugar
½	teaspoon salt (optional)
¼	teaspoon ground black pepper
1	cup 2% low-fat milk
¼	cup finely chopped fresh cilantro
	Fat-free or reduced-fat plain yogurt (optional)

Cut the squash in half lengthwise. Scoop out and discard the seeds and surrounding strings. Cut each half into 4 pieces.

Place half of the squash pieces, peel side down, in a large, microwave-safe casserole. Add ½ cup of the water. Cover with the casserole lid. Microwave on high power for 5 minutes. Turn the pieces over. Cover and microwave for 5 minutes more, or until the squash is tender when tested with a fork. Transfer the squash and liquid to a bowl; set aside to cool.

Repeat with the remaining squash and water.

When the first batch of squash is cool enough to handle, remove and discard the peel. Cut the squash into ½" pieces. Reserve the cooking liquid.

Warm the oil in a large saucepan over medium heat. Add the onions and celery. Cook, stirring, for 5 minutes. Then add the ginger and garlic; cook, stirring, for 2 minutes.

Add the ½" pieces of squash and the reserved cooking liquid, broth, curry powder, sugar, salt (if using) and pepper. Stir until well-combined. Cover and cook over medium heat for 10 minutes.

Meanwhile, remove and discard the peel from the remaining batch of squash. Working in batches, puree the pieces with the milk in a blender or food processor. Stir into the saucepan.

Cook the soup over medium heat for 5 minutes. Stir in the cilantro. Cover and let stand for 5 minutes.

To serve, ladle the soup into bowls. Top each serving with a spoonful of the yogurt (if using).

THINK AHEAD: If you are using a squash or pumpkin that's bigger than 2½ pounds, microwave the remainder. Peel and cut it into cubes. You can easily reheat it the next night to serve as a side-dish vegetable.

Per serving: 132 calories, 5 g. total fat (30% of calories), 1 g. saturated fat,
3 mg. cholesterol, 201 mg. sodium

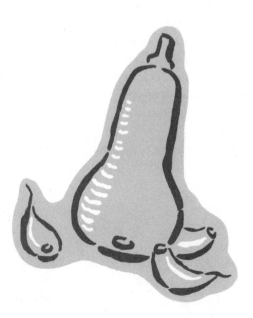

Creamy Porcini Mushroom Soup

*P*orcini mushrooms, also called cèpes, add a rich, hazelnut flavor to this thick, creamy soup. Look for these dried mushrooms in well-stocked supermarkets, specialty produce markets or health food stores. If you can't find them or feel they're too expensive, substitute other dried mushrooms.

MAKES 6 SERVINGS

½ ounce dried porcini mushrooms
1 cup boiling water
1 large potato, peeled and cubed
1 tablespoon nondiet tub-style margarine or butter
1 tablespoon olive oil
1 cup chopped onions
1 pound small fresh mushrooms, sliced
4 cloves garlic, minced
1½ tablespoons all-purpose flour
3 cups skim or 1% low-fat milk
¾ teaspoon salt (optional)
¼ teaspoon ground black pepper
¼ teaspoon dried marjoram
¼ teaspoon dried thyme
    Pinch of ground red pepper
1 bay leaf
¼ cup dry red wine or nonalcoholic red wine (optional)
2 tablespoons grated Parmesan cheese

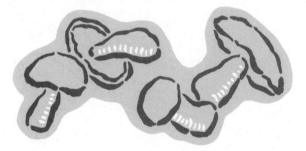

Place the dried mushrooms in a small bowl. Cover them with the boiling water and let stand for at least 20 minutes, until softened.

Place the potatoes in a medium saucepan. Add cold water to cover. Bring to a boil and cook for 15 minutes, or until the potatoes are tender. Drain and mash well.

Drain the mushrooms, reserving the liquid. Coarsely chop the mushrooms and set aside. If the liquid has a lot of sediment in it, pour it into another container, leaving the sediment behind; set aside.

Melt the margarine or butter in a large saucepan over medium heat. Add the oil and onions. Cook, stirring, for 3 minutes, or until the onions are tender. Add the fresh mushrooms and garlic. Gently toss until mixed. Cover and cook for 1 to 2 minutes, or until the mushrooms are tender.

In a small bowl, use a wire whisk to stir together the flour and ½ cup of the milk until smooth. Stir the mixture into the pan. Add the chopped mushrooms, reserved mushroom liquid, potatoes, salt (if using), black pepper, marjoram, thyme, red pepper, bay leaf and the remaining 2½ cups milk. Cook, stirring, over medium heat until the mixture becomes hot and begins to slightly thicken. Remove and discard the bay leaf.

Working in batches, puree the mixture in a blender or food processor. Return the mixture to the saucepan. Stir in the wine (if using) and cheese. Cook over low heat, stirring, for 5 minutes, or until heated. (Do not bring to a boil.)

THINK AHEAD: While you're cooking the potatoes, make extras to serve as mashed potatoes tomorrow. Mash with milk, salt and pepper. If desired, mix in some minced parsley. Place in a microwave-safe bowl, cover and refrigerate. To reheat, cover the bowl with vented plastic wrap and microwave on high power for 2 minutes. Stir. Continue microwaving at 1-minute intervals until heated through.

Per serving: 170 calories, 5.5 g. total fat (28% of calories), 2.1 g. saturated fat, 4 mg. cholesterol, 127 mg. sodium

---

Classic Minestrone

$\mathcal{C}$hock-full of assorted vegetables, beans and pasta, this Italian soup is a meal in a bowl. Round it out with garlic bread and a big tossed salad.

MAKES 6 SERVINGS

1	tablespoon olive oil
1½	cups chopped onions
1½	cups chopped celery
2	medium carrots, halved lengthwise and thinly sliced
1	small green pepper, chopped
7	cups vegetable or defatted chicken broth
1	can (16 ounces) tomatoes (with juice), cut up
1	bay leaf
4	ounces medium ziti or other medium pasta
4	large cloves garlic, minced
1	teaspoon dried basil
½	teaspoon salt (optional)
1	can (19 ounces) cannellini beans, rinsed and drained
¼	cup finely chopped fresh flat-leaf parsley
	Finely shredded fresh Parmesan cheese (optional)

In a large saucepan over medium heat, combine the oil, onions, celery and carrots. Cook, stirring, for 4 minutes. Add the peppers; cook, stirring, for 4 minutes.

Add the broth, tomatoes (with juice) and bay leaf. Stir until combined. Bring to a boil. Reduce the heat, cover and simmer for 5 minutes.

Add the pasta, garlic, basil and salt (if using). Return to a simmer. Simmer, uncovered, for 5 minutes. Add the beans. Simmer for 5 to 10 minutes, or until the pasta is tender but firm.

Remove from the heat. Stir in the parsley. Cover and let stand for 5 minutes. Remove and discard the bay leaf before serving. Ladle into bowls and top each serving with the cheese (if using).

THINK AHEAD: Most soups reheat well and actually improve in flavor if made a day or so ahead. Minestrone is no exception. Be aware, however, that the pasta will tend to absorb some of the liquid as the soup stands. Stir in extra water when reheating the soup to compensate.

Per serving: 192 calories, 3.7 g. total fat (15% of calories), 0.4 g. saturated fat, 0 mg. cholesterol, 490 mg. sodium

---

Potato-Carrot Soup

*T*he carrots add a hint of sweetness to this elegant soup. Serve it hot as an entrée or chilled as an appetizer. We've used whole milk here to give the soup extra body—and it works out to only ¼ cup per person, so you're not getting an excessive amount of fat. But if you prefer, you can cut back to a low-fat type.

Makes 6 servings

- 2 teaspoons nondiet tub-style margarine or butter
- 2 cups chopped onions
- 1 large clove garlic, minced
- 3 cups defatted chicken broth
- 1½ pounds potatoes, peeled and cut into ¾" cubes (about 3½ cups)
- 2 large carrots, chopped
- ½ teaspoon dried basil
- ½ teaspoon dried thyme
- ½ teaspoon salt (optional)
- ¼ teaspoon ground black pepper
- 1½ cups milk
- 1 tablespoon chopped fresh parsley

Melt the margarine or butter in a Dutch oven or large saucepan over medium heat. Add the onions, garlic and 3 tablespoons of the broth. Cook, stirring, for 5 minutes, or until the onions are tender. (If necessary, add more broth during cooking.)

(continued)

Add the potatoes, carrots, basil, thyme, salt (if using), pepper and the remaining broth. Bring to a boil. Reduce the heat, cover and simmer for 15 minutes, or until the potatoes and carrots are tender.

Transfer about half of the mixture to a blender and process until thoroughly pureed and smooth.

Return the mixture to the pan. Stir in the milk. Simmer, stirring occasionally, for 3 minutes. Serve sprinkled with the parsley.

THINK AHEAD: When reheating creamy soups, especially those containing milk, use medium-low heat and stir often to prevent sticking. You can also reheat single servings in a microwave. Use a large enough container so that if the soup boils up, it won't overflow the dish.

Per serving: 189 calories, 4.2 g. total fat (19% of calories), 1.4 g. saturated fat, 8 mg. cholesterol, 230 mg. sodium

---

Slow-Simmered Split-Pea Soup

*W*hen you want a simple, meatless meal, serve this pea soup with crusty bread. This version is flavored with lots of vegetables and seasonings instead of ham. Because it's prepared in a slow-cooker, you can toss everything together before you go to work and come home to ready-made soup.

MAKES 6 SERVINGS

6 cups boiling water or vegetable broth
1 pound dried green or yellow split peas, sorted and rinsed
1 medium onion, diced
1 carrot, diced
1 stalk celery, diced
2 large cloves garlic, minced
1 teaspoon dried thyme
1 teaspoon olive oil
½ teaspoon salt
¼ teaspoon ground black pepper
1 bay leaf
2 dashes hot-pepper sauce
   Dash of Worcestershire sauce

In a 6-quart Crock-Pot or other slow-cooker, combine the water or broth, split peas, onions, carrots, celery, garlic, thyme, oil, salt, pepper, bay leaf, hot-pepper sauce and Worcestershire sauce. Stir until well-mixed.

Cover and cook on high heat for 7 to 8 hours. (If you are home while the soup is cooking, stir it occasionally.) Remove and discard the bay leaf before serving.

Per serving: 280 calories, 1.7 g. total fat (5% of calories), 0.2 g. saturated fat, 0 mg. cholesterol, 200 mg. sodium

---

Italian Bread Soup

*T*he concept of bread soup is very old and has long been a way for Europeans to use up stale bread. We Americanized this tradition by topping each serving with toasted bread cubes. And, for an extra-special treat, we sprinkled the bread with fresh Parmesan cheese. Although the ingredient list is long, the soup really is easy to prepare. You can customize it according to what vegetables you like or have on hand.

MAKES 6 SERVINGS

- 2 cups cubed Italian bread
- 2 teaspoons olive oil
- 1 large onion, chopped
- 1 large stalk celery (with leaves), finely chopped
- 2 cloves garlic, minced
- 4 cups defatted chicken broth
- 1 can (19 ounces) cannellini beans, rinsed and drained
- 1 large carrot, chopped
- 1 cup frozen whole kernel corn
- 1 cup chopped cabbage
- 1 cup chopped zucchini or yellow summer squash
- 1 broccoli stem, peeled and chopped
- ½ green pepper, chopped
- 2 tablespoons chopped fresh parsley
- 2½ teaspoons dried Italian seasoning
- ¼ teaspoon ground black pepper
- 1 can (8 ounces) reduced-sodium tomato sauce
- 5 tablespoons finely shredded fresh Parmesan cheese

Place the bread cubes on a baking sheet in a single layer. Broil 3″ to 4″ from the heat until lightly toasted. Set aside.

Warm the oil in a Dutch oven or very large saucepan over medium heat. Add the onions, celery, garlic and 3 tablespoons of the broth. Cook, stirring, for 5 minutes, or until the onions are tender. (If necessary, add more broth during cooking.)

Add the beans, carrots, corn, cabbage, zucchini or summer squash, broccoli, green peppers, parsley, Italian seasoning, black pepper and remaining broth. Bring to a boil. Reduce the heat, cover and simmer for 30 minutes.

Stir in the tomato sauce and simmer for 10 minutes, or until the vegetables are tender.

To serve, ladle the soup into bowls. Top with the bread cubes and sprinkle with the cheese.

Per serving: 213 calories, 5.1 g. total fat (18% of calories), 1.3 g. saturated fat, 4 mg. cholesterol, 580 mg. sodium

---

≋ Tips from the Family Chef ≋

FLAVOR IN A FLASH

*H*erbs, spices and chili peppers add instant flavor to low-fat dishes, says Steven Raichlen, author of *High-Flavor, Low-Fat Cooking* and *High-Flavor, Low-Fat Vegetarian Cooking*.

"If food is intensely flavorful, you won't miss the fat," says Steven. "I use fresh herbs with gusto. In fact, if I have a choice between using a dried herb and an entirely different fresh one, I'll always go with the fresh herb."

As for spices, Steven recommends that you buy them whole, rather than ground or otherwise processed.

"Whole spices contain more flavor and will keep longer," he says, noting that the volatile oils that give spices their characteristic flavor lose potency over time. To maximize flavor, he recommends toasting your spices for a few minutes in an oven, under a broiler or even in a dry frying pan before using them.

Florentine Soup with Pasta and Mushrooms

Served with Italian bread and a fruit salad, this vegetable soup makes a perfect light supper entrée. It's also good as a first-course soup with crackers.

MAKES 6 SERVINGS

1 tablespoon olive oil
3 cups sliced mushrooms
1 cup chopped onions
1 large clove garlic, chopped
1 package (10 ounces) frozen spinach, thawed
6 cups defatted chicken broth
½ cup water
1⅓ cups spaghettini broken into 1½" pieces
¼ cup chopped fresh basil
¼ teaspoon ground black pepper
3 tablespoons grated Parmesan cheese

Warm the oil in a Dutch oven or large saucepan over medium-high heat. Add the mushrooms, onions and garlic. Cook, stirring, for 8 to 10 minutes, or until the onions are tender and lightly browned.

Meanwhile, drain and squeeze the spinach to remove excess moisture. If using whole-leaf spinach, remove and discard any tough stems and finely chop the spinach.

Add the spinach, broth and water to the pan. Bring to a boil. Add the spaghettini, basil and pepper to the pot. Cook, stirring occasionally, for 3 minutes, or until the spaghettini is tender but firm. Serve sprinkled with the cheese.

THINK AHEAD: Because this soup contains pasta, which absorbs liquid as it stands, leftovers will thicken considerably. When reheating, add extra water to compensate for what the pasta has soaked up.

Per serving: 152 calories, 4 g. total fat (22% of calories), 0.4 g. saturated fat, 0 mg. cholesterol, 378 mg. sodium

Potato and Leek Soup

*a*lthough regular white potatoes work well in this soup, a yellow-fleshed variety such as Yukon Gold gives the soup a buttery look and flavor without adding extra fat. If you'd rather not peel your potatoes, just scrub them well before cutting.

MAKES 6 SERVINGS

4 leeks, halved lengthwise
1 tablespoon nondiet tub-style margarine or butter
4–5 medium potatoes (1½ pounds total), peeled and cut into ½" cubes
3 cloves garlic, minced
4 cups vegetable or defatted chicken broth
1 bay leaf
½ teaspoon dried thyme
½ teaspoon dried marjoram
1 cup 2% low-fat milk
⅛ teaspoon salt (optional)
Pinch of ground black pepper
2 dashes of angostura bitters (optional)

Wash the leeks well under cold running water, removing any dirt. Cut crosswise into ¼" thick slices.

Melt the margarine or butter in a large saucepan. Add the leeks. Cook, stirring, for 3 minutes. Then add the potatoes; cook, stirring, for 3 minutes. Add the garlic and stir for 1 minute.

Stir in the broth and bay leaf. Bring to a boil, then reduce the heat. Gently simmer for 10 minutes. Add the thyme and marjoram. Cover and gently simmer for 10 minutes, or until the potatoes are tender.

Remove and discard the bay leaf. Working in batches, puree half of the mixture in a blender. Return the pureed mixture to the saucepan. Stir in the milk, salt (if using), pepper and bitters (if using). Gently simmer for 5 minutes.

Per serving: 186 calories, 1.9 g. total fat (9% of calories), 0.6 g. saturated fat, 3 mg. cholesterol, 267 mg. sodium

---

Gazpacho

*W*hen fresh tomatoes are at their peak, serve this simple, refreshing soup with French bread and an assortment of reduced-fat cheeses. It's a cooling refresher for lunch or dinner on a hot summer day.

MAKES 6 SERVINGS

- 1 sweet red pepper
- 2–3 large tomatoes, quartered
- 1 sweet white onion (such as Vidalia or Walla Walla), quartered
- 1 cucumber, peeled and coarsely chopped
- 1 large clove garlic, minced
- 1 tablespoon olive oil (optional)
- 8–10 fresh basil leaves, finely chopped
- 1 teaspoon angostura bitters
- ½ teaspoon salt
- 1 tablespoon + 2 teaspoons balsamic vinegar
- Ground black pepper
- Garlic croutons (optional)

Cut the red pepper in half lengthwise and remove the stem, seeds and inner membranes. Place the pieces, cut side down, on a baking sheet lined with foil. Broil 5″ from the heat for 10 to 15 minutes, or until the skin blackens. Remove from the oven, wrap in the foil and set aside until cool enough to handle. Peel off the skin and chop the peppers. Transfer to a food processor.

Add the tomatoes, onions, cucumbers and garlic. Process with on/off turns until almost pureed (the vegetables will be in tiny pieces). Transfer to a bowl.

Stir in the oil (if using), basil, bitters, salt and 1 tablespoon of the vinegar. Cover and refrigerate for at least 30 minutes to blend the flavors.

About 20 minutes before serving, remove the soup from the refrigerator and allow it to stand at room temperature. Taste and add black pepper and as much of the remaining 2 teaspoons vinegar as needed. Ladle into bowls and top with a few croutons (if using).

THINK AHEAD: You can roast red peppers ahead and keep them in the refrigerator for a few days so you can throw this soup together quickly. In a pinch, you can use a large, canned pimento.

Per serving: 31 calories, 0.3 g. total fat (8% of calories), 0.1 g. saturated fat, 0 mg. cholesterol, 184 mg. sodium

≫ Tips from the Family Chef ≪

MOTHER WONDERFUL'S SECRETS

*M*yra Chanin is a Philadelphia writer who's known as Mother Wonderful. Her book, *The Secret Life of Mother Wonderful*, is a collection of humorous essays about her culinary adventures.

"I have learned to lie a lot, especially when I am entertaining," Myra laughs. "For instance, my guests think I make the best hot-and-sour gazpacho. What they don't know is that it comes from a can." She starts with a can of ordinary low-fat gazpacho and jazzes it up with some hot-and-sour soup from the local Chinese market and maybe some bamboo shoots.

Mixing flavors is one of Myra's tricks. "I never pass an ethnic market without going in and buying something. I must have a dozen different flavored vinegars." She uses them to improve the taste of bottled salad dressings or to add some zip to skinless baked chicken.

"I just splash a sweet vinegar on the chicken, sprinkle on some herbs and bake it," she says.

One way she saves time is by making large quantities of dishes, freezing them and then seasoning them to her whim when she reheats them. In addition to changing flavors with spices, Myra often changes textures, letting couscous or barley, for instance, transform a favorite soup or stew into a new dish.

Zesty Cheddar Cheese Soup

Depending on your choice of chili peppers, this vegetable soup can range from mild to quite piquant. If you like really spicy-hot foods, choose chopped canned jalapeño peppers.

MAKES 6 SERVINGS

      2 teaspoons canola oil
      2 medium onions, chopped
      1 medium stalk celery, chopped
      1 small carrot, chopped
    3½ cups defatted reduced-sodium chicken broth
      4 cups peeled and cubed potatoes
    ¾ teaspoon prepared mustard
    ½ teaspoon dried marjoram
    ⅛ teaspoon ground black pepper
    1¼ cups skim milk
    1¼ cups (5 ounces) coarsely shredded reduced-fat sharp
          Cheddar cheese
      1 can (4 ounces) diced green chili peppers, drained

Warm the oil in a large, heavy saucepan over medium-high heat. Add the onions, celery and carrots. Cook, stirring, for 8 to 10 minutes, or until the onions are tender and lightly browned.

Stir in the broth, potatoes, mustard, marjoram and black pepper. Bring to a boil, then reduce the heat. Simmer, stirring frequently, for 10 to 15 minutes, or until the potatoes and carrots are almost tender.

Transfer about 2 cups of the mixture to a blender. Add the milk and cheese. Blend until the vegetables are pureed.

Return the mixture to the saucepan. Stir in the chili peppers. Cook, stirring, over medium heat until heated. Do not boil.

Per serving: 257 calories, 5.5 g. total fat (19% of calories), 1.9 g. saturated fat, 13 mg. cholesterol, 614 mg. sodium

---

Salmon and Vegetable Chowder

This chowder gets rich flavor and creamy texture from pureed vegetables.

MAKES 6 SERVINGS

- 1 large onion, chopped
- 2 tablespoons dry sherry or nonalcoholic wine
- 1 clove garlic, minced
- 3½ cups defatted chicken broth
- 3½ cups peeled and cubed potatoes
- 2 large carrots, sliced
- 1 teaspoon dried thyme
- 1 teaspoon dried dill
- ½ teaspoon dry mustard
- ¼ teaspoon ground black pepper
- ⅛ teaspoon ground celery seeds
- 2½ cups frozen whole kernel yellow corn
- 1 cup whole or 2% low-fat milk
- 12 ounces skinless salmon fillets, cut into ½" cubes
- ½ teaspoon salt (optional)

In a large saucepan, combine the onions, sherry or wine, garlic and 2 tablespoons of the broth. Cook, stirring, over medium heat for 6 to 8 minutes, or until the onions are very tender. (If necessary, add more broth during cooking.)

Add the potatoes, carrots, thyme, dill, mustard, pepper, celery seeds and the remaining broth. Bring to a boil. Reduce the heat, cover and simmer for 10 to 15 minutes, or until the potatoes are almost tender, stirring occasionally.

Stir in the corn and ½ cup of the milk. Cover and simmer for 5 to 10 minutes, or until the potatoes are tender.

Transfer about half of the mixture to a blender. Process on medium speed until pureed. Return the pureed mixture to the saucepan. Stir in the salmon and the remaining ½ cup milk. Gently simmer for 6 to 8 minutes, or until the salmon flakes easily when tested with a fork. Season with the salt (if using).

Per serving: 252 calories, 4.3 g. total fat (14% of calories), 1.3 g. saturated fat, 16 mg. cholesterol, 268 mg. sodium

---

Clam and Corn Chowder

*T*his is a hybrid of two American favorites: corn chowder and New England clam chowder.

   2 cans (10 ounces each) minced clams (with juice)
   1 tablespoon nondiet tub-style margarine or butter
   2 medium onions, finely chopped
   1 stalk celery, chopped
   1 small carrot, chopped
   1 tablespoon all-purpose flour
   1 cup bottled clam juice or defatted chicken broth
   1 tablespoon Worcestershire sauce
1½ teaspoons dried basil
   1 teaspoon dry mustard
   ½ teaspoon dried marjoram
   ¼ teaspoon celery salt
   ¼ teaspoon ground black pepper
2½ cups whole or 2% low-fat milk
   3 cups peeled and cubed potatoes
   2 cups frozen whole kernel corn
   3 tablespoons finely chopped fresh chives or scallion tops

Drain the clams, reserving the juice. Set aside.

In a large, heavy saucepan over medium-high heat, melt the margarine or butter. Add the onions, celery and carrots. Cook, stirring, until the onions are lightly browned. Stir in the flour; cook, stirring, for 1 minute.

Add the reserved clam juice and stir until smooth. Then stir in the bottled clam juice or broth, Worcestershire sauce, basil, mustard, marjoram, celery salt, pepper and 1½ cups of the milk. Stir in the potatoes and corn. Bring to a boil. Reduce the heat, cover and simmer for 20 minutes, or until the potatoes are tender.

Using a slotted spoon, transfer about 3 cups of the vegetables to a blender. Add the remaining 1 cup milk and blend until the vegetables are pureed. Return the puree to the pan.

Stir in the reserved clams and chives or scallions. Bring to a boil over medium-high heat, stirring frequently. Reduce the heat and simmer, stirring occasionally, for 5 to 8 minutes, or until the flavors are well-blended.

Per serving: 319 calories, 6.8 g. total fat (18% of calories), 2.7 g. saturated fat, 72 mg. cholesterol, 302 mg. sodium

---

New England Clam Chowder

*C*lam chowder is typically made with heavy cream and contains bacon for flavor. In this healthier version, we use milk and lean ham to keep the fat content low and still retain the classic flavor of this favorite. This recipe is for those who like whole, freshly cooked clams in their chowder rather than chopped clams.

MAKES 6 SERVINGS

- 2 cups water
- 3 dozen littleneck clams, scrubbed
- 3 medium potatoes, peeled and diced
- 2 medium onions, chopped
- 4 stalks celery, chopped
- 2 large carrots, halved lengthwise and thinly sliced
- ¼ cup minced fully cooked ham
- 1 clove garlic, minced
- 2 teaspoons canola oil
- 2 bottles (8 ounces each) clam juice
- ½ teaspoon dried thyme
- 2 cups 2% low-fat milk
- ½ teaspoon ground red pepper
- ⅓ cup chopped fresh parsley
- 1 scallion, thinly sliced

In a Dutch oven or large saucepan over high heat, bring the water to a boil. Add the clams. Reduce the heat. Cover and simmer for 5 minutes, or until the clams open. Use a slotted spoon to remove the clams; discard any that did not open. Strain the liquid through a fine-mesh strainer. Set the liquid aside.

Remove the clams from their shells and set aside.

Using the same pot, combine the potatoes, onions, celery, carrots, ham, garlic and oil. Cook, stirring, over medium heat for 5 minutes.

Stir in the reserved clam liquid, bottled clam juice and thyme. Bring to a boil, then reduce the heat, cover and gently simmer for 10 minutes, or until the potatoes are tender.

Working in batches, puree the mixture in a blender. Return the pureed mixture to the pan. Stir in the milk. Bring to a simmer. (Do not boil.) Then stir in the pepper and the reserved clams.

Serve sprinkled with the parsley and scallions.

Per serving: 193 calories, 4 g. total fat (19% of calories), 1.3 g. saturated fat, 23 mg. cholesterol, 268 mg. sodium

---

Manhattan-Style Clam Chowder

If a tomato-based clam chowder is more your style, try this easy variation on the all-American classic. Supplement it with a big leafy salad and some crusty bread for an easy low-fat dinner that's on the table in 45 minutes or less.

MAKES 6 SERVINGS

1 tablespoon olive oil
1 large onion, finely chopped
2 large stalks celery (with leaves), chopped
1 small clove garlic, minced
1 bottle (8 ounces) clam juice
2 cans (6½ ounces each) chopped clams (with juice)
2 large potatoes, peeled and diced

> 1 green pepper, chopped
> 2 cans (14½ ounces each) reduced-sodium stewed tomatoes (with juice)
> 1½ cups frozen whole kernel corn
> ¾ teaspoon dried thyme
> ½ teaspoon dried basil
> ½ teaspoon chili powder
> ¼ teaspoon salt (optional)
> ⅛ teaspoon ground black pepper
> 2–3 drops hot-pepper sauce
> 1 bay leaf

Warm the oil in a Dutch oven or large saucepan over medium heat. Add the onions, celery, garlic and 3 tablespoons of the bottled clam juice. Cook, stirring, for 5 minutes, or until the onions are tender. (If necessary, add more juice during cooking.)

Drain the juice from the clams into a small bowl. Set the clams aside and add the juice to the onion mixture. Then stir in the potatoes, green peppers and the remaining bottled clam juice. Bring to a boil. Reduce the heat, cover and simmer, stirring occasionally, for 10 to 12 minutes or until the potatoes are tender.

Add the tomatoes (with juice), corn, thyme, basil, chili powder, salt (if using), black pepper, hot-pepper sauce, bay leaf and the reserved clams. Bring to a boil. Cover and simmer for 5 minutes, or until the flavors are well-blended. Remove and discard the bay leaf.

Per serving: 193 calories, 3.6 g. total fat (15% of calories), 0.5 g. saturated fat, 38 mg. cholesterol, 120 mg. sodium

---

Slow-Simmered Creole Chicken Soup

*H*ere's a spicy chicken soup with Creole antecedents. It can simmer away in a slow-cooker while you're at work so dinner is just about ready when you walk in the door. Be sure to use large chicken breast halves, because smaller ones will cook too quickly.

MAKES 6 SERVINGS

- 6 cups defatted chicken broth
- 1 can (15 ounces) reduced-sodium tomato sauce
- 1½ cups sliced fresh or frozen okra
- 1 large onion, chopped
- 1 large green pepper, chopped
- ¼ cup ketchup
- 1 tablespoon Dijon mustard
- 2 teaspoons sugar
- 2 teaspoons dried thyme
- 2 teaspoons dried basil
- 2 large cloves garlic, minced
- 1 teaspoon lemon juice
- ¼ teaspoon ground black pepper
- 3–4 drops hot-pepper sauce
- 2 pounds bone-in chicken breast halves, skin and visible fat removed
- 1½ cups frozen whole kernel corn
- ½ cup long-grain white rice
- ¼ teaspoon salt (optional)

In a 6-quart Crock-Pot or other slow-cooker, combine the broth, tomato sauce, okra, onions, green peppers, ketchup, mustard, sugar, thyme, basil, garlic, lemon juice, black pepper and hot-pepper sauce. Stir until well-mixed.

Add the chicken, corn and rice. Cover and cook on high heat setting for 1 hour. Stir, then reduce the heat to low. Cook for 7 to 9 hours or until the chicken is very tender.

Remove the chicken from the pot and set aside until cool enough to handle. Remove the meat from the bones and cut into bite-size pieces. Return the chicken to the soup. Cook for 5 minutes, or until heated through. Season with the salt (if using).

THINK AHEAD: Save yourself some time in the morning by chopping and otherwise preparing ingredients the night before. You can, for instance, mix all the ingredients from the first step and place them in a bowl. Cover and refrigerate. You can also make sure the chicken is well-trimmed; place on a plate, cover with plastic wrap and refrigerate. First thing in the morning, you can toss everything into the slow-cooker so it can cook on high for the required 1 hour before you have to leave home.

Per serving: 310 calories, 4.3 g. total fat (12% of calories), 0.8 g. saturated fat, 61 mg. cholesterol, 583 mg. sodium

---

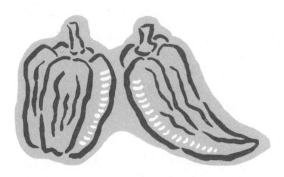

Southern Chicken Gumbo

*T*he name *gumbo* comes from an African word for okra. This stewlike dish has in it not only okra but also plenty of other hearty ingredients, like rice and black-eyed peas. Using frozen black-eyed peas rather than dried peas cuts down on the preparation time for this dish. Using a well-trimmed ham bone or ham hocks gives traditional flavor without all the fat that smoky bacon usually adds to gumbo.

MAKES 6 SERVINGS

4½ cups water

3 cups defatted chicken broth

1 small, well-trimmed smoked ham bone or 2 medium smoked pork hocks (about 1½ pounds total)

2 boneless, skinless chicken breast halves (about 8 ounces)

1 package (10 ounces) frozen black-eyed peas

¾ cup coarsely chopped sweet red or green peppers

⅓ cup chopped fresh parsley

⅓ cup long-grain white rice

5 scallions, sliced

1 large onion, chopped

1 large stalk celery, sliced

2 large cloves garlic, minced

½ teaspoon dried thyme

1 can (16 ounces) stewed tomatoes (with juice)

1 cup sliced fresh or frozen okra

¼ teaspoon ground black pepper

⅛ teaspoon ground red pepper (optional)

Salt (optional)

In a Dutch oven or large saucepan, combine the water, broth, ham bone or pork hocks, chicken, black-eyed peas, red or green peppers, parsley, rice, scallions, onions, celery, garlic and thyme. Bring to a boil over medium-high heat. Reduce the heat, cover and simmer, stirring occasionally, for 20 minutes.

Using tongs, remove the chicken breasts and transfer them to a plate to cool. Let the gumbo simmer for 10 minutes more.

Stir in the tomatoes (with juice), okra, black pepper and red pepper (if using). Cover and simmer, stirring occasionally, for 10 minutes.

Meanwhile, cut the chicken into bite-size pieces. Add the meat to the pan. Remove and discard the ham bone or pork hocks. Skim off and discard any visible fat from the surface of the mixture. Simmer for 5 minutes, or just until the chicken is heated through. Season to taste with the salt (if using).

Per serving: 255 calories, 2.8 g. total fat (10% of calories), 0.6 g. saturated fat, 38 mg. cholesterol, 407 mg. sodium

Black Bean and Rice Soup

*M*ake good use of your pressure cooker to prepare dried beans. Done in this time-saving appliance, black beans take only 9 minutes. Compare that with the minimum 1½ hours they need when cooked conventionally.

MAKES 8 SERVINGS

1 **pound dried black beans, sorted, rinsed and soaked overnight**
6 **cups water**
1½ **cups chopped red onions**
3–4 **cloves garlic, minced**
1 **tablespoon chili powder**
2 **teaspoons olive oil**
1 **teaspoon salt (optional)**
1 **teaspoon ground cumin**
1 **teaspoon dried sage**
1 **bay leaf**
3 **cups cooked long-grain white or brown rice**
1 **tablespoon lemon or lime juice**
  Ground black pepper
  Reduced-fat sour cream (optional)

Drain the beans and place them in a pressure cooker. Add enough cold water to cover the beans by 1". Follow the manufacturer's directions to cover the pot and cook the beans for 9 minutes.

Remove the pressure cooker from the heat. Let stand for 5 minutes. Set the cooker under cold running water for several minutes to reduce pressure rapidly. Loosen and remove the lid following the manufacturer's directions.

Add the water, onions, garlic, chili powder, oil, salt (if using), cumin, sage and bay leaf. Bring to a boil, then reduce the heat. Simmer, uncovered, for 10 minutes. Add the rice. Cover but do not seal the lid. Cook over medium heat, stirring occasionally, for 10 minutes.

Stir in the lemon or lime juice. Season to taste with the pepper. Remove and discard the bay leaf.

Serve topped with spoonfuls of the sour cream (if using).

THINK AHEAD: Give yourself time to soak the dried beans. You can do them overnight if you're planning to cook in the morning, or they can soak all day if you prepare the soup just before dinner. If you're pressed for time, a quicker method is to place the beans in a large saucepan, add cold water to cover generously and bring to a boil. Boil for 2 minutes, then set aside for 1 hour.

Per serving: 179 calories, 1.8 g. total fat (9% of calories), 0.3 g. saturated fat, 0 mg. cholesterol, 9 mg. sodium

---

Quick and Easy Bean and Pasta Soup

*H*ere's an Italian bean soup that's so rich and flavorful, you'd swear it simmered on the stove all afternoon. Yet it cooks for only half an hour because canned beans replace dried ones.

MAKES 6 SERVINGS

2 teaspoons olive oil
1 large onion, chopped
1 large carrot, chopped
1 clove garlic, minced
5 cups defatted reduced-sodium chicken broth
1 can (19 ounces) cannellini beans, rinsed and drained
1 can (15 ounces) no-salt-added red kidney beans, rinsed and drained
1 can (15 ounces) reduced-sodium tomato sauce
1 fully cooked ham steak (8 ounces), trimmed of all visible fat
   and cut into bite-size pieces
½ teaspoon dried basil
½ teaspoon dried oregano
½ teaspoon dried thyme
⅛ teaspoon ground black pepper
2 cups spaghettini broken into 2″ pieces
   Grated Parmesan cheese

Warm the oil in a Dutch oven or large saucepan over medium heat. Add the onions, carrots, garlic and ¼ cup of the broth. Cook, stirring, for 5 minutes, or until the onions are tender.

Add the cannellini beans, kidney beans, tomato sauce, ham, basil, oregano, thyme, pepper and the remaining 4¾ cups broth. Bring to a boil. Reduce the heat, cover and simmer, stirring occasionally, for 20 minutes.

Meanwhile, cook the spaghettini in a large pot of water for 5 minutes, or until tender. Drain, rinse with hot water and drain again.

Add the spaghettini to the soup and heat. Serve sprinkled with the cheese.

(continued)

THINK AHEAD: Leftovers of this soup make a wonderful hearty lunch. Store the soup in a covered container in the refrigerator for up to 4 days. Before reheating, you may want to add a small amount of water to the soup to slightly thin it. (During storage, the pasta will absorb some of the liquid.)

Per serving: 315 calories, 6.4 g. total fat (17% of calories), 1.2 g. saturated fat, 4 mg. cholesterol, 553 mg. sodium

≋ Tips from the Family Chef ≋

A HEARTY BEAN AND MUSHROOM STEW

*Y*ears of training in traditional French cuisine had taken their caloric toll on Jimmy Sneed, co-owner and chef of The Frog and the Redneck restaurant in Richmond, Virginia.

So he went on a major diet. But lowering his calorie and fat intake didn't mean sacrificing flavor. One of his favorite creations is a hearty bean and mushroom stew that fits right into his more healthful eating style.

The dish is low in fat and high in fiber. Best of all, it can be assembled quickly and left to simmer all day in a slow-cooker for an evening dinner. Just add a salad to round out the meal.

"Start with a very flavorful chicken stock. Add beans—I especially like lentils and white beans. Throw in some sliced shiitake mushrooms and crushed garlic. Then let it simmer all day," Jimmy says.

Tomato, Pasta and Lentil Soup

$\mathcal{T}$he pork hock adds a rich smoky, yet salty, flavor to this soup. So, to keep the sodium level down, we use reduced-sodium beef broth. You could cut the level even more by replacing part of the broth with water and by using reduced-sodium tomatoes.

MAKES 4 SERVINGS

- 4 teaspoons olive oil
- 3 large onions, chopped
- 1 large clove garlic, minced
- 4½ cups defatted reduced-sodium beef broth
- 1 small smoked pork hock (about 8 ounces)
- ¼ cup brown lentils, sorted and rinsed
- 1½ teaspoons dried basil
- 1½ teaspoons dried marjoram
- ¼ teaspoon dried thyme
- ¼ teaspoon ground black pepper
  Pinch of crushed red pepper (optional)
- 1 can (32 ounces) plum tomatoes (with juice)
- ½ cup water
- ¼ cup vermicelli broken into 1″ pieces

Warm the oil in a Dutch oven or in a large saucepan over medium-high heat. Add the onions and garlic. Cook, stirring, for 8 to 10 minutes, or until the onions are lightly browned.

Add the broth, pork hock, lentils, basil, marjoram, thyme, black pepper and red pepper (if using). Bring to a boil, stirring occasionally. Reduce the heat. Cover and simmer for 30 to 40 minutes, or until the lentils are tender.

Remove and discard the pork hock. Stir in the tomatoes (with juice), breaking them up with a spoon. Add the water and vermicelli. Bring to a boil. Reduce the heat, cover and simmer for 5 to 8 minutes, or until the vermicelli is just tender.

Per serving: 219 calories, 6 g. total fat (23% of calories), 0.8 g. saturated fat,
0 mg. cholesterol, 683 mg. sodium

30-Minute Beef and Vegetable Soup

*P*ressed for time? A pressure cooker lets you have a traditionally long-cooking soup on the table in short order.

Makes 6 servings

1 pound beef top round, trimmed of all visible fat and cut into ¾" cubes
2 large onions, coarsely chopped
2 large stalks celery, cut into ¼" slices
2 large carrots, cut into ¼" slices
4½ cups defatted beef broth
⅔ cup brown lentils, sorted and rinsed
¾ teaspoon dried thyme
¾ teaspoon dried marjoram
1 large bay leaf
2½ cups frozen whole kernel corn
1 can (16 ounces) stewed tomatoes (with juice)
2½ teaspoons Worcestershire sauce
¼ teaspoon ground black pepper

In a 6-quart pressure cooker, combine the beef, onions, celery, carrots, broth, lentils, thyme, marjoram and bay leaf. Follow the manufacturer's directions to cover the pot and set the gauge on medium. Cook over high heat until the gauge jiggles. Then adjust the heat so the pressure gauge jiggles 3 or 4 times each minute; cook for 12 minutes.

Remove the pressure cooker from the heat. Let stand for 5 minutes. Set the cooker under cold running water for several minutes to reduce pressure rapidly. Loosen and remove the lid following the manufacturer's directions.

Remove and discard the bay leaf. Stir in the corn, tomatoes (with juice), Worcestershire sauce and pepper.

Cook, uncovered, over high heat for 5 minutes, or until the corn is hot.

Per serving: 264 calories, 5 g. total fat (14% of calories), 1.1 g. saturated fat, 48 mg. cholesterol, 495 mg. sodium

---

GOOD FLAVOR EQUALS GOOD HEALTH

*I*f you have a diet that is boring, you are going to die of boredom," says Jeff Smith, whose popular television show, *The Frugal Gourmet*, is also the inspiration for several cookbooks.

Jeff is serious about flavor. "If you have a diet that is bland and unexciting, you are going to stop eating properly." But don't reach for the salt to perk up food, he says, when there are so many healthier flavor enhancers.

Lemon juice is one (make it real lemon juice, Jeff insists). He also believes in increasing the amount of spices and herbs in recipes in order to pep up flavor. Pepper in its various forms is one of his favorites—so much so that he has been known to carry a small bottle of pepper sauce on airplanes to spice up the meals they serve.

Jeff calls herbs and spices the treasures of the kitchen. "Those treasures will help you reduce your desire for fat because they add a richness to food that we have come to associate with fat."

And, he says, nothing robs food of its exciting flavors more than overcooking. He prefers quick stir-fries and simple steaming to keep vegetables exciting.

Beef Minestrone

This one-dish dinner also makes a great portable lunch. Either pack the soup hot in an insulated container or heat it in a microwave at work.

MAKES 6 SERVINGS

- 4 teaspoons olive oil
- 1 pound beef top round, trimmed of all visible fat and cut into ½" cubes
- 1 large onion, chopped
- 1 large stalk celery, sliced
- ⅓ cup coarsely chopped sweet red peppers
- 1 large clove garlic, minced
- 4 cups defatted beef broth
- 1 cup water
- 1 large carrot, thinly sliced
- 1 teaspoon dried basil
- 1 teaspoon dried marjoram
- ¼ teaspoon dried oregano
- ¼ teaspoon dried thyme
- ½ cup elbow macaroni
- 1 medium zucchini, thinly sliced
- 1 can (19 ounces) cannellini beans, rinsed and drained
- 1 can (8 ounces) reduced-sodium tomato sauce
- ¼ teaspoon ground black pepper
- Pinch of crushed red pepper (optional)
- Salt (optional)

Heat 2 teaspoons of the oil in a Dutch oven or large saucepan over medium-high heat. Add half of the beef. Cook, stirring, until browned; remove from the pan and set aside. Repeat with the remaining oil and beef.

Return the reserved beef to the pan. Add the onions, celery, red peppers and garlic. Cook, stirring, for 3 minutes, or until the onions are tender.

Stir in the broth, water, carrots, basil, marjoram, oregano and thyme. Bring to a boil, stirring occasionally. Reduce the heat, cover and simmer for 25 minutes.

Stir in the macaroni. Cover and simmer for 15 minutes. Add the zucchini, beans, tomato sauce, black pepper and crushed red pepper (if using). Bring to a boil. Reduce the heat, cover and simmer for 10 to 15 minutes, or until the zucchini is tender. Season with the salt (if using).

Per serving: 249 calories, 6.2 g. total fat (20% of calories), 0.9 g. saturated fat, 33 mg. cholesterol, 218 mg. sodium

---

Spicy Ground Beef and Vegetable Soup

*H*ere's another slow-cooked soup that can simmer on its own sweet time while you're away or doing other things.

MAKES 6 SERVINGS

- 12 ounces ground beef round
- 2 cups finely chopped onions
- 2 cloves garlic, minced
- 6 cups defatted reduced-sodium chicken broth
- 3 cups finely shredded cabbage
- 2 cups frozen whole kernel corn
- 1 can (8 ounces) tomato sauce
- ¼ cup long-grain white rice
- ¼ cup ketchup
- 1 large carrot, chopped
- 1 tablespoon packed brown sugar
- 1 tablespoon cider vinegar
- 2 teaspoons dried thyme
- ¼ teaspoon ground cinnamon
- ¼ teaspoon ground black pepper
- ⅛ teaspoon ground cloves
- 1 bay leaf

In a large skillet over medium heat, cook the beef, onions and garlic, stirring often, until the meat is browned. Drain the beef mixture in a strainer or colander, then transfer it to a large plate lined with paper towels. Blot the top of the beef mixture with additional paper towels to remove any remaining fat.

Transfer the mixture to a 6-quart Crock-Pot or other slow-cooker. Add the broth, cabbage, corn, tomato sauce, rice, ketchup, carrots, sugar, vinegar, thyme, cinnamon, pepper, cloves and bay leaf. Stir until well-mixed.

Cover and cook on the low heat setting for 7½ to 9 hours, or until the rice is tender.

Remove and discard the bay leaf. Using a large spoon, skim off and discard any fat from the surface of the soup.

Think ahead: After a long, hard day at work, there is nothing more enjoyable than coming home to dinner that's ready and waiting. To make your day even easier, mix together all of the ingredients—except for the rice—the night before and refrigerate them. In the morning, all you need to do is transfer the soup to the slow-cooker, stir in the rice and turn the heat setting on low.

Per serving: 272 calories, 8.4 g. total fat (26% of calories), 2.8 g. saturated fat, 35 mg. cholesterol, 753 mg. sodium

Creamy Vegetable Chowder with Ham

*T*his chowder is so loaded with rich taste that you won't believe it's a reduced-fat recipe.

MAKES 6 SERVINGS

    2 medium onions, chopped
    2 medium stalks celery, diced
    1 tablespoon olive oil
    2 medium carrots, diced

2 tablespoons all-purpose flour

2 cans (14½ ounces each) defatted chicken broth

4 large potatoes, peeled and cubed

1 teaspoon dried marjoram

1 teaspoon dry mustard

¼ teaspoon curry powder

¼ teaspoon ground black pepper

1⅓ cups 2% low-fat milk

1¼ cups trimmed and diced fully cooked smoked ham

1 can (16 ounces) tomatoes (with juice)

⅓ cup thinly sliced scallions

In a Dutch oven or large saucepan, combine the onions, celery and oil. Sauté over medium-high heat for 6 minutes, or until the vegetables begin to brown. Stir in the carrots and flour; stir for 1 minute more. Stir in the broth until well-blended.

Add the potatoes, marjoram, mustard, curry powder and pepper. Bring the mixture to a boil. Reduce the heat. Simmer, stirring occasionally, for 12 to 14 minutes, or until the potatoes and carrots are almost tender.

Using a ladle, transfer 1¼ cups of the vegetables to a blender. Add about half of the milk. Blend until the vegetables are smoothly pureed. Pour into a large bowl. Repeat the process with 1¼ cups more vegetables and the remaining milk. Return all the puree to the pot, along with the ham, tomatoes (with juice) and scallions.

Simmer, stirring occasionally, for 5 to 8 minutes, or until the remaining vegetable pieces are tender.

Per serving: 220 calories, 5.4 g. total fat (20% of calories), 1.3 g. saturated fat, 17 mg. cholesterol, 629 mg. sodium

---

Red Lentil, Ham and Vegetable Soup

*G*ood things come in small packages, as in the case of red lentils. They're inexpensive, high in protein and low in fat. Further, they cook quickly—and don't need presoaking—so you can have this hearty soup on the table in less than 45 minutes. Red lentils are available in some supermarkets and most health food stores.

MAKES 6 SERVINGS

2 teaspoons olive oil

2 large onions, chopped

2 large cloves garlic, minced

7 cups water

4 reduced-sodium chicken bouillon cubes

2 cups chopped cabbage

1 large stalk celery, thinly sliced

1 large carrot, thinly sliced

1 fully cooked reduced-sodium ham steak (8 ounces), trimmed of all visible fat and cut into bite-size pieces

1 cup red lentils, sorted and rinsed

1 teaspoon dried thyme

1 teaspoon dried basil

½ teaspoon chili powder

¼ teaspoon ground black pepper

⅛ teaspoon ground celery seeds

1 large bay leaf

2–3 drops hot-pepper sauce (optional)

1 can (16 ounces) reduced-sodium tomatoes (with juice), cut up

1½ cups frozen whole kernel corn

⅓ cup orzo

Warm the oil in a Dutch oven or large saucepan over medium heat. Add the onions, garlic and 3 tablespoons of the water. Cook, stirring, over medium heat for 5 minutes, or until the onions are tender. (If necessary, add more water during cooking.)

Add the bouillon cubes and break them apart with a large spoon. Add the cabbage, celery, carrots, ham, lentils, thyme, basil, chili powder, black pepper, celery seeds, bay leaf, hot-pepper sauce (if using) and the remaining water.

Bring to a boil, then reduce the heat. Cover and simmer for 20 minutes, or until the lentils are almost tender.

Add the tomatoes (with juice), corn and orzo. Bring to a boil, then reduce the heat. Cover and simmer for 15 minutes, or until the orzo is tender. Remove and discard the bay leaf.

THINK AHEAD: This soup also makes an excellent hot lunch. Store leftovers in a covered container in the refrigerator for up to 3 days. The lentils will soak up liquid as they stand, so add some extra water when reheating the soup to achieve the desired consistency.

Per serving: 292 calories, 4.4 g. total fat (13% of calories), 0.8 g. saturated fat, 9 mg. cholesterol, 863 mg. sodium

---

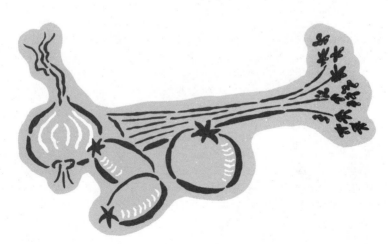

Favorite Salads

Southwestern Slaw

*F*ull of flavor and low in fat, this spicy slaw is a crunchy accompaniment to grilled meats and burgers.

MAKES 8 SERVINGS

¼ cup water
2 tablespoons rice wine vinegar
1 tablespoon balsamic vinegar
1 tablespoon olive oil
2 teaspoons sugar
1 teaspoon salt
1 teaspoon ground cumin
1 clove garlic, minced
¼ teaspoon dried oregano
¼ teaspoon ground black pepper
8 cups coarsely grated cabbage
1 small red onion, thinly sliced
2 carrots, coarsely shredded
1 small sweet red pepper, thinly sliced
1 jalapeño or serrano pepper, thinly sliced
　　(wear disposable gloves when handling)

In a small bowl, whisk together the water, rice wine vinegar, balsamic vinegar, oil, sugar, salt, cumin, garlic, oregano and black pepper.

In a large bowl, combine the cabbage, onions, carrots, red peppers and jalapeño or serrano peppers. Toss until mixed. Add the dressing and toss until well-coated.

Cover and chill in the refrigerator for at least 30 minutes to blend the flavors. Store leftovers, covered, in the refrigerator for up to 3 days; toss before serving.

Per serving: 60 calories, 2 g. total fat (27% of calories), 0.3 g. saturated fat, 0 mg. cholesterol, 290 mg. sodium

---

Creamy Cabbage Slaw with Dill

The dressing used here contains yogurt and cottage cheese, making it rich in calcium and low in fat and calories. It's also delicious over chilled lean beef or seafood served on a bed of greens. This recipe makes a large quantity that's good for a picnic or potluck. For a family dinner, you could halve the recipe—although leftovers keep well and are certainly appropriate for lunch the next day.

MAKES 8 SERVINGS

- ⅔ cup fat-free or reduced-fat plain yogurt
- ⅓ cup reduced-fat cottage cheese
- ¼ cup chopped fresh dill
- ¼ cup fat-free buttermilk
- 2 teaspoons Dijon mustard
- 1 teaspoon sugar
- ½ teaspoon salt
- ½ teaspoon paprika
- 1 clove garlic, minced
- ¼ teaspoon ground black pepper
- 3 dashes angostura bitters
- 1–2 teaspoons fresh lemon juice
- 10 cups shredded cabbage
- 2 cups finely shredded carrots
- 3 tablespoons finely chopped onions

In a blender or small food processor, puree the yogurt, cottage cheese, dill, buttermilk, mustard, sugar, salt, paprika, garlic, pepper, bitters and 1 teaspoon of the lemon juice. Taste; if needed, add the remaining 1 teaspoon lemon juice.

In a large bowl, combine the cabbage, carrots and onions. Add the dressing and toss until well-coated.

Cover and chill in the refrigerator for at least 20 minutes to blend the flavors.

Per serving: 55 calories, 0.5 g. total fat (8% of calories), 0.1 g. saturated fat,
1 mg. cholesterol, 236 mg. sodium

Greek Cabbage Salad

*F*or a quick lunch, serve this international slaw in a pita bread with slices of tomato. For variety, add some leftover roasted chicken.

MAKES 8 SERVINGS

2	tablespoons water
1½	tablespoons lemon juice
1	tablespoon olive oil
¼	teaspoon ground black pepper
¼	cup chopped fresh dill
8	cups shredded cabbage
1	medium Vidalia or other sweet onion, thinly sliced
1	green pepper, cut into thin strips
1	large carrot, coarsely shredded
¼	cup (1 ounce) crumbled feta cheese (optional)
	Kalamata olives, pitted and sliced (optional)

In a small bowl, whisk together the water, lemon juice, oil and black pepper. Stir in the dill.

In a large bowl, combine the cabbage, onions, green peppers, carrots and cheese (if using). Add the dressing and toss until well-coated.

Cover and let stand at room temperature for 15 minutes to blend the flavors. Sprinkle with the olives (if using).

Per serving: 45 calories, 1.9 g. total fat (34% of calories), 0.3 g. saturated fat, 0 mg. cholesterol, 17 mg. sodium

---

Carrot and Squash Slaw

*N*obody says that slaw has to be made with cabbage. This version replaces the cabbage with zucchini and yellow summer squash. It is best when served immediately. But if you would like to make it ahead, prepare the vegetables and dressing and store them separately in the refrigerator. Then just toss them together at the last minute.

MAKES 4 SERVINGS

- 3 tablespoons reduced-fat mayonnaise
- 3 tablespoons fat-free buttermilk
- 1 tablespoon finely chopped scallion tops
- ½ teaspoon sugar
- ¼ teaspoon onion salt
- ¼ teaspoon dried dill
- ⅛ teaspoon dry mustard
- ⅛ teaspoon ground black pepper
- 2 large carrots, shredded
- 1 medium yellow summer squash, shredded
- 1 medium zucchini, shredded

In a medium bowl, whisk together the mayonnaise, buttermilk, scallions, sugar, onion salt, dill, mustard and pepper.

Add the carrots, squash and zucchini. Toss until well-coated.

Per serving: 68 calories, 3.3 g. total fat (41% of calories), 0.4 g. saturated fat, 4 mg. cholesterol, 171 mg. sodium

---

Sweet-and-Sour Eggplant Salad

In Italy, this dish is known as caponata. Traditionally, it is served for the salad course or as an appetizer with toasted Italian bread that has been rubbed with garlic.

MAKES 8 SERVINGS

1 medium eggplant (about 1¼ pounds)
1 tablespoon olive oil
1 red onion, diced
1 green or sweet red pepper, cut into ½" pieces
2 large stalks celery, thinly sliced
1 can (16 ounces) tomatoes (with juice), cut up
4 cloves garlic, minced
2 tablespoons capers, drained
¼ cup water
¼ cup tomato paste
3 tablespoons red wine vinegar
4 teaspoons sugar
¾ teaspoon dried basil
½ teaspoon salt

Use a meat fork to pierce the skin of the eggplant 6 to 8 times. Place on a paper towel on the turntable of a microwave. Microwave on high power for a total of 6 minutes; turn the eggplant over after 4 minutes. Transfer to a plate and set aside to cool.

Warm the oil in a large no-stick skillet over medium heat. Add the onions, peppers and celery. Sauté for 2 minutes. Then cover and cook for 4 minutes.

Add the tomatoes (with juice) and garlic. Cover and cook, stirring occasionally, for 5 minutes. Remove from the heat and stir in the capers.

In a small bowl, whisk together the water, tomato paste, vinegar, sugar, basil and salt. Stir into the onion mixture.

Cut the eggplant in half lengthwise. Scrape out and discard most of the seeds (a grapefruit spoon works well for this). Hold the eggplant by its skin and use a sharp paring knife to scrape the pulp from the skin. Coarsely chop the pulp and add to the onion mixture.

Cover and cook over medium heat for 5 minutes. Reduce heat to medium-low and cook for 5 minutes more. Cool to room temperature before serving.

THINK AHEAD: You can prepare this dish up to 3 days ahead. Store it in the refrigerator. Let it warm to room temperature before serving.

Per serving: 73 calories, 2.2 g. total fat (24% of calories), 0.3 g. saturated fat, 0 mg. cholesterol, 235 mg. sodium

---

CULTIVATE THE GARDEN HABIT

*G*et your kids involved in selecting their own food, says Alice Waters, whose Chez Panisse restaurant in Berkeley, California, is the backdrop of her numerous cookbooks. If she had her way, every youngster would have his or her own garden plot to grow fresh fruits and vegetables to enjoy at the height of their flavor.

Tomatoes, she says, make a good first gardening project for youngsters because they are easily grown—even in pots—and are so versatile, especially for youngsters who want to concoct their own recipes. Kids can easily throw together a salad with tomatoes, a little shredded basil and a vinaigrette made from red wine vinegar, shallots, salt and olive oil.

If you can't garden, at least take the kids along with you to the supermarket or a farmers' market. Let them pick out their prizes and take them home to try out some interesting but simple dishes, Alice says.

"They can put some lettuce and boiled new potatoes on a platter with some chicken breast or fish that you've grilled or pan-sautéed," she says. "Then they can pour vinaigrette on everything." Variations of this little-person's meal can involve green beans, grilled squash or any vegetable that is at the peak of its flavor.

"You can end a meal with a bowl of cherries or some bright, ripe peaches," she says. "You can slice the peaches and make a compote of them by adding some tangerine or orange juice."

Oriental Cucumber Salad

Serve these sweet-and-sour cucumbers as a cooling side dish with spicy Asian meals. Or offer them as an appetizer, as they do in Chinese restaurants.

MAKES 4 SERVINGS

- 2 **large cucumbers, peeled**
- ½ **teaspoon salt**
- ½ **cup rice wine vinegar**
- 2 **tablespoons sugar**
- 1 **tablespoon reduced-sodium soy sauce**
- 1 **small carrot, shredded**

Cut each cucumber lengthwise into 8 pieces; cut each piece crosswise into 2"-long sections. Place the cucumbers flat in a colander. Sprinkle with the salt and toss to mix well. Let stand for 20 minutes.

In a medium bowl, whisk together the vinegar, sugar and soy sauce until the sugar dissolves.

Press down on the cucumbers to remove as much juice as possible. Then rinse well under cold running water to remove the salt. Drain well. Blot dry with paper towels.

Add the cucumbers and carrots to the vinegar mixture. Toss until coated. Cover and chill in the refrigerator for at least 15 minutes to blend the flavors.

Per serving: 57 calories, 0.2 g. total fat (3% of calories), 0 g. saturated fat,
0 mg. cholesterol, 231 mg. sodium

Creamy Cucumber Salad

*T*ypically, this classic salad is made by dressing the cucumbers with full-fat sour cream or heavy cream. We lighten the salad by using reduced-fat sour cream and mixing it with yogurt. If your market carries sour half-and-half, which is a lower-fat substitute for sour cream, you could use that also.

MAKES 4 SERVINGS

- ¼ cup reduced-fat sour cream
- ⅓ cup fat-free or reduced-fat plain yogurt
- 1½ tablespoons tarragon or white wine vinegar
- 1½ teaspoons sugar
- ½ teaspoon salt (optional)
- ⅛ teaspoon ground black pepper
- 3 large cucumbers, thinly sliced
- 1 medium Vidalia or other sweet onion, thinly sliced

In a small bowl, whisk together the sour cream, yogurt, vinegar, sugar, salt (if using) and pepper.

In a medium bowl, combine the cucumbers and onions. Add the dressing and toss to coat well.

Cover and chill in the refrigerator for at least 15 minutes to blend all the flavors.

Per serving: 80 calories, 2.1 g. total fat (21% of calories), 1.1 g. saturated fat, 5 mg. cholesterol, 27 mg. sodium

---

Marinated Italian Salad

*S*erve this colorful, chunky vegetable salad with lasagna or other pasta dishes. If you like, it can be made up to a day ahead.

MAKES 8 SERVINGS

¼	cup defatted chicken broth
2	tablespoons olive oil
2	tablespoons thinly sliced scallion tops
2	teaspoons dried Italian seasoning
2	teaspoons lemon juice
2	teaspoons cider vinegar
¼	teaspoon salt (optional)
⅛	teaspoon ground black pepper
2–3	drops hot-pepper sauce
4	cups small broccoli florets
1	cup water
1	jar (14½ ounces) water-packed artichoke heart quarters, well-drained
6	plum tomatoes, quartered
1	large sweet red pepper, chopped

In a large bowl, whisk together the broth, oil, scallions, Italian seasoning, lemon juice, vinegar, salt (if using), black pepper and hot-pepper sauce.

In a medium saucepan, combine the broccoli and water. Cover and bring to a boil over high heat. Reduce the heat and simmer for 1 to 2 minutes, or just until the broccoli is bright green. Drain in a colander and rinse with cold running water. Drain well and add to the bowl with the dressing.

Add the artichokes, tomatoes and red peppers. Toss to coat the vegetables well. Cover and marinate at room temperature for 20 minutes.

Per serving: 92 calories, 4.1 g. total fat (35% of calories), 0.6 g. saturated fat, 0 mg. cholesterol, 92 mg. sodium

---

Mixed-Vegetable Salad

*T*his tangy, colorful salad features a variety of very healthful vegetables and little fat. It keeps for up to a week in the refrigerator and makes a nice addition to a buffet or picnic.

MAKES 6 SERVINGS

6½	tablespoons red wine vinegar
1	tablespoon canola oil
1	tablespoon sugar
2	teaspoons Worcestershire sauce
1¼	teaspoons Dijon mustard
2	tablespoons finely chopped scallion tops
¼	teaspoon celery seeds
¼	teaspoon celery salt
⅛	teaspoon ground black pepper
2½	cups mixed green and red cabbage chopped into 1¼" pieces
2	carrots, thinly sliced
1	cup sweet red pepper, cut into 1¼" pieces
1	cup small cauliflower florets
1	stalk celery, sliced

In a large bowl, whisk together the vinegar, oil, sugar, Worcestershire sauce, mustard, scallions, celery seeds, celery salt and black pepper.

Add the cabbage, carrots, red peppers, cauliflower and celery. Mix well.

Cover and refrigerate for at least 20 minutes to blend the flavors. Mix again before serving.

Per serving: 68 calories, 2.6 g. total fat (31% of calories), 0.2 g. saturated fat, 0 mg. cholesterol, 143 mg. sodium

---

Ranch Potato Salad

*T*he trick to making this potato salad in a hurry is to cube the potatoes before cooking them. That way, they'll only take half as long to cook.

MAKES 8 SERVINGS

- 8 cups potatoes cut into ¾" cubes (about 2½ pounds)
- 1 medium onion, chopped
- ⅓ cup reduced-fat mayonnaise
- ⅔ cup fat-free buttermilk
- 1½ teaspoons dried basil
- 1½ teaspoons dried marjoram
- ¾ teaspoon salt (optional)
- ½ teaspoon dried oregano
- ¼ teaspoon celery seeds
- ¼ teaspoon dry mustard
- ⅛ teaspoon ground black pepper
- 2–3 drops hot-pepper sauce
- 3 stalks celery, sliced
- 2 tablespoons finely chopped scallion tops

Place the potatoes and onions in a Dutch oven or large saucepan. Add cold water to cover. Cover the pan and bring to a boil over high heat. Reduce the heat and gently boil for 8 to 11 minutes, or until the potatoes are tender but firm. (Do not overcook.) Drain in a colander and rinse with cold running water. Drain well.

Place the mayonnaise in a large bowl. Using a wire whisk, slowly stir in the buttermilk until smooth. Stir in the basil, marjoram, salt (if using), oregano, celery seeds, mustard, black pepper and hot-pepper sauce. Add the celery and scallions. Gently stir in the potatoes and onions.

Cover and refrigerate for 1 to 2 hours or chill in the freezer for 15 to 20 minutes.

THINK AHEAD: This recipe makes a large amount that's great for a picnic or potluck dinner. If you do have leftovers, however, store them in a covered container in the refrigerator for no more than 3 days. Stir in a small amount of milk before serving if the salad appears dry.

Per serving: 164 calories, 2.9 g. total fat (16% of calories), 0.4 g. saturated fat, 3 mg. cholesterol, 53 mg. sodium

≋ *Tips from the Family Chef* ≋

BAKED SALADS

*H*ere's an unusual idea that combines the flavors of a cold salad with the comforting warmth of a hot entrée. Baked salads are an old concept that's due for a comeback, says culinary historian William Woys Weaver, author of *Pennsylvania Dutch Country Cooking*.

"In the old Pennsylvania Dutch cooking, they were called schales, which means 'a shell,' after the shallow pans they were baked in. They were one-course meals made not with wilty vegetables like lettuce but with such hearty ingredients as shredded cabbage, leeks, kohlrabi and root vegetables. They fell out of fashion in the Victorian era because they were considered too rustic," says William.

Today baked salads can be made with any number of ingredients, he says. "I start by brushing a shallow glass plate with garlic-flavored oil and put in some chopped fresh vegetables. I like to use cabbage and beans with fresh herbs. Add a little cooked lean meat if you want to or some cooked grains. I use everything under the sun, from eggplant to snake gourds."

Then cover and pop the dish into a hot oven for 20 to 30 minutes to heat. Or microwave for about 10 minutes for an even faster meal.

Because these one-pot meals tend to be low in fat and high in fiber, they might just be the meal for the 1990s—a hundred years after they fell from favor because they weren't fancy enough, William says.

Microwave Potato Salad with Mustard Dressing

You can serve this side dish warm or cold. Potatoes turn out well when microwaved, so you can have this dish on the table quickly. To save even more time, simply scrub the potatoes instead of peeling them.

MAKES 6 SERVINGS

2 tablespoons olive oil
2 tablespoons lemon juice
1 teaspoon Dijon mustard
½ teaspoon paprika
1¼ pounds red-skin or yellow-flesh potatoes, peeled and cubed
1 cup water
1 sweet red or yellow pepper, thinly sliced
¾ cup thinly sliced scallions
¼ cup chopped fresh dill
½ teaspoon salt
⅛ teaspoon ground black pepper

In a small bowl, whisk together the oil, lemon juice, mustard and paprika.

Place the potatoes and water in a 2-quart microwave-safe casserole. Cover and microwave on high power for a total of 9 to 10 minutes, or until the potatoes are tender but firm; stop and stir after 4 minutes. Let stand, covered, for 5 minutes.

Drain the potatoes, reserving 2 tablespoons of the cooking water. Add the red or yellow peppers, scallions and dill. Gently toss until mixed. Season with the salt and black pepper.

Add the dressing. Toss until well-coated. Cover and let stand at room temperature for 10 minutes to blend the flavors.

Per serving: 140 calories, 4.7 g. total fat (29% of calories), 0.6 g. saturated fat, 0 mg. cholesterol, 196 mg. sodium

---

German Potato Salad

*M*ost German potato salads use quite a bit of bacon to create their characteristic flavor. Surprisingly, we were able to reduce the amount of bacon and still get that same robust taste—with less than 2 grams of fat per serving.

MAKES 8 SERVINGS

- 3 slices bacon
- 1 large onion, chopped
- 2 stalks celery, chopped
- 1 tablespoon all-purpose flour
- ⅔ cup cider vinegar
- ¼ cup water
- 3 tablespoons sugar
- ¾ teaspoon dry mustard
- ¼ teaspoon celery salt
- ¼ teaspoon ground black pepper
- 6 cups boiled and peeled red-skin or yellow-flesh potatoes cut into thick slices

Cook the bacon in a large no-stick skillet until crisp. Transfer to a plate lined with paper towels. Blot well with paper towels to remove all surface fat. Finely crumble the bacon and set aside.

Discard all but 1 tablespoon of the bacon drippings in the skillet. Add the onions and celery. Sauté over medium heat for 3 minutes, or until the onions are tender.

Add the flour and stir until smooth. Stir over heat for 1½ minutes. Stir in the vinegar, then stir in the water until smooth. Add the sugar, mustard, celery salt, pepper and the reserved bacon. Remove the skillet from the heat.

Add the potatoes, then gently toss until well-coated. Serve warm or at room temperature.

Per serving: 196 calories, 1.5 g. fat (7% of calories), 0.5 g. saturated fat, 2 mg. cholesterol, 120 mg. sodium

---

Mediterranean White Bean Salad

*L*ooking for a quick side-dish salad? This marinated bean salad uses canned beans, rather than freshly cooked ones, and has a full-flavored dressing so that you don't need to marinate it for hours.

MAKES 4 SERVINGS

- 4 teaspoons lemon juice
- 1 tablespoon olive oil
- 1 teaspoon Dijon mustard
- ¼ teaspoon dried savory or marjoram
- 1 clove garlic, minced
- ¼ teaspoon ground black pepper
- 1 can (19 ounces) cannellini beans, rinsed and drained
- ½ cup chopped onions
- ½ cup chopped celery
- 1 ripe medium tomato, chopped
- 2 tablespoons finely chopped fresh parsley
- 12 romaine or leaf lettuce leaves
- 1 ripe tomato, cored and cut into 12 wedges

In a small bowl, whisk together the lemon juice, oil, mustard, savory or marjoram, garlic and pepper.

In a medium bowl, combine the beans, onions, celery, chopped tomatoes and parsley. Add the dressing and toss to coat well. Cover and chill in the refrigerator until serving time.

Line 4 salad plates with the lettuce. Spoon the bean mixture on top and garnish with the tomato wedges.

Per serving: 178 calories, 4.2 g. total fat (20% of calories), 0.6 g. saturated fat, 0 mg. cholesterol, 47 mg. sodium

---

Three-Bean Salad

Kidney beans and chick-peas add a new twist to this picnic favorite. If you make the salad ahead of time and chill it, let it come to room temperature before serving.

MAKES 8 SERVINGS

1	pound green beans, cut in half
2	tablespoons olive oil
1	clove garlic, minced
1	can (15 ounces) kidney beans, rinsed and drained
1	can (15 ounces) chick-peas, rinsed and drained
1	small red onion, thinly sliced
4	teaspoons balsamic vinegar
¾	teaspoon dried rosemary, crushed
2–3	dashes angostura bitters
¼	teaspoon salt (optional)
¼	teaspoon ground black pepper

Steam the beans for 5 to 10 minutes, or until crisp-tender. Transfer to a colander and cool under cold running water. Drain well, then transfer to a large bowl. Add the oil and garlic. Toss well. Set aside until cool.

Add the kidney beans, chick-peas and onions. Toss until mixed.

In a small bowl, whisk together the vinegar, rosemary, bitters, salt (if using) and pepper. Pour over the bean mixture and toss until coated. Cover and let stand at room temperature for 30 minutes to blend the flavors.

Per serving: 152 calories, 4.7 g. total fat (27% of calories), 0.6 g. saturated fat, 0 mg. cholesterol, 399 mg. sodium

---

Tabbouleh Salad

*T*his Middle Eastern grain salad has all the characteristics of a great dish for a summertime picnic: It's easy to prepare and tote, and you don't need to worry about keeping it cold or hot because it doesn't contain eggs or other ingredients that spoil easily. Best of all, it's a delicious, low-fat accompaniment to grilled chicken or fish.

MAKES 8 SERVINGS

2	cups bulgur
4	cups water
1	ripe tomato, chopped
1	small cucumber, chopped
1	small Vidalia or sweet onion, chopped
½	sweet red or green pepper, chopped
3	tablespoons lemon juice
1½	tablespoons olive oil
1	clove garlic, minced
½	teaspoon salt
¼	teaspoon ground black pepper
⅓	cup chopped fresh parsley
¼	cup chopped fresh mint

Place the bulgur in a large bowl. Add the water and let stand at room temperature for 40 minutes. Drain and return the bulgur to the bowl.

Add the tomatoes, cucumbers, onions and red or green peppers. Toss to mix well.

In a small bowl, whisk together the lemon juice, oil, garlic, salt and black pepper. Stir in the parsley and mint. Pour over the bulgur mixture. Use a fork to toss until all is coated.

Cover and let stand at room temperature for 30 minutes to blend the flavors.

Per serving: 159 calories, 3.2 g. total fat (17% of calories), 0.4 g. saturated fat,
0 mg. cholesterol, 143 mg. sodium

Mixed Fruit
with Orange-Yogurt Dressing

*W*ith the addition of cardamom, this fruit salad tastes delightfully exotic, even though the fruit selection is nothing out of the ordinary. Cardamom has a subtle, slightly sweet flavor and is commonly used in Indian, Middle Eastern and Scandinavian dishes.

MAKES 4 SERVINGS

½ cup fat-free vanilla yogurt
½ teaspoon lime juice
    Pinch of finely shredded orange peel
⅛ teaspoon ground cardamom
1½ cups pineapple chunks
 1 cup green grapes
⅔ cup orange segments
½ cup cubed apples

In a medium bowl, stir together the yogurt, lime juice, orange peel and cardamom.

Add the pineapple, grapes and oranges. Gently toss until the fruit is well-coated. Cover and chill in the refrigerator for at least 15 minutes. Just before serving, stir in the apples.

Per serving: 117 calories, 0.2 g. total fat (2% of calories), 0 g. saturated fat,
0 mg. cholesterol, 16 mg. sodium

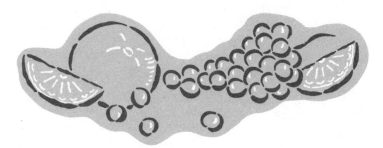

Molded Pineapple and Mandarin Orange Salad

*B*right, refreshing and virtually fat-free, this delicious salad makes a great warm-weather side dish. And because it can be prepared up to 2 days in advance, it's good for entertaining.

MAKES 8 SERVINGS

1¼	cups orange juice
1	envelope + 2 teaspoons unflavored gelatin
6	tablespoons sugar
1½	teaspoons lemon juice
1¼	teaspoons finely shredded orange peel
1	can (20 ounces) crushed pineapple (packed in juice)
1	can (11 ounces) mandarin orange sections (packed in juice), well-drained
2½	cups shredded carrots

Place ½ cup of the orange juice in a 2-cup glass measure. Sprinkle on the gelatin and let stand for 5 minutes to soften.

Microwave on high power for a total of 1 minute, or until the gelatin is dissolved; stop and stir after 30 seconds.

In a large bowl, stir together the sugar, lemon juice and orange peel. Stir in the gelatin mixture. Continue stirring until the sugar dissolves. Then stir in the remaining ¾ cup orange juice.

Add the pineapple (with juice), mandarin oranges and carrots. Mix well. Transfer to a 6- to 8-cup ring mold or other decorative mold. Refrigerate for 1 hour, stirring often. Then refrigerate, without stirring, for 3 to 4 hours, or until set.

To unmold, dip the bottom of the mold for a few seconds in a sink filled with hot water. Run a knife around the edge of the mold, then invert onto a serving plate. Remove the mold. Cut into wedges to serve.

Per serving: 137 calories, 0.2 g. total fat (1% of calories), 0 g. saturated fat, 0 mg. cholesterol, 18 mg. sodium

---

Molded Berry and Fruit Salad

$\mathcal{C}$hock full of raspberries, blueberries and oranges, this make-ahead salad can also double as a dessert for a busy weekday dinner. It stores well in the refrigerator for up to 4 days.

MAKES 8 SERVINGS

1	package (10 ounces) frozen red raspberries (packed in syrup), thawed
3	tablespoons water
1	envelope + 1½ teaspoons unflavored gelatin
⅓	cup red raspberry jelly
1	can (30 ounces) plums (packed in heavy syrup), drained, pitted and chopped
1⅔	cups fresh or thawed frozen blueberries
1	cup orange segments
¼	teaspoon finely shredded lemon peel
1½	teaspoons lemon juice

Drain the syrup from the raspberries into a 2-cup glass measure. Set the berries aside. Stir the water into the syrup. Sprinkle the gelatin over the mixture and let stand for 5 minutes to soften.

Microwave on high power for 1 to 1½ minutes, or until the gelatin is dissolved and the mixture is warm; stop and stir every 30 seconds.

Stir in the jelly. Microwave for 30 seconds. Stir until the jelly is completely melted. Set aside to cool slightly.

In a large bowl combine the raspberries, plums, blueberries, oranges, lemon peel and lemon juice.

Pour the gelatin mixture over the fruit. Gently stir until combined. Transfer to a 6- to 8-cup ring mold or other decorative mold. Refrigerate for 4 hours, or until set.

To unmold, dip the bottom of the mold for a few seconds in a sink filled with hot water. Run a knife around the edge of the mold, then invert the mold onto a serving plate. Remove the mold. Cut into wedges to serve.

Per serving: 200 calories, 0.3 g. total fat (1% of calories), 0 g. saturated fat, 0 mg. cholesterol, 25 mg. sodium

---

Individual Taco Salads

Here we used a mixture of ground beef and turkey breast to reduce the fat while keeping the flavor of beef. Try doing that with your own ground beef recipes—your family won't taste the difference. Just be sure to use pure ground turkey breast. Many brands of ground turkey contain both the dark meat and the fatty skin.

MAKES 4 SERVINGS

½ teaspoon olive oil
8 ounces ground beef round
8 ounces ground turkey breast
1 medium onion, chopped
1 can (15 ounces) kidney beans, rinsed and drained
1 can (8 ounces) tomato sauce
1 tablespoon chili powder
¼ teaspoon ground cumin
¼ teaspoon dried oregano
4 ounces no-oil, unsalted tortilla chips
1 cup (4 ounces) shredded reduced-fat sharp Cheddar cheese
1 cup chopped tomatoes
1 cup shredded iceberg lettuce
Taco sauce or salsa (optional)
Chopped scallions
Chopped fresh cilantro

Warm the oil in a large no-stick skillet over medium heat. Add the beef, turkey and onions. Sauté for 5 minutes, or until the beef and turkey are browned and the onions are tender.

Stir in the beans, tomato sauce, chili powder, cumin and oregano. Bring to a boil, then reduce the heat. Simmer for 5 to 8 minutes, or until the liquid is reduced to a desired consistency and the flavors are well-blended.

Divide the chips among 4 dinner plates. Spoon the meat mixture on top. Top with the cheese, tomatoes and lettuce. Spoon on taco sauce or salsa (if using) and sprinkle with the scallions and cilantro.

THINK AHEAD: The filling keeps well for up to 3 days. Just reheat it before using.

Per serving: 311 calories, 12.9 g. total fat (35% of calories), 3.9 g. saturated fat, 56 mg. cholesterol, 629 mg. sodium

---

≈ Tips from the Family Chef ≈

ROOM-TEMPERATURE DINNERS

*F*or fast, easy-to-make family meals, don't cook at all, says Dorie Greenspan, author of *Waffles from Morning to Midnight*.

"My mother used to say that I was lucky to have a husband who calls salad a meal," Dorie jokes. Actually, her salads are really meals in themselves, all artistically assembled and served at room temperature.

Dorie sometimes serves her family a platter of raw vegetables and cooked chick-peas. She accompanies this with a crusty loaf of bread and some olive oil as a dip. "You can cut the vegetables the night before and store them in a plastic bag in the refrigerator," she says.

With a busy career, Dorie doesn't cook much during the week. Instead, she uses weekends to prepare ingredients for workday meals. "My family likes grain salads," she says. "So over the weekend I'll cook up enough rice for six or eight people, even though there are only three of us. Or I'll cook lentils and store them for a future salad."

To assemble her salads, she might mix some chopped onions, shallots or scallions with zucchini, red peppers and beans. She then mixes in some room-temperature rice or lentils.

Another room-temperature meal is a salad made of tuna, chick-peas, apples and raisins and dressed with olive oil or a mustard vinaigrette. "I just experiment with whatever I have on hand."

Nacho Salad

*N*o need to feel guilty with these nachos—we turned this traditionally fat-laden appetizer into a healthy, no-meat entrée. To keep the fat down, be sure to use baked rather than fried tortilla chips. You can find these in the snack section of well-stocked supermarkets or in health food stores.

MAKES 4 SERVINGS

1 teaspoon olive oil
3 tablespoons finely chopped onions
1 large clove garlic, minced
1 can (15 ounces) pinto beans, rinsed and drained
2 jalapeño peppers, seeded and finely chopped
   (wear disposable gloves when handling)
1 teaspoon ground cumin
4 ounces no-oil tortilla chips
8 cups shredded lettuce
⅓ cup (about 1½ ounces) shredded Monterey Jack
   or Cheddar cheese
1 medium carrot, finely shredded
¼ cup salsa
4 scallions, thinly sliced

Warm the oil in a medium no-stick skillet over medium heat. Add the onions and garlic. Sauté for 3 minutes, or until tender. Add the beans, peppers and cumin. Cook over medium-low heat, stirring occasionally, for 10 minutes or until heated through.

Divide the tortilla chips among 4 dinner plates. Spoon the bean mixture evenly on top of the chips. Top with the lettuce, cheese, carrots, salsa and scallions.

Per serving: 368 calories, 6.7 g. total fat (16% of calories), 0.3 g. saturated fat, 11 mg. cholesterol, 606 mg. sodium

---

Chicken, Bean and Orzo Salad

*T*ry this interesting chicken salad. It's a hearty main-dish medley rich in contrasting flavors, colors and textures. Serve it either warm or chilled.

MAKES 6 SERVINGS

½ cup orzo
1½ cups frozen whole kernel corn
1 pound skinless, boneless chicken breast halves, cut into bite-size pieces
1 teaspoon chili powder
½ teaspoon salt (optional)
¼ teaspoon ground black pepper
1 jar (16 ounces) mild salsa
2 tablespoons olive oil
2 tablespoons honey
1 can (15 ounces) no-salt-added kidney beans, rinsed and drained
1 large sweet red pepper, cubed
1 large tomato, cubed
1 large cucumber, peeled, seeded and sliced
¼ cup thinly sliced scallions

Bring a large pot of water to a boil. Add the orzo. Cook for 7 minutes. Add the corn and cook for 4 minutes, or until the orzo is tender. Drain in a colander and cool under cold running water. Drain well.

Sprinkle the chicken with the chili powder, salt (if using) and black pepper. Coat a large no-stick skillet with no-stick spray and place over medium heat until hot. Add the chicken and sauté, stirring frequently, for 7 to 10 minutes, or until it is cooked through and lightly browned.

In a large bowl, mix the salsa, oil and honey. Add the chicken, beans, red peppers, tomatoes, cucumbers, scallions and the orzo mixture. Toss to mix well.

Per serving: 281 calories, 6.5 g. total fat (20% of calories), 1 g. saturated fat, 33 mg. cholesterol, 586 mg. sodium

Shrimp and Ham Salad

Simple enough for a convenient family supper, yet fancy enough for company fare, this warm-weather meal is perfect for almost any occasion. Cooking the corn and broccoli along with the orzo saves time (and pot washing).

MAKES 4 SERVINGS

1	cup orzo
2	cups frozen whole kernel corn
3	cups small broccoli florets and sliced tender stem pieces
½	cup defatted chicken broth
2	tablespoons olive oil
1	tablespoon cider vinegar
1	tablespoon lemon juice
½	teaspoon Dijon mustard
1½	teaspoons dried marjoram
1	teaspoon dried thyme
¼	teaspoon ground black pepper
2–3	drops hot-pepper sauce
1	large stalk celery, thinly sliced
¼	cup chopped red onions
8	ounces cooked and deveined medium shrimp
4	ounces fully cooked ham, cut into julienne strips
1	large tomato, chopped

Bring a large pot of water to a boil. Add the orzo. Cook for 6 minutes. Add the corn and cook for 4 minutes. Add the broccoli and cook for 1 minute, or until the broccoli turns bright green and the orzo is tender. Drain in a colander and cool under cold running water. Drain well.

In a large bowl, whisk together the broth, oil, vinegar, lemon juice, mustard, marjoram, thyme, black pepper and hot-pepper sauce. Stir in the celery and onions. Add the orzo mixture, shrimp, ham and tomatoes. Cover and refrigerate for 20 minutes to blend the flavors.

Per serving: 357 calories, 8.8 g. total fat (21% of calories), 1.5 g. saturated fat, 82 mg. cholesterol, 455 mg. sodium

---

Summertime Shrimp-and-Pasta Salad

*W*hen you're watching your waistline, here's a complete one-dish meal that'll easily fit your fat and calorie budgets and still satisfy your family's hearty appetites.

MAKES 4 SERVINGS

6	tablespoons reduced-fat mayonnaise
⅓	cup fat-free buttermilk
3	tablespoons ketchup
3	tablespoons finely chopped sweet gherkin pickles
2	tablespoons sweet gherkin pickle juice
2	tablespoons finely chopped scallion tops
2½	teaspoons dried dill
1½	teaspoons Worcestershire sauce
1¼	teaspoons Dijon mustard
4	cups cooked small shells
2½	cups cooked tiny shrimp
1½	cups chopped cauliflower
1	cup chopped celery

In a small bowl, stir together the mayonnaise, buttermilk, ketchup, pickles, pickle juice, scallions, dill, Worcestershire sauce and mustard.

In a large bowl, combine the pasta, shrimp, cauliflower and celery. Add the dressing and toss until the mixture is well-coated. Cover and chill in the refrigerator for at least 30 minutes to blend the flavors.

Per serving: 380 calories, 8.6 g. total fat (20% of calories), 1.2 g. saturated fat, 146 mg. cholesterol, 9 mg. sodium

Italian Turkey and Tortelloni Salad

*T*ortelloni are larger versions of tortellini. Look for the reduced-fat cheese-and-tomato variety used in this salad in the refrigerated section of your supermarket.

MAKES 4 SERVINGS

1 package (9 ounces) reduced-fat cheese-and-tomato tortelloni
1½ cups small cauliflower florets
½ cup water
1 can (15 ounces) kidney beans, rinsed and drained
1 jar (14½ ounces) water-packed artichoke heart quarters, well-drained
1 large tomato, seeded and cubed
½ medium sweet red pepper, chopped
6 ounces fully cooked smoked turkey breast or turkey ham slices, cut into thin strips
¼ cup thinly sliced scallion tops
⅓ cup defatted chicken broth
¼ cup ketchup
1½ tablespoons olive oil
2 teaspoons dried Italian seasoning
2 teaspoons balsamic vinegar
¼ teaspoon dry mustard
⅛ teaspoon ground black pepper
2–3 drops hot-pepper sauce

Cook the tortelloni according to the package directions, but without adding salt. Drain in a colander, rinse with cold water and drain again. Place in a large bowl.

In a small saucepan, combine the cauliflower and water. Cover and bring to a boil. Reduce the heat and simmer for 2 minutes. Then drain in a colander and cool under cold running water. Drain well and add to the bowl with the tortelloni.

Add the beans, artichokes, tomatoes, red peppers, turkey and scallions. Toss to mix well.

In a small bowl, whisk together the broth, ketchup, oil, Italian seasoning, vinegar, mustard, black pepper and hot-pepper sauce. Pour over the salad and toss to mix well. Cover and refrigerate for 20 minutes to blend the flavors.

Per serving: 466 calories, 8.4 g. total fat (16% of calories), 1.8 g. saturated fat, 25 mg. cholesterol, 1,104 mg. sodium

---

Waldorf Salad

*W*e reduced the fat—but not the flavor—of this old-time favorite. Serve the salad as a side dish to a poultry or fish entrée or as a healthy dessert.

MAKES 8 SERVINGS

- ½ **cup fat-free or reduced-fat plain yogurt**
- 1 **tablespoon mayonnaise**
- 1 **tablespoon lemon juice**
- 1 **teaspoon sugar**
- ⅛ **teaspoon salt (optional)**
- 3 **large apples, chopped**
- 4 **large stalks celery, cut into ½" pieces**
- ¼ **cup currants**
- ¼ **cup toasted and chopped walnuts**

In a small bowl, stir together the yogurt, mayonnaise, lemon juice, sugar and salt (if using).

In a medium bowl, mix the apples, celery, currants and walnuts. Add the dressing and toss until well-coated. Cover and let stand at room temperature for 15 minutes to blend the flavors.

Per serving: 79 calories, 4 g. total fat (41% of calories), 0.4 g. saturated fat, 1 mg. cholesterol, 37 mg. sodium

---

Fresh Salmon and Fusilli Salad

*D*ill and cucumber team up with salmon for a delicious main-dish salad. For variety, substitute shrimp or chicken breasts for the salmon.

MAKES 4 SERVINGS

3	tablespoons defatted chicken broth
2	tablespoons olive oil
¼	teaspoon ground black pepper
2–3	drops hot-pepper sauce
3	teaspoons lemon juice
¼	cup thinly sliced scallions
3	teaspoons finely chopped fresh dill
1½	cups fusilli
12	ounces salmon steaks, cut ½" thick
1	large green pepper, chopped
1	large tomato, cubed
1	large cucumber, peeled, seeded and sliced

In a large bowl, whisk together the broth, oil, black pepper, hot-pepper sauce and 2 teaspoons of the lemon juice. Stir in the scallions and 2 teaspoons of the dill.

Cook the fusilli in a large pot of boiling water for 8 minutes, or until just tender. Drain, rinse with cold water and drain again. Add to the bowl with the dressing and mix well.

While the fusilli is cooking, coat the rack of a broiling pan with no-stick spray. Place the salmon on the rack. Brush with the remaining 1 teaspoon lemon juice and sprinkle with the remaining 1 teaspoon dill. Broil 4" from the heat for 4 to 8 minutes, or until the salmon flakes easily when tested with a fork. Let cool for a few minutes. Remove and discard the skin and bones. Then break the salmon into bite-size pieces. Add to the bowl.

Add the green peppers, tomatoes and cucumbers. Gently toss until well-mixed.

Per serving: 308 calories, 10.5 g. total fat (31% of calories), 1.6 g. saturated fat, 15 mg. cholesterol, 90 mg. sodium

Herbed Turkey-Pasta Salad

*H*ere's an ideal way to use leftover turkey or chicken.

MAKES 4 SERVINGS

½   cup defatted chicken broth
¼   cup olive oil
¼   cup lemon juice
¼   cup finely chopped fresh dill
¼   cup chopped scallion tops
1½ tablespoons Dijon mustard
1¼ teaspoons dried tarragon
½   teaspoon salt (optional)
¼   teaspoon ground black pepper
3   cups cooked ziti
3   cups cubed cooked turkey breast
1   cup chopped sweet red or yellow peppers
1   cup chopped celery

In a small bowl, whisk together the broth, oil, lemon juice, dill, scallions, mustard, tarragon, salt (if using) and black pepper.

In a large bowl, combine the ziti, turkey, red or yellow peppers and celery. Toss until mixed. Add the dressing and toss until mixed well. Cover and chill in the refrigerator for at least 30 minutes to blend the flavors.

Per serving: 305 calories, 3.3 g. total fat (10% of calories), 0.6 g. saturated fat, 71 mg. cholesterol, 278 mg. sodium

---

Poultry's a Big Hit

Easy Chicken and Stuffing

*Y*ou don't have to roast a whole chicken to enjoy chicken and stuffing. This version is not only convenient but also lower in fat than standard recipes.

MAKES 6 SERVINGS

Stuffing
- 1 tablespoon nondiet tub-style margarine or butter
- 1 large onion, chopped
- 2 large stalks celery, chopped
- 1 large carrot, chopped
- ¼ cup chopped fresh parsley
- 1 clove garlic, minced
- ¾ cup defatted chicken broth
- ½ teaspoon dried thyme
- ⅛ teaspoon ground black pepper
- 2½ cups herb-seasoned stuffing mix

Chicken
- 6 skinless, boneless chicken breast halves (4 ounces each)
- 1 teaspoon nondiet tub-style margarine or butter, melted
- ¼ teaspoon salt (optional)
- ¼ teaspoon dried basil
- ¼ teaspoon dried thyme
- ⅛ teaspoon ground black pepper

To make the stuffing: Melt the margarine or butter in a large no-stick skillet over medium heat. Add the onions, celery, carrots, parsley, garlic and ¼ cup of the broth. Cook, stirring, for 5 minutes, or until the onions are tender. Stir in the thyme and pepper. Remove from the heat.

Stir in the stuffing mix and the remaining ½ cup broth. Transfer to a 13″ × 9″ baking pan.

To make the chicken: Lay the chicken on top of the stuffing. Brush with the margarine or butter and sprinkle with the salt (if using), basil, thyme and pepper. Bake at 350° for 25 to 30 minutes, or until the chicken is tender and no longer pink when cut with a sharp knife.

Per serving: 184 calories, 5.2 g. total fat (26% of calories), 2.4 g. saturated fat, 53 mg. cholesterol, 347 mg. sodium

≫ Tips from the Family Chef ≪

BIG FAT DIFFERENCES

It is a myth that fat *carries* flavor, according to Lynn Fischer, author and host of the very successful television show, *The Low Cholesterol Gourmet*. "Fat has its own flavor, but if you use lots of other good food, you won't miss it."

"Whenever you would normally use oil, you can use water or another liquid instead," Lynn suggests. "You eliminate extra fat and calories and end up with a fresher taste."

She suggests using a little water to start the cooking process when making such things as spaghetti sauce, chili, soups and, of course, all vegetables.

Lynn has other easy ways to cut out a lot of fat. "You can still enjoy fried chicken, for instance," she says. "You just remove the skin, season the meat with salt and pepper, flour it and cook it in a nonstick pan with a little vegetable oil spray." The chicken will brown as usual and be almost indistinguishable from its fat-fried counterpart. In fact, she says, it will have a better flavor and a nice crust.

When shopping for ground turkey, she suggests, select a piece of boneless turkey breast. Ask the butcher to remove the skin and any visible fat and then grind the meat fresh. You'll avoid the skin and fat sometimes found in preground turkey. And because the turkey hasn't been stored without the skin on it—which dries it out—it will have a better flavor.

Chicken and Rice Skillet Dinner

*H*ere's a complete meal—chicken, rice and vegetables—in one easy, homestyle skillet dish. If you like, serve a tossed salad on the side and frozen yogurt for dessert.

MAKES 6 SERVINGS

- 6 skinless, boneless chicken breast halves (4 ounces each)
- 1½ teaspoons dried thyme
- ½ teaspoon ground black pepper
- 2 teaspoons olive oil
- 1 large onion, chopped
- 1 small clove garlic, minced
- 2¾ cups defatted chicken broth
- 1¼ cups long-grain white rice
- 1 medium carrot, chopped
- 1 cup chopped zucchini
- ¼ cup chopped fresh parsley
- 1 large bay leaf
- 1 teaspoon dried basil
- ¼ teaspoon salt (optional)

Sprinkle the chicken with ½ teaspoon of the thyme and ¼ teaspoon of the pepper.

Lightly coat a large no-stick skillet with no-stick spray. Place over medium heat and add the chicken. Brown the pieces on both sides. Remove from the pan and set aside.

Warm the oil in the same skillet. Add the onions, garlic and 3 tablespoons of the broth. Cook, stirring, over medium heat for 5 minutes, or until the onions are tender. Stir in the rice, carrots, zucchini, parsley, bay leaf, basil, salt (if using) and the remaining 1 teaspoon thyme, remaining ¼ teaspoon pepper and remaining broth.

Place the chicken on top of the rice mixture. Bring to a boil, then reduce the heat. Cover and simmer for 20 minutes, or until the rice is tender and the liquid is absorbed.

Remove and discard the bay leaf. Move the chicken to one side of the skillet. Stir the rice, then transfer it to a serving platter. Arrange the chicken on top.

Per serving: 329 calories, 5.5 g. total fat (15% of calories), 1.2 g. saturated fat, 73 mg. cholesterol, 315 mg. sodium

---

Apricot-Mustard Chicken Breasts

*H*ere's the perfect dish for unexpected company. It's fast and elegant—and you can easily double the recipe (use an extra-large skillet to hold all the chicken). If you accompany the chicken with cooked couscous and steamed asparagus or green beans, you can have dinner on the table in less than 30 minutes.

MAKES 4 SERVINGS

⅔ cup water
¼ cup Dijon mustard
3 tablespoons apricot preserves
1 tablespoon reduced-sodium soy sauce
1 tablespoon finely chopped scallions
4 skinless, boneless chicken breast halves (4 ounces each)

In a large no-stick skillet, stir together the water, mustard, preserves, soy sauce and scallions. Add the chicken.

Bring to a simmer over medium-high heat, then reduce the heat. Gently simmer for 15 to 18 minutes, or until the chicken is tender. (If the sauce becomes too thick, add more water during cooking.)

Per serving: 147 calories, 2.9 g. total fat (18% of calories), 0.7 g. saturated fat, 45 mg. cholesterol, 374 mg. sodium

---

Mandarin Chicken Breasts with Rice

Mandarin oranges and Asian spices give these chicken breasts the flavor of the Orient—with less than 4 grams of fat per serving.

MAKES 4 SERVINGS

- 1⅓ cups long-grain white rice
- 1 teaspoon peanut oil
- 3–4 scallions, chopped
- 4 skinless, boneless chicken breast halves (4 ounces each)
- 1 can (11 ounces) mandarin orange sections (packed in syrup)
- ¼ cup orange juice
- 2½ tablespoons reduced-sodium soy sauce
- 1 teaspoon sugar
- 1 teaspoon grated ginger root
- ½ teaspoon finely shredded orange peel
- 2 tablespoons water
- ¾ teaspoon cornstarch

Cook the rice according to the package directions.

While the rice is cooking, warm the oil in a large no-stick skillet over medium heat. Add the scallions. Cook, stirring, for 3 minutes, or until tender. Add the chicken and brown the pieces on both sides.

Drain the oranges, reserving the syrup; set the oranges aside. Add the syrup to the skillet. Stir in the orange juice, soy sauce, sugar, ginger and orange peel. Bring to a simmer. Cook, turning the chicken occasionally, for 12 minutes.

In a custard cup, stir together the water and cornstarch. Add to the skillet. Cook, stirring, until the mixture comes to a boil and thickens. Stir in the reserved oranges. Simmer for 2 minutes. Serve over the rice.

Per serving: 304 calories, 3.4 g. total fat (10% of calories), 0.8 g. saturated fat, 46 mg. cholesterol, 375 mg. sodium

---

Basil Marinara Chicken with Vermicelli

*I*talians have traditionally used olive oil in their cooking because of its distinctive taste. Today, we value it for the heart-healthy monounsaturated fat it contains. To get the richest, full-bodied flavor in this sauce, use extra-virgin olive oil; it's the highest grade available.

MAKES 6 SERVINGS

1½	tablespoons olive oil
2	tablespoons chopped onions
1	large clove garlic, minced
6	skinless, boneless chicken breast halves (4 ounces each)
1	cup water
1	can (6 ounces) tomato paste
1	can (16 ounces) tomato sauce
⅓	cup chopped fresh basil
¼	teaspoon ground black pepper
¼	teaspoon salt (optional)
	Pinch of crushed red pepper
12	ounces vermicelli

Warm the oil in a large no-stick skillet over medium heat. Add the onions and garlic. Cook, stirring, for 3 minutes, or until the onions are tender. Add the chicken. Cook for 5 minutes, turning the pieces occasionally, until surfaces begin to brown.

In a medium bowl, stir together the water and tomato paste until smooth. Add the tomato sauce, basil, black pepper, salt (if using) and red pepper; mix well.

Pour the tomato mixture over the chicken. Bring the mixture to a simmer. Cover and gently simmer for 15 to 18 minutes, or until the chicken is tender.

Cook the vermicelli in a large pot of boiling water for 5 minutes, or until just tender. Drain and divide among plates. Top with the chicken and sauce.

Per serving: 368 calories, 6.9 g. total fat (17% of calories), 1.3 g. saturated fat, 46 mg. cholesterol, 726 mg. sodium

---

Gingered Chicken with Vegetables

$\mathcal{F}$resh ginger gives this dish its signature flavor. Be aware that it's not interchangeable with powdered ginger and is much more pungent. For best flavor, buy fresh ginger that is firm and not shriveled. Store it in a resealable storage bag in the refrigerator or freezer. To use, scrape off its peel with a sharp knife and grate the amount you need (you don't need to thaw the ginger if it's frozen).

MAKES 4 SERVINGS

- 1⅓ cups long-grain white rice
- 3 tablespoons reduced-sodium soy sauce
- 3 tablespoons dry sherry or nonalcoholic wine
- 1 teaspoon honey
- 1 teaspoon grated ginger root
- 1 teaspoon peanut oil
- ⅛ teaspoon chili powder
- 1 pound skinless, boneless chicken breast halves, cut lengthwise into thirds
- 1 large onion, cut into eighths
- 1 small sweet red pepper, cut into 1" pieces
- 1 cup small fresh mushrooms

Cook the rice according to the package directions.

Line a 15" × 10" baking pan with foil and set aside.

In a large bowl, use a wire whisk to stir together the soy sauce, sherry or wine, honey, ginger, oil and chili powder. Add the chicken, onions, peppers and mushrooms. Mix until well-coated; let stand at room temperature for 5 minutes.

Using a slotted spoon, transfer the chicken and vegetables to the prepared pan and spread out evenly. Set aside the soy sauce mixture remaining in the pan.

Bake the chicken and vegetables at 400° for 7 minutes. Using a wide spatula, turn the pieces over and brush with the reserved soy sauce mixture. Bake for 7 to 11 minutes more, or until the chicken is tender.

Discard any of the remaining soy sauce mixture. Serve the chicken and vegetables over the rice.

THINK AHEAD: Cook a double amount of rice. Rice stores well in the refrigerator for a few days. To use, either microwave it until hot or place in a fine-mesh steaming basket and steam until heated through.

Per serving: 276 calories, 3.1 g. total fat (11% of calories), 0.8 g. saturated fat, 46 mg. cholesterol, 308 mg. sodium

Curried Chicken in a Hurry

*T*his chicken entrée can be on the table in less than 20 minutes. Serve the chicken over white rice, quick-cooking brown rice or couscous.

MAKES 4 SERVINGS

- 1½ teaspoons canola oil
- 1 small onion, chopped
- ½ cup cubed sweet red peppers
- 4 skinless, boneless chicken breast halves, cut lengthwise in half
- 1 can (12 ounces) tomato sauce
- ½ cup water
- ⅓ cup raisins
- 1½ teaspoons curry powder
- ½ teaspoon ground allspice
- ½ teaspoon sugar

Warm the oil in a large no-stick skillet over medium heat. Add the onions and peppers. Cook, stirring, for 3 minutes, or until the onions are tender.

Add the chicken and brown both sides of each piece. Stir in the tomato sauce, water, raisins, curry powder, allspice and sugar. Bring to a simmer. Cover and gently simmer for 12 minutes, or until the chicken is tender. (If the sauce becomes too thick, add more water during cooking.)

Per serving: 184 calories, 4 g. total fat (19% of calories), 0.7 g. saturated fat, 46 mg. cholesterol, 557 mg. sodium

Jamaican-Style Chicken with Black Beans and Rice

*D*on't be alarmed—even though the ingredient list looks long, this skillet dinner actually goes together quite quickly. (If you take a second glance, you'll notice that most of the ingredients are just spices from your cupboard.)

MAKES 4 SERVINGS

- 1 tablespoon olive oil
- 1 pound skinless, boneless chicken breast halves, cut into ¾" cubes
- 1 cup chopped scallions
- ½ cup chopped sweet red peppers
- ¼ cup chopped celery
- 1 large clove garlic, minced
- 1 cup defatted chicken broth
- 1 can (15 ounces) tomatoes (with juice)
- 1 can (4 ounces) diced green chili peppers, drained
- ¼ cup chopped fresh cilantro or parsley
- 1 teaspoon curry powder
- ½ teaspoon chili powder
- ½ teaspoon dried thyme
- ½ teaspoon dried oregano
- ½ teaspoon ground allspice
- 1 can (15 ounces) black beans, rinsed and drained
- 1 cup quick-cooking white rice

Warm the oil in a large no-stick skillet over medium heat. Add the chicken, scallions, red peppers, celery and garlic. Cook, stirring, for 3 minutes, or until the scallions are tender.

Stir in the broth and tomatoes (with juice); use a spoon to break up the tomatoes. Then stir in the chili peppers, cilantro or parsley, curry powder, chili powder, thyme, oregano and allspice. Simmer for 5 minutes.

Stir in the beans and rice. Reduce the heat. Cover and gently simmer, stirring occasionally, for 10 minutes, or until the liquid is absorbed and the rice is tender.

Per serving: 356 calories, 7.3 g. total fat (17% of calories), 1 g. saturated fat, 46 mg. cholesterol, 975 mg. sodium

---

≋ Tips from the Family Chef ≋

SPICE RUBS

*a*n invigorating spice rub can be a no-fuss way to punch up your low-fat chicken dinners, says John Willoughby, a Cambridge, Massachusetts, food writer and coauthor of *Big Flavors of the Hot Sun.*

Chicken thighs are an ideal candidate for this treatment, he says. Remove the skin, rub the flesh with a spice blend and bake them until tender.

"You can find a variety of spice mixtures in supermarkets, specialty stores and ethnic markets. But you can easily make them yourself, too," he says.

When he is in the mood for a Latin dish, John rubs the chicken with a combination of chili powder, cinnamon, cumin, coriander, a touch of brown sugar and red-pepper flakes.

Another aromatic rub combines allspice, cinnamon, ginger and cloves. Still a third gives barbecue flavor to lean meats, including pork tenderloin. It's a blend of cumin, paprika, brown sugar, chili powder, salt and pepper. "It gives the meat an outdoor flavor," says John.

Easy Chicken Jambalaya

*T*his jiffy Cajun-style meal takes only 15 minutes to cook. Part of the secret lies in the use of quick-cooking rice.

MAKES 6 SERVINGS

- 1 tablespoon peanut oil
- 1 cup chopped scallions
- 1 large stalk celery, sliced
- ⅓ cup coarsely chopped sweet red or green peppers
- ⅓ cup chopped fresh parsley
- 1 pound skinless, boneless chicken breast halves, cut into ¾" cubes
- 2 cups defatted chicken broth
- 1¼ cups quick-cooking white rice
- ½ cup chopped smoked ham
- ½ teaspoon dried thyme
- ½ teaspoon ground allspice
- ⅛ teaspoon ground black pepper
- 1 large bay leaf
- 1 can (16 ounces) stewed tomatoes (with juice)

Warm the oil in a large no-stick skillet over medium heat. Add the scallions, celery, red or green peppers and parsley. Cook, stirring, for 3 minutes, or until the onions are tender.

Add the chicken. Cook, stirring, for 4 minutes. Stir in the broth, rice, ham, thyme, allspice, black pepper and bay leaf. Bring to a simmer. Reduce the heat and gently simmer, stirring occasionally, for 3 minutes.

Stir in the tomatoes (with juice) and use a spoon to break them up. Cook until very hot. Turn off the heat. Cover and let stand for 5 minutes.

Remove and discard the bay leaf. Stir well.

Per serving: 202 calories, 4.3 g. total fat (19% of calories), 0.8 g. saturated fat, 35 mg. cholesterol, 430 mg. sodium

---

Chicken Picante Pronto

*P*icante sauce is similar to salsa, except it is smoother. For just a little heat in this saucy chicken dish, use a mild picante sauce. And for more fire, use a medium-hot version.

MAKES 4 SERVINGS

- 1⅓ cups long-grain white rice
- ½ teaspoon chili powder
- ½ cup mild or medium picante sauce
- 1 pound skinless, boneless chicken breast halves, cut into 1″ pieces
- 1½ teaspoons canola oil
- 2 cups small mushrooms
- 1 large onion, cut into eighths
- 1 small sweet red or green pepper, cut into 1″ pieces
- ¼ cup chopped fresh cilantro
- 3 tablespoons reduced-fat sour cream
- ¼ teaspoon salt (optional)

Cook the rice according to the package directions.

While the rice is cooking, mix the chili powder and ¼ cup of the picante sauce in a medium bowl. Add the chicken and stir until coated. Let stand at room temperature for 5 minutes.

Warm the oil in a large no-stick skillet over medium heat. Add the chicken mixture. Cook, stirring, for 2 minutes. Add the mushrooms, onions, peppers, cilantro and the remaining ¼ cup picante sauce. Cook, stirring, for 3 minutes, or until the chicken is tender. Remove the skillet from the heat.

Stir in the sour cream and salt (if using).

To serve, arrange the rice on a serving platter. Spoon the chicken mixture on top.

Per serving: 295 calories, 6.1 g. total fat (18% of calories), 1.6 g. saturated fat, 50 mg. cholesterol, 270 mg. sodium

---

Moroccan Chicken Breasts

*T*his super-quick skillet dinner is redolent with the flavors of the Middle East. Be sure to cut the chicken into small pieces so that it cooks quickly.

MAKES 4 SERVINGS

- 1⅓ cups long-grain white rice
- 1 pound skinless, boneless chicken breast halves, cut into bite-size pieces
- 2 teaspoons olive oil
- 1½ cups chopped onions
- 1 clove garlic, minced
- ¾ cup defatted chicken broth
- 2 large carrots, thinly sliced
- 1 can (14½ ounces) reduced-sodium stewed tomatoes (with juice)
- ½ cup raisins
- ¼ cup chopped fresh parsley
- 1½ teaspoons dried thyme
- 1 teaspoon ground cumin
- ¼ teaspoon ground cinnamon
- ⅛ teaspoon ground cloves
- ⅛ teaspoon ground black pepper
- ¼ teaspoon salt (optional)

Cook the rice according to the package directions.

Lightly coat a large no-stick skillet with no-stick spray. Place over medium heat and add the chicken. Cook, stirring, for 7 to 10 minutes, or until the pieces begin to brown. Transfer to a medium bowl.

Warm the oil in the same skillet. Add the onions, garlic and 3 tablespoons of the broth. Cook, stirring, for 5 minutes, or until the onions are tender. (If necessary, add more broth during cooking.)

Return the chicken to the skillet. Stir in the carrots, tomatoes (with juice), raisins, parsley, thyme, cumin, cinnamon, cloves, pepper, salt (if using) and the remaining broth. Bring to a boil, then reduce the heat. Simmer, stirring occasionally, for 15 to 20 minutes, or until the chicken is tender and the sauce thickens slightly.

To serve, arrange the rice on a serving platter. Spoon the chicken mixture on top.

Per serving: 458 calories, 5.5 g. total fat (11% of calories), 1.1 g. saturated fat, 46 mg. cholesterol, 139 mg. sodium

---

Chicken Paprikash

*I*n this special Hungarian dish, fat-free sour cream lends richness and creaminess to the sauce usually associated with regular sour cream. Round out the menu with French or Italian bread and a tossed salad served with a low-fat dressing.

MAKES 4 SERVINGS

1 pound skinless, boneless chicken breast halves,
   cut into bite-size pieces
½ teaspoon salt (optional)
¼ teaspoon ground black pepper
2 teaspoons olive oil
1 large onion, chopped
1 clove garlic, minced
¾ cup defatted chicken broth
2 teaspoons paprika
1 large sweet red pepper, chopped
1½ cups cauliflower florets
12 ounces yolk-free egg noodles
1 cup fat-free sour cream

Sprinkle the chicken with the salt (if using) and the black pepper.

Lightly coat a large skillet with no-stick spray. Place over medium heat and add the chicken. Cook, stirring, for 7 to 8 minutes, or until the pieces begin to brown. Remove the chicken from the pan.

Warm the oil in the same skillet. Add the onions, garlic and 3 tablespoons

(continued)

of the broth. Cook, stirring, for 5 minutes, or until the onions are tender. (If necessary, add more broth during cooking.)

Stir in the paprika and cook for 1 minute more. Stir in the remaining broth. Then add the chicken, red peppers and cauliflower. Bring to a boil, then reduce the heat. Cover and simmer for 20 minutes, or until the vegetables are tender.

Meanwhile, cook the noodles according to the package directions. Drain, rinse with hot water and drain again. If necessary, cover the noodles to keep them warm.

Stir the sour cream into the chicken mixture. Cook, stirring, over low heat for 1 to 2 minutes, or until heated through. (Do not boil.) Serve the chicken mixture on top of the noodles.

THINK AHEAD: Cook extra noodles to have for tomorrow's lunch or dinner. To reheat them, either microwave a single serving for 1 to 2 minutes or bring a medium pot of water to a boil, add the noodles and drain after about 10 seconds.

Per serving: 431 calories, 4.8 g. total fat (10% of calories), 0.9 g. saturated fat, 46 mg. cholesterol, 192 mg. sodium

---

Chicken and Asparagus Stir-Fry

*T*his easy stir-fry is a great way to enjoy asparagus when it is in season. The asparagus complements the chicken in both color and flavor. For a colorful dessert, top off the meal with orange wedges and fortune cookies.

MAKES 4 SERVINGS

1⅓ cups long-grain white rice
1 tablespoon rice wine vinegar
1 tablespoon ketchup
½ teaspoon sugar
1 teaspoon grated ginger root

1 large clove garlic, minced

2 tablespoons reduced-sodium soy sauce

1 pound skinless, boneless chicken breasts, cut into 1½" × ¼" strips

⅓ cup defatted chicken broth

1½ teaspoons cornstarch

½ teaspoon oriental sesame oil

2 teaspoons peanut oil

1 pound asparagus, diagonally cut into 1" pieces

Cook the rice according to the package directions.

While the rice is cooking, place the vinegar, ketchup, sugar, ginger, garlic and 1 tablespoon of the soy sauce in a large bowl; whisk to combine. Add the chicken and stir until coated. Let stand at room temperature for 5 minutes.

In a custard cup, stir together the broth, cornstarch, sesame oil and the remaining 1 tablespoon soy sauce. Set aside.

Heat the peanut oil in a large no-stick skillet. Add the chicken mixture. Cook, stirring, for 3 minutes. Add the asparagus. Cook, stirring, for 2 minutes.

Stir in the cornstarch mixture. Continue cooking and stirring until the sauce begins to thicken and just comes to a boil. Cook, stirring, for 2 minutes more, or until the asparagus is crisp-tender. Immediately remove the skillet from the heat. Serve over the rice.

Per serving: 296 calories, 5.5 g. total fat (17% of calories), 1.1 g. saturated fat, 46 mg. cholesterol, 387 mg. sodium

Saucy Italian Chicken on Rice

*T*his skillet dinner gets a splash of color from both zucchini and yellow squash.

MAKES 4 SERVINGS

- 2 cups long-grain white rice
- 1 pound skinless, boneless chicken breast halves, cut into bite-size pieces
- ½ teaspoon salt (optional)
- ¼ teaspoon ground black pepper
- 2 teaspoons olive oil
- 1 large onion, chopped
- 3 tablespoons defatted chicken broth
- 1 clove garlic, minced
- ¼ cup dry sherry or nonalcoholic wine
- 1 can (16 ounces) stewed tomatoes (with juice)
- ½ large sweet red pepper, chopped
- ¼ cup chopped fresh parsley
- 1 teaspoon dried basil
- 1 teaspoon dried thyme
- 1 cup cubed zucchini
- 1 cup cubed yellow squash
- ¼ cup cold water
- 1 teaspoon cornstarch

Cook the rice according to the package directions.

While the rice is cooking, sprinkle the chicken with the salt (if using) and the black pepper.

Lightly coat a large skillet with no-stick spray. Place over medium heat and add the chicken. Cook, stirring, for 7 to 8 minutes, or until the pieces begin to brown. Remove the chicken and set aside.

Add the oil, onions, broth and garlic to the skillet. Cook, stirring, for 5 minutes, or until the onions are tender. (If necessary, add more broth during cooking.)

Stir in the sherry or wine and cook for 1 minute more. Stir in the chicken, tomatoes (with juice), red peppers, parsley, basil and thyme. Bring to a boil, then reduce the heat. Cover and simmer for 10 minutes. Add the zucchini and squash. Cover and simmer for 10 minutes more.

In a custard cup, stir together the water and cornstarch. Slowly stir the mixture into the skillet. Cook, stirring, for 2 minutes, or until the liquid thickens.

Place the rice on a large serving platter. Top with the chicken mixture.

Per serving: 275 calories, 4.9 g. total fat (16% of calories), 1 g. saturated fat, 46 mg. cholesterol, 335 mg. sodium

It's So Easy... It's Kid Stuff

HOMEMADE TV DINNERS

Catherine Alexandrou comes from a restaurant family in Normandy, and she did almost everything she could to escape the long hours preparing meals in a commercial kitchen.

But after working as an au pair in England and as a translator for the United Nations, Catherine was drawn back into the restaurant business. She opened Chez Catherine's in Westfield, New Jersey.

She's sympathetic toward her teenage daughter, who has to fend for herself at dinner while her mother works at the restaurant. "It was hard for me not to be home at night for her. And finding healthy food for her to make for herself was a big problem for me," she says.

But Catherine solved the problem by copying the success of frozen TV dinners—only hers aren't frozen, and they contain fresh, healthy ingredients.

"I make up dinners for her in advance," she says. "I can do three days' worth at a time. I put them in rectangular ceramic dishes and cover them with aluminum foil. My daughter can choose whatever she wants, put it in the oven and just warm it up."

The dishes are simple. One favorite is baked or broiled fish, boiled potatoes and some sautéed vegetables. When she's feeling more ambitious, Catherine does a roast, which she cooks with vegetables, potatoes and fruit, such as apples or nectarines. The fruit adds a touch of Normandy to the dish and cooks down into a tasty sauce.

Chicken Vermicelli
with Sun-Dried Tomatoes

*V*ermicelli is very thin spaghetti that cooks quickly. If you have other ready-cooked pasta on hand, feel free to substitute it.

Makes 4 servings

2	teaspoons olive oil
⅓	cup chopped onions
1	pound skinless, boneless chicken breast halves, cut into 2″ × ¼″ strips
1	small zucchini, coarsely chopped
1	large tomato, chopped
1¼	teaspoons dried marjoram
½	teaspoon chili powder
½	cup drained and chopped pimentos
½	cup defatted chicken broth
3	tablespoons diced oil-packed sun-dried tomatoes
1	tablespoon finely chopped pitted black olives
¼	teaspoon salt (optional)
2½	cups cooked vermicelli cut into 3″ pieces

Warm the oil in a large no-stick skillet over medium heat. Add the onions and cook, stirring, for 3 minutes. Add the chicken and cook, stirring, for 3 minutes, or until the chicken begins to brown. Add the zucchini, chopped tomatoes, marjoram and chili powder. Cook, stirring, for 1 minute.

Stir in the pimentos, broth, sun-dried tomatoes, olives and salt (if using). Then stir in the vermicelli. Cover and cook for 5 minutes, or until heated through.

Per serving: 279 calories, 7.1 g. total fat (23% of calories), 1.3 g. saturated fat, 46 mg. cholesterol, 254 mg. sodium

---

New-Fashioned Paella

*P*aella is like a Spanish grab-bag dinner, since it's often made with whatever the cook has on hand. This version uses skinless chicken breasts and lean ham.

MAKES 6 SERVINGS

1 pound skinless, boneless chicken breast halves,
cut into bite-size pieces

2 teaspoons olive oil

4 ounces fully cooked ham, trimmed of all visible fat
and cut into thin strips

1 cup chopped onions

2 cloves garlic, minced

2½ cups defatted reduced-sodium chicken broth

¼ teaspoon crushed saffron threads

1 can (14½ ounces) tomatoes (with juice)

1 large sweet red or green pepper, chopped

1 package (10 ounces) frozen peas, partially thawed

1½ teaspoons dried thyme

1 teaspoon dried basil

⅛ teaspoon ground red pepper

⅛ teaspoon ground black pepper

1¼ cups long-grain white rice

Lightly coat a Dutch oven or large saucepan with no-stick spray. Place over medium heat. Add the chicken and brown well. Remove the chicken and set aside.

Warm the oil in the same pan. Add the ham, onions, garlic and 3 tablespoons of the broth. Cook, stirring, for 5 minutes.

Stir the saffron into the remaining broth, then stir the mixture into the pan. Add the tomatoes (with juice) and use a spoon to break up the tomatoes. Stir in the chicken, red or green peppers, peas, thyme, basil, ground red pepper and black pepper.

Stir in the rice. Bring to a boil, then reduce the heat. Cover and simmer for 20 minutes, or until the rice is tender and the liquid is absorbed.

Per serving: 312 calories, 4.8 g. total fat (14% of calories), 1 g. saturated fat,
36 mg. cholesterol, 532 mg. sodium

Chicken and Noodle Stir-Fry

$\mathcal{H}$ere's a super-fast skillet meal. It features Chinese noodles, called rice sticks, that cook in only 4 minutes. Look for these at oriental markets or large supermarkets.

MAKES 4 SERVINGS

3½	ounces rice sticks
1	pound skinless, boneless chicken breast halves, cut into thin strips
2	teaspoons canola oil
1	large onion, finely chopped
1	large clove garlic, minced
3	tablespoons + ½ cup defatted chicken broth
2	tablespoons reduced-sodium soy sauce
1	tablespoon rice wine vinegar
2–3	drops hot chili oil (optional)
4	cups sliced bok choy
1	can (8 ounces) sliced water chestnuts, well-drained
¼	cup chopped fresh cilantro
½	sweet red pepper, chopped
¼	teaspoon salt (optional)

Cook the rice sticks according to the package directions. Drain and set aside.

Lightly coat a large skillet with no-stick spray. Place over medium heat and add the chicken. Cook, stirring, until the pieces begin to brown. Remove the chicken from the pan.

Heat the canola oil in the same skillet. Add the onions, garlic and 3 tablespoons of the broth. Cook, stirring, over medium heat for 5 minutes, or until the onions are tender.

Stir in the soy sauce, vinegar, chili oil (if using) and the remaining ½ cup broth. Return the chicken to the skillet. Bring to a boil, then reduce the heat. Cover and simmer for 10 minutes. Add the bok choy, water chestnuts, cilantro and peppers. Cook for 5 minutes, or until the vegetables are crisp-tender. Stir in the salt (if using) and the noodles. Cook for 1 minute more.

Per serving: 269 calories, 4.8 g. total fat (16% of calories), 0.9 g. saturated fat, 46 mg. cholesterol, 456 mg. sodium

⋙ Tips from the Family Chef ⋙

GET ORGANIZED!

*I*f you want to get cooking fast, get organized, says chef, author and television cooking show host Nathalie Dupree.

"Every kitchen is different, so you should get it organized and plan ahead for meals," she says. That can include keeping individual-size portions of entrées frozen and ready to thaw on a moment's notice.

"Some fresh things that should be on hand in every kitchen are onions, garlic, rice and potatoes," says Nathalie. "If you have just those things, you can make yourself a meal."

One way to save time is to cook two meals at once. This is especially efficient if one of the dishes has to simmer or bake for a while. As long as you're already in the kitchen, you can make efficient use of your time by cooking a second entrée.

For instance, says Nathalie, while you are roasting a chicken for Sunday dinner, prepare a stir-fry for Monday. You'll spend less time in the kitchen the next day.

Chicken and Chick-Peas with Polenta

*W*e blended the past with the present for this Italian fare. Polenta is a traditional peasant dish made from cornmeal that generally requires long cooking and lots of stirring. But with the use of the microwave, polenta can be ready in no time.

MAKES 6 SERVINGS

- 12 ounces skinless, boneless chicken breast halves, cut into bite-size pieces
- 1 large onion, chopped
- 3 tablespoons defatted chicken broth
- 2 teaspoons olive oil
- 1 clove garlic, minced
- 1 can (15 ounces) reduced-sodium tomato sauce
- 1 can (15 ounces) chick-peas, rinsed and drained
- 1 can (14½ ounces) reduced-sodium stewed tomatoes (with juice)
- 1 large green pepper, chopped
- 1 teaspoon dried basil
- 1 teaspoon dried thyme
- ¼ teaspoon ground black pepper
- 1⅓ cups yellow cornmeal
- 1 tablespoon sugar
- ½ teaspoon salt (optional)
- 3 cups water
- 1 cup 1% low-fat milk
- 1 medium onion, diced

Lightly coat a Dutch oven or large saucepan with no-stick spray. Place over medium heat and add the chicken. Cook, stirring, for 7 to 8 minutes, or until the pieces begin to brown. Remove the chicken from the pan.

Add the chopped onions, broth, oil and garlic to the same pan. Cook, stirring, for 5 minutes, or until the onions are tender.

Stir in the tomato sauce, chick-peas, tomatoes (with juice), green peppers, basil, thyme, black pepper and chicken. Bring to a boil, then reduce the heat. Cover and simmer, stirring occasionally, for 25 minutes.

Meanwhile, in a 2½-quart microwave-safe casserole, stir together the cornmeal, sugar and salt (if using). Then stir in the water, milk and diced onions.

Microwave on high power for a total of 9 minutes; stop and stir every 3 minutes with a wire whisk. Whisk again until the mixture is smooth. Cover and microwave for 6 minutes more. Let stand, covered, for 3 minutes.

Divide the cornmeal among serving plates and top with the chicken mixture.

Per serving: 413 calories, 10.8 g. total fat (23% of calories), 2.8 g. saturated fat, 29 mg. cholesterol, 343 mg. sodium

---

51 Fast Ways to Prepare Chicken

You can serve dinner on the double by choosing any of our fast-fixing chicken entrées. Skinless, boneless chicken breasts are among the easiest, quickest and healthiest items to prepare. And almost everyone—even finicky eaters—likes them.

Many of our ideas start with ready-cooked chicken, making them ideal ways to use up leftovers. If you don't have any cooked chicken on hand, the quick preparation methods below will solve that problem.

But first a few words about handling and storing raw chicken: To maintain peak freshness, store chicken in its original package in the coldest part of your refrigerator for no more than two days. If you can't cook the chicken within this time, freeze it for up to six months. Thaw the chicken in the refrigerator. If you will be cooking it *immediately*, you may also defrost it in the microwave following the manufacturer's instructions.

Both before and after handling raw poultry, wash your hands, rubber gloves (if using) and utensils thoroughly with hot soapy water. Use a separate cutting board for the raw meat and choose one that can go into the dishwasher. Also use different platters for raw and cooked poultry.

Before cooking boneless, skinless chicken breasts, you might want to slightly pound them to a uniform thickness so they cook evenly. Use the flat side of a meat mallet. If you don't have a meat mallet, a heavy ice-cream scoop or even a rolling pin can be used. Then use one of these cooking methods.

- *To pan-fry:* Coat an unheated no-stick skillet with no-stick spray. Place the skillet over medium heat and let it get hot. Add the chicken and cook for 8 to 12 minutes, or until cooked through; turn the pieces over halfway through cooking .

- *To poach:* Bring about an inch of water to a boil in a large skillet. Carefully add the chicken and simmer, covered, for 15 to 20 minutes.

- *To microwave:* Use 1 pound of skinless, boneless chicken breast halves. (You'll get the best results if the pieces are all similar in size.) Arrange the pieces, spoke-fashion, in a microwave-safe dish with the thicker parts facing the rim. Cover with plastic wrap and vent by pulling back a small corner. Microwave on high power for a total of 6 minutes, or until the pieces are cooked through; stop and rotate the dish a half-turn after 3 minutes.

- *To broil:* Preheat the broiler. Coat the rack of a broiling pan with no-stick spray. Place the chicken on the rack. Broil 4″ from the heat for 9 to 11 minutes, turning the chicken over halfway through cooking.
- *To grill:* Coat the unheated grill rack with no-stick spray. Light the grill according to the manufacturer's directions. Place the rack on the grill and arrange the chicken on the rack, directly over medium-hot coals. Grill, uncovered, for 15 to 18 minutes, turning the chicken over halfway through cooking.

In all cases, the chicken will be done when it is tender and the juices run clear when you pierce the thickest part with a fork.

Here are some ways to use the cooked chicken, followed by more ideas for ready-to-cook skinless, boneless breasts. (Don't forget that turkey breast—cooked or not, as appropriate—is interchangeable with chicken white meat.)

Black Bean Chicken Salad: Mix rinsed and drained canned *black beans* with cubes of *cooked chicken*, thawed frozen *whole kernel corn*, chopped *tomatoes* and chopped *scallions*. Moisten with *lime juice* and a small amount of *olive oil*. Season to taste with chopped fresh *cilantro*.

Honey-Dijon Chicken Slaw: Mix shredded *cabbage* with cubes of *cooked chicken* and chopped *apples*. Moisten with *fat-free honey-Dijon salad dressing*. Serve in *pita bread* pockets.

Italian Chicken Pasta Salad: Mix cooked *radiatore* or *corkscrew pasta*, cubed *cooked chicken*, cubed *reduced-fat mozzarella cheese*, sliced *zucchini*, thin *tomato wedges*, sliced pitted *ripe olives* and sliced *scallions*. Moisten with *fat-free Italian salad dressing* and season to taste with finely chopped

(continued)

fresh *basil* or *oregano* or crushed dried *Italian seasoning*. Marinate in the refrigerator for 30 minutes to blend the flavors. Sprinkle with a small amount of grated *Parmesan cheese* before serving.

Russian Waldorf Chicken Salad: Mix chopped *red apples* with chopped *cooked chicken* and chopped *celery*. Moisten with *reduced-calorie creamy Russian salad dressing*. Serve on *lettuce leaves*. Top each serving with a few broken toasted *walnuts*.

In-a-Hurry Curried Chicken Salad: Combine cooked *rice* or *orzo*, cubed *cooked chicken*, chopped *apples*, *raisins* and sliced *scallions*. Moisten with a mixture of equal parts *fat-free mayonnaise* and *fat-free plain yogurt*. Season to taste with *curry powder*. If desired, top with a small amount of chopped *lightly salted peanuts*.

Dill Chicken Slaw: Mix together shredded *carrots*, cubed *cooked chicken* and *raisins*. Moisten with a dressing made of four parts *lemon juice* to one part *olive oil*. Season to taste with finely chopped fresh *dill*.

Chicken and Spinach Salad: Toss together torn *spinach*, *cooked chicken* cut into bite-size pieces, thinly sliced *red onion rings* and cooked and chopped *turkey bacon*. Serve with a *reduced-fat salad dressing* such as blue cheese, ranch or honey-Dijon.

Chicken and Couscous Tabbouleh: Prepare *couscous* according to the package directions, then cool it to room temperature. Stir in chopped *cooked chicken*, chopped fresh *parsley* and chopped fresh *mint*. Flavor with *lemon juice*.

Greek Chicken Salad: Toss together torn *iceberg lettuce*, *cooked chicken* cut into bite-size pieces, thinly sliced *onion rings*, sliced *cucumbers*, halved *cherry tomatoes* and sliced pitted *ripe olives*. Lightly moisten with *reduced-calorie Italian* or *Caesar salad dressing*. Season to taste with crushed dried *oregano*. Sprinkle with crumbled *feta cheese*.

Chicken Tostada Salad: Lightly coat both sides of white or yellow *corn tortillas* with no-stick spray; place on a baking sheet and bake at 400° for 10 minutes. Spread the tortillas with canned *fat-free refried beans*. Layer with shredded *lettuce*, chopped *tomatoes*, cubed *cooked chicken* and canned *whole kernel corn*. Drizzle with *salsa*.

Creamy Taters: Heat 1 can *low-fat condensed cream of chicken soup* with ½ soup can *skim milk*, cubes of *cooked chicken* and chopped leftover *vegetables* (such as broccoli, corn or peas). Serve on top of baked *potatoes*.

Crispy Pita Pizzas: Split *pita breads* horizontally. Broil, cut side up, until toasted. Spread with *pizza sauce*. Top with finely shredded *reduced-fat mozzarella cheese*, shredded *cooked chicken* and chopped *vegetables* (such as green or sweet red peppers, mushrooms, onions, cooked broccoli or spinach). Broil until the cheese melts.

Cracker Bread Roll-Ups: Stir chopped fresh *dill*, *chives* or *basil* into soft-style *light cream cheese*. Spread the mixture on soft *Armenian cracker bread* (or large *flour tortillas*). Top with a mixture of finely chopped *cooked chicken* or *smoked chicken* and finely chopped raw *broccoli*, *cauliflower* and *carrots*. Roll up jelly-roll fashion, then cut into 1½″ slices. (If necessary, use toothpicks to hold the slices together.)

Shortcut Chicken Chili: Stir together equal parts *Mexican-style stewed tomatoes* (with juice) and rinsed and drained canned *beans*. Season to taste with *chili powder*. Simmer for 5 minutes. Add chopped *cooked chicken* and simmer for 5 minutes more. Garnish with *fat-free sour cream* and serve with *no-oil tortilla chips*.

Chicken Quesadillas: On a *flour tortilla*, layer finely shredded *reduced-*

(continued)

fat Monterey Jack cheese or *Cheddar cheese,* shredded *cooked chicken* and chopped, canned *green chili peppers* or *jalapeño peppers.* Sprinkle with a *salt-free seasoning* (such as Mexican), ground *cumin* or chopped *cilantro.* Top with a second tortilla and heat in a no-stick skillet until the cheese melts and both sides are lightly browned. Cut into wedges and serve with *salsa.*

Chicken and Bean Burritos: Stir *chili powder* into canned *fat-free refried beans.* Spoon the mixture onto a *flour tortilla* in a strip, slightly off-center. Top with chopped *cooked chicken* and *reduced-fat Cheddar cheese.* Roll up, jelly-roll fashion, and slightly flatten with your hand. Heat in a no-stick skillet coated with no-stick spray until the cheese melts and the tortilla is lightly browned.

Grilled Chicken with Red-Pepper Sauce: Drain bottled *roasted red peppers* and puree them with fresh *basil* and *garlic.* If desired, stir in a small amount of *tomato paste* to make a thicker consistency. Serve at room temperature over *grilled chicken breast halves.*

Peanut Chicken: In a saucepan, mix two parts *reduced-fat peanut butter,* two parts unsweetened *pineapple juice* and one part *skim milk.* Cook and stir until heated and smooth. Flavor with *reduced-sodium soy sauce,* grated fresh *ginger* and ground *red pepper.* Serve over *broiled or grilled chicken breast halves.* Garnish with finely chopped fresh *chives* or *scallions.*

Chunky Chicken Corn Chowder: In a saucepan, stir together 1 can *low-fat condensed cream of chicken soup,* 1 soup can *skim milk,* cubed *cooked* *chicken*, cubed cooked *potatoes* and frozen *whole kernel corn*. Heat through. Serve sprinkled with cooked and chopped *turkey bacon*.

Ginger, Carrot and Chicken Soup: Cook sliced *carrots* until very tender. Drain and puree with a small amount of defatted *reduced-sodium chicken broth*. Transfer to a saucepan and stir in equal amounts of the *broth* and *evaporated skim milk*. Stir in chopped *cooked chicken* and flavor with ground *ginger* and grated *orange peel*. Heat just until warm.

Chicken Tortellini and Spinach Soup: Bring defatted *reduced-sodium chicken broth* to a boil. Add frozen *cheese tortellini* (5 per person). Simmer for 5 minutes. Then add chopped *cooked chicken* and a few chopped *sun-dried tomatoes* (without oil). Season to taste with crushed dried *oregano* and *basil*. Cook for a few minutes more, until the tortellini is tender but firm. Stir in torn fresh *spinach* and let wilt. Serve garnished with finely shredded fresh *Parmesan cheese*.

Creamy Chicken and Noodle Bake: Stir together 1 can *low-fat condensed cream of chicken soup*, ½ soup can *evaporated skim milk*, ¼ cup soft-style *light cream cheese*, ¼ teaspoon crushed dried *thyme* and ⅛ teaspoon *pepper*. Stir in 3 cups cooked *yolk-free egg noodles*, 2 cups cubed *cooked chicken* and ⅔ cup frozen *mixed carrots and peas*. Transfer to a 1½-quart casserole coated with no-stick spray. Cover and bake at 350° for 20 minutes.

(continued)

51 Fast Ways to Prepare Chicken—Continued

CLT: For this version of a BLT, pound *chicken breast halves* to make them an even thickness. Pan-fry in a no-stick skillet coated with no-stick spray. Serve in toasted, split *kaiser rolls* with *lettuce* and *tomato slices*; drizzle with *reduced-fat ranch salad dressing with bacon.*

Hot Chicken Hoagies: Pound *chicken breast halves* to make them an even thickness. Lightly coat the chicken with all-purpose *flour.* Pan-fry in a no-stick skillet coated with no-stick spray. Serve in split *hoagie* or *French rolls* spread with *fat-free mayonnaise* and *Dijon mustard.* Top with very thin slices of *tomatoes*, *onions* and *green pepper rings.*

Holiday Chicken Sandwiches: Pound *chicken breast halves* to ¼" thickness. Pan-fry in a no-stick skillet coated with no-stick spray. Serve between toasted *whole-grain bread* spread with *fat-free mayonnaise* and lined with *lettuce.* Top with *cranberry-orange sauce* flavored with grated fresh *ginger.*

Parmesan Chicken Sandwiches: Pound *chicken breast halves* to make them an even thickness. Lightly coat with olive oil no-stick spray, then roll in fine dry seasoned *bread crumbs.* Pan-fry the chicken in a no-stick skillet coated with no-stick spray. Serve in split *hoagie* or *French rolls.* Top with heated *reduced-fat spaghetti sauce.* Sprinkle with grated *Parmesan cheese.*

Barbecued Chicken Sandwiches: Cut *chicken breasts* into strips. Coat a no-stick skillet with no-stick spray. Add the chicken and thin slices of *onions* and chopped *green peppers.* Stir in *fat-free, low-sodium barbecue sauce.* Serve in split *hoagie rolls.*

Chicken Caesar Salad: Grill or broil *chicken breast halves*, brushing them occasionally with *reduced-fat Caesar salad dressing.* Cut the chicken into strips and toss with torn *romaine lettuce* and toasted *Italian* or *French bread cubes.* Moisten with additional dressing and top with a small amount of shredded fresh *Parmesan cheese.*

Seasoned Chicken with Slaw: Pound *chicken breast halves* to make them an even thickness. Lightly coat with olive oil no-stick spray, then sprinkle with a *salt-free seasoning* (such as lemon-herb, garlic-and-herb, Cajun/creole, fajita, Japanese, mesquite or Thai). Grill or broil the chicken and serve with shredded *cabbage* mixed with *fat-free mayonnaise* and a dash of *lemon juice*.

Grilled Citrus-Tarragon Chicken: Pound *chicken breast halves* to an even thickness. Marinate for 1 hour in the refrigerator in a mixture of two parts *orange juice*, one part *lemon juice* and one part *lime juice* with chopped fresh *tarragon*. Discard the marinade. Grill the chicken until done.

Hot-and-Sour Chicken Noodle Soup: Cut *chicken breasts* into bite-size strips. Cook with *ramen noodles* (discard the seasoning package) and a pinch of *ground red pepper* in defatted *reduced-sodium chicken broth*. Season to taste with grated fresh *ginger*, *rice wine vinegar* and *soy sauce*.

Chicken Piccata: Pound *chicken breast halves* to make them an even thickness. Lightly coat the chicken with all-purpose *flour* seasoned with *salt* and *pepper*. Pan-fry in a no-stick skillet coated with no-stick spray. Serve drizzled with *lemon juice* and sprinkled with *capers*.

Chicken Stuffed with Herbed Cheese: Pound *chicken breast halves* to ⅛" thickness. Place 2 tablespoons of soft-style *light herbed cheese* (or *light cream cheese* mixed with your favorite *herb*) in a strip, slightly off-center, on each breast. Fold to enclose the cheese and secure with wooden toothpicks. Dip in *fat-free egg substitute*, then in fine dry plain *bread crumbs*. Pan-fry, turning the pieces occasionally, in a no-stick skillet coated with no-stick spray. Remove the toothpicks before serving.

(continued)

51 Fast Ways to Prepare Chicken—Continued

Chicken Breasts with Apple-Walnut Stuffing: Cook peeled and finely chopped *apples*, minced *onions* and finely chopped *celery* in a small amount of defatted *reduced-sodium chicken broth* until tender. Stir in coarse dry plain *bread crumbs*, chopped *walnuts* and dried *sage*. Moisten with boiling *broth*; cover to keep warm. Cook *chicken breast halves* with a spoonful of *apple juice concentrate* in a no-stick skillet coated with no-stick spray. Serve the chicken with the stuffing.

Cornflake-Coated Chicken: Dip *chicken breast halves* in all-purpose *flour* and shake off the excess. Then dip in *fat-free egg substitute* and finally in fine *cornflake crumbs*. Place on a baking sheet coated with no-stick spray. Bake at 375° for 20 minutes.

Dijon Chicken Cordon Bleu: Pound *chicken breast halves* to ⅛" thickness. Lightly spread one side of each with *Dijon mustard*; top with 1 very thin slice *97% fat-free ham* and 1 slice *fat-free Swiss cheese*. Fold to enclose the filling and secure with wooden toothpicks. Dip in *fat-free egg substitute*, then in fine dry plain *bread crumbs*. Pan-fry in a no-stick skillet coated with no-stick spray. Remove the toothpicks before serving.

Chicken in a Packet: Pound *chicken breast halves* to ½" thickness. Place each on a large piece of heavy foil. Top with very thinly sliced *potatoes* and *carrots*. Lightly sprinkle with *salt* and *pepper*; top with finely chopped fresh *dill*, *marjoram* or *basil*. Wrap tightly, crumpling the edges of the foil to seal. Place on a baking sheet and bake at 400° for 15 minutes, or until the chicken is done and the vegetables are tender.

Italian Chicken: Pound *chicken breast halves* to make them an even thickness. Dip the chicken in *fat-free* or *reduced-fat Italian salad dressing*; shake off the excess. Dip in a mixture of all-purpose *flour* and crushed dried *Italian seasoning*. Pan-fry in a no-stick skillet coated with no-stick spray.

Chicken Diane: Pound *chicken breast halves* to make them an even thickness. Pan-fry in a no-stick skillet coated with no-stick spray. Remove the chicken and cover to keep warm. To the skillet, add sliced *mushrooms*, finely chopped *onions*, minced *garlic* and a small amount of a mixture of equal parts *white wine Worcestershire sauce* and *lemon juice*. Cook and stir until the mushrooms are tender. Flavor with a small amount of *reduced-calorie tub-style margarine* or *light butter*. Serve over the chicken.

Indian Chicken: Cut *chicken breast halves* into bite-size strips. Cook, stirring, in a no-stick skillet coated with no-stick spray. Stir in a mixture of *fat-free plain yogurt* and all-purpose *flour* (use 2 teaspoons flour for each ½ cup yogurt). Season to taste with *curry powder* and *garlic powder*. Then stir in chopped *raisins* or *currants*. Heat just until warm (do not boil). Serve over cooked *rice*; garnish with a few *chopped cashews*.

Quick-Fix Fajitas: Cut *chicken breasts* into strips and sprinkle lightly with ground *cumin*. Cook and stir in a no-stick skillet coated with no-stick spray along with strips of *sweet red peppers*, *green peppers* and *onions*. Serve in *flour tortillas* with *salsa*.

Skillet Shish Kabobs: Cut *chicken breasts* into cubes; marinate in the refrigerator in a small amount of *red wine vinegar* or *balsamic vinegar* mixed with chopped *scallions*, finely chopped fresh *mint* and a dash of *olive oil*. Cook and stir in a no-stick skillet with slices of *zucchini* and halved *cherry tomatoes*.

Red-Hot Chicken Dippers: Cut *chicken breasts* into ½"-wide strips. Thread onto bamboo skewers in a loose accordion fashion. Marinate in defatted *reduced-sodium chicken broth* seasoned to taste with *hot-pepper sauce* for 2 hours in the refrigerator. Drain and discard the marinade. Broil the chicken until done. Serve with *reduced-fat blue cheese salad dressing*.

Teriyaki Chicken Kabobs: Cut *chicken breasts* into ¾" cubes. Cover with a mixture of equal parts *reduced-sodium teriyaki sauce* and unsweetened *pineapple juice*. Marinate for 30 minutes in the refrigerator. On bamboo skewers, alternately thread the chicken with *pineapple chunks* and cubes of *sweet red*

(continued)

51 Fast Ways to Prepare Chicken—Continued

peppers. Generously brush with the teriyaki marinade (discard the remaining marinade). Broil, occasionally turning the kabobs, until the chicken is cooked through.

Spanish Stuffed Sweet Potatoes: Cut *chicken breasts* into bite-size strips. Cook and stir in a no-stick skillet coated with no-stick spray along with julienne strips of *sweet red peppers*, sliced *scallions*, minced *garlic* and a small amount of defatted *reduced-sodium chicken broth*. Serve over split baked *sweet potatoes*.

Baked Potatoes with Pesto Chicken: Cut *chicken breasts* into cubes. Sauté the chicken and chopped *sweet red peppers* in a no-stick skillet coated with no-stick spray. Toss with a small amount of store-bought *pesto*. Serve over hot split baked *potatoes*.

Mandarin Chicken: Cut *chicken breasts* into thin bite-size strips. Cook and stir in a no-stick skillet coated with no-stick spray. Add *mandarin orange sections*, frozen *snow peas* and just enough *orange marmalade* to lightly coat the mixture. Stir-fry until the peas are hot. Flavor with a dash of *rice wine vinegar* and *soy sauce*.

Chicken Creole: Cut *chicken breasts* into ¾" cubes. Mix the chicken with canned *Cajun-style stewed tomatoes* (with juice) in a saucepan. Cover and simmer until the chicken is cooked through. Serve over cooked *rice*.

Chicken Stroganoff: Cut 12 ounces *chicken breasts* into bite-size strips. Cook and stir with sliced *mushrooms* and minced *garlic* in a no-stick skillet coated with no-stick spray. Stir in 1 can *low-fat condensed cream of mushroom soup* and ½ soup can *fat-free sour cream* or *fat-free plain yogurt*. Serve over cooked *yolk-free egg noodles*.

Shortcut Cacciatore: Cut *chicken breasts* into bite-size chunks. Cook and stir with sliced *mushrooms*, chopped *onions* and minced *garlic* in a no-stick skillet coated with no-stick spray. Remove the chicken and set aside. Add *Italian stewed tomatoes* (with juice) to the skillet. Flavor with dry *red wine* or *nonalcoholic wine*. Simmer, uncovered, for 15 minutes, or until thickened to a sauce consistency. Stir in the chicken and heat through. Serve over cooked *yolk-free egg noodles*.

Chicken and Potato Hash: Finely chop *chicken breasts*. Cook and stir with chopped *scallions* and *sweet red peppers* in a no-stick skillet coated with olive oil no-stick spray. Remove the skillet from the heat and add frozen *fat-free hash brown potatoes*, then lightly coat with the no-stick spray. Season with *pepper* and a *salt-free seasoning* (such as garlic-and-herb, Cajun/Creole, Greek or herbes de Provence). Cook and stir until the potatoes are hot and golden.

Turkey and Black Bean Stir-Fry

Black beans add extra fiber and a slightly different flavor to this Thai-style stir-fry. To save time, we use canned black beans, but if you prefer, you can substitute 1⅔ cups cooked beans.

MAKES 4 SERVINGS

- 3 tablespoons reduced-sodium soy sauce
- 3 tablespoons dry sherry or nonalcoholic wine
- 2 teaspoons cider vinegar
- ¾ teaspoon ground ginger
- 2–3 drops hot chili oil (optional)
- 8 ounces turkey breast cutlets, cut into thin strips
- 1⅓ cups long-grain white rice
- 1 medium onion, finely chopped
- 2 teaspoons oriental sesame oil
- 1 large clove garlic, minced
- ¾ cup defatted chicken broth
- 3 cups sliced Chinese cabbage
- 1 can (15 ounces) black beans, rinsed and drained
- 1 sweet red or green pepper, chopped
- 2 tablespoons chopped scallions
- ¼ teaspoon salt (optional)

In a medium bowl, stir together the soy sauce, sherry or wine, vinegar, ginger and chili oil (if using). Add the turkey and stir until coated. Cover and marinate in the refrigerator for 20 minutes.

Meanwhile, cook the rice according to the package directions.

Lightly coat a large skillet with no-stick spray. Place over medium heat. Use a slotted spoon to remove the turkey from the marinade; reserve the marinade. Add the turkey to the skillet. Cook, stirring, just until the turkey is no longer pink on the surface. Remove the turkey from the pan.

In the same skillet, combine the onions, sesame oil, garlic and 3 tablespoons of the broth. Cook, stirring, for 5 minutes, or until the onions are tender. Stir in the reserved marinade and the remaining broth. Cook, stirring, for 2 minutes.

Add the cabbage, beans, peppers and scallions. Stir until mixed, then stir in the turkey and salt (if using). Cook, stirring occasionally, for 5 or 6 minutes, or until the turkey is no longer pink and the vegetables are crisp-tender.

To serve, fluff the rice with a fork. Serve the turkey mixture over the rice.

Per serving: 441 calories, 5.3 g. total fat (10% of calories), 0.9 g. saturated fat, 25 mg. cholesterol, 824 mg. sodium

≫ Tips from the Family Chef ≪

A CLEVER WAY TO CUT FAT

Here's a slick little trick for keeping store-bought meats, poultry and fish fresh in the refrigerator and reducing the amount of fat needed to cook them. It comes from Damian Grismer, formerly chef and general manager at Kramer Books and Afterwords Cafe in Washington, D.C.

"Unwrap the items as soon as you get them home," he says. "Then coat plastic wrap with a little vegetable oil, wrap the food with it and put it in the refrigerator." Damian says the oil coating will keep the food from turning brown and will be just the right amount for browning the meat, fish or poultry without any additional oil.

Cajun-Seasoned Turkey Cutlets

*T*hese cutlets are extra-lean, with only 6.5 grams of fat per serving.

MAKES 4 SERVINGS

1	pound turkey breast cutlets
2½	teaspoons chili powder
1½	teaspoons paprika
1	teaspoon dried thyme
⅛	teaspoon garlic salt
⅛	teaspoon celery salt
⅛	teaspoon ground black pepper
⅛	teaspoon ground red pepper (optional)
4	teaspoons nondiet tub-style margarine or butter, melted

Line a 15″ × 10″ baking pan with foil. Coat the foil with no-stick spray and set aside.

Place each turkey cutlet between 2 pieces of plastic wrap. Working from the center to the edges, lightly pound with the flat side of a meat mallet or the back of a large, heavy spoon to ⅛″ thickness. Remove the turkey from the plastic and lay the slices, in a single layer, on the prepared baking sheet.

In a custard cup, stir together the chili powder, paprika, thyme, garlic salt, celery salt, black pepper and red pepper (if using).

Lightly brush the turkey with 2 teaspoons of the margarine or butter. Sprinkle with half of the chili mixture. Turn the turkey slices over. Brush with the remaining 2 teaspoons margarine or butter and sprinkle with the remaining chili mixture.

Bake at 425° for 9 or 10 minutes, or until the turkey is tender and cooked through.

Per serving: 154 calories, 6.5 g. total fat (38% of calories), 3.1 g. saturated fat, 52 mg. cholesterol, 229 mg. sodium

---

Curried Orange Turkey Cutlets

*W*ith this easy recipe, you have the option of marinating the turkey for just a few minutes or as long as 24 hours. Either way, these cutlets make a tasty, healthy, fuss-free main dish.

MAKES 4 SERVINGS

1	pound turkey breast cutlets
3	tablespoons orange marmalade
1½	tablespoons reduced-sodium soy sauce
1	tablespoon ketchup
1	tablespoon finely chopped fresh ginger
1	teaspoon canola oil
½	teaspoon curry powder
½	teaspoon chili powder
⅛	teaspoon salt (optional)

Place each turkey cutlet between 2 pieces of plastic wrap. Working from the center to the edges, lightly pound with the flat side of a meat mallet or the back of a large, heavy spoon to ⅛" thickness. Remove the turkey from the plastic and set aside.

In a large, shallow bowl or baking dish, stir together the marmalade, soy sauce, ketchup, ginger, oil, curry powder, chili powder and salt (if using). Add the cutlets, turning them over to evenly coat them. Cover and marinate in the refrigerator for at least 15 minutes or for up to 24 hours, turning them over occasionally.

Line a 15" × 10" baking pan with foil. Spray the foil with no-stick spray. Place the turkey, in a single layer, in the pan. Discard the marinade. Bake at 425° for 9 to 10 minutes, or until the turkey is tender and cooked through.

Per serving: 171 calories, 3.6 g. total fat (19% of calories), 0.8 g. saturated fat, 50 mg. cholesterol, 300 mg. sodium

Barbecued Turkey Sandwich

We took classic barbecued pork and replaced the meat with turkey to create a family favorite that'll meet today's healthy eating guidelines. Serve the barbecued turkey on toasted English muffins, as we did here, or use toasted hamburger buns or kaiser rolls.

MAKES 4 SERVINGS

- 1 pound turkey breast cutlets
- ¼ teaspoon dried thyme
- ¼ teaspoon ground black pepper
- ¼ teaspoon salt (optional)
- 2 teaspoons nondiet tub-style margarine or butter
- 1 teaspoon olive oil
- 1 medium onion, chopped
- 1 small green pepper, chopped
- 1 small clove garlic, minced
- ½ cup ketchup
- ¼ cup water
- 1 tablespoon Worcestershire sauce
- ½ teaspoon sugar
- ⅛ teaspoon dry mustard
  Pinch of ground cloves
- 4 English muffins, split and toasted

Place each turkey cutlet between 2 pieces of plastic wrap. Working from the center to the edges, lightly pound with the flat side of a meat mallet or the back of a large, heavy spoon to ¼" thickness. Remove the turkey from the plastic and sprinkle with the thyme, black pepper and salt (if using).

Melt the margarine or butter in a large no-stick skillet over medium heat. Cook the turkey for 2 minutes per side, or until tender and cooked through. (Do not overcook.) Cover and set aside.

In a 4-cup glass measure, mix the oil, onions, green peppers and garlic. Cover with a piece of wax paper. Microwave on high power for a total of 3 to 4 minutes, or until the vegetables are almost tender; stop and stir after 2 minutes.

Stir in the ketchup, water, Worcestershire sauce, sugar, mustard and cloves. Cover and microwave for 2 to 3 minutes, or until the vegetables are tender.

Pour the sauce over the turkey in the skillet. Stir until the turkey is coated. Spoon the turkey mixture over the English muffin halves.

Per serving: 352 calories, 6.8 g. total fat (17% of calories), 1.4 g. saturated fat, 50 mg. cholesterol, 918 mg. sodium

---

≫ Tips from the Family Chef ≪

THE DAILY GRILL

*I*f you think the outdoor grill should be reserved for lazy summer weekends, take a tip from chef Emeril Lagasse, author of *Emeril's New New Orleans Cooking.*

"I look at the grill as a nightly convenience during the week," he says. "Grilling is a fast and easy way to prepare more than just hot dogs, hamburgers and steaks. It lends itself to chicken, turkey breasts and fish. And it is wonderful for giving a new dimension to certain vegetables."

You can make a quick meal from chicken breasts that you marinate for ten minutes in a little olive oil and fresh herbs. Or you can experiment with blends of herbs and other seasonings, such as lemon juice. The key is simplicity.

For a side dish, grill some vegetables. "Take some peeled whole onions," says Emeril, "drizzle them with a little olive oil and wrap them individually in aluminum foil. Put them on the grill for 15 or 20 minutes before adding the entrée to the grill. They come out caramelized, with a wonderful flavor." The same technique works with whole heads of garlic and ears of sweet corn.

Picante Turkey Sauce and Baked Potatoes

*F*or variety, serve the turkey mixture over rice, noodles or couscous. Garnish with chopped tomatoes, shredded lettuce, chopped scallions or picante sauce.

MAKES 4 SERVINGS

- 2 teaspoons olive oil
- 1 large onion, finely chopped
- 2 medium stalks celery, finely chopped
- ½ cup finely chopped green peppers
- 1 pound ground turkey breast
- 1½ cups tomato sauce
- ½ cup picante sauce
- 2 teaspoons cider vinegar
- 1½ teaspoons Worcestershire sauce
- ½ teaspoon ground allspice
- 1–4 tablespoons water
- 4 large baking potatoes (8 ounces each)

Warm the oil in a large saucepan over medium heat. Add the onions, celery and peppers. Cook, stirring, for 6 minutes, or until the celery is almost tender.

Add the turkey. Cook, breaking up the turkey with a spoon, until it is no longer pink. Stir in the tomato sauce, picante sauce, vinegar, Worcestershire sauce and allspice. Reduce the heat. Cover and simmer for 15 to 20 minutes. Stir in enough of the water to thin to the desired consistency.

While the sauce is cooking, pierce each potato in several places with a fork. Arrange on a microwave-safe plate like the spokes of a wheel. Microwave on high power for a total of 15 minutes, or until the potatoes are easily pierced with a sharp knife; stop and turn each potato over after 10 minutes. Let stand for 5 minutes.

Cut a lengthwise slit in each potato, then gently push in on the ends of the potato to slightly open the slit. Fluff the potato pulp with a fork. Spoon the turkey mixture on top of each potato.

Per serving: 389 calories, 5.6 g. fat (13% of calories), 1.1 g. saturated fat, 50 mg. cholesterol, 868 mg. sodium

---

Turkey Chili Con Carne

Does someone in your family think he doesn't like ground turkey? He won't be able to tell the difference in this hearty chili that tastes just like beef chili. Serve the chili over rice for a one-dish meal.

MAKES 4 SERVINGS

- 1 tablespoon olive oil
- 2 medium onions, chopped
- 1 large stalk celery, finely chopped
- 1 clove garlic, minced
- 1 pound ground turkey breast
- 1 can (16 ounces) stewed tomatoes (with juice)
- 2 cans (15 ounces each) no-salt-added kidney beans, rinsed and drained
- 1 can (8 ounces) tomato sauce
- 1 can (4 ounces) diced green chili peppers, drained
- 3 tablespoons chili powder
- ½ teaspoon dried oregano
- ⅛ teaspoon dried thyme
- ¼ cup water (optional)

Warm the oil in a large saucepan over medium-high heat. Add the onions, celery and garlic. Cook, stirring, for 8 to 10 minutes, or until the onions are tender and lightly browned.

Add the turkey. Cook, breaking up the turkey with a spoon, until it is no longer pink. Stir in the tomatoes (with juice) and break them up with the spoon. Add the beans, tomato sauce, chili peppers, chili powder, oregano and thyme.

Simmer for 15 to 20 minutes, or until the flavors are well-blended. If a thinner chili is desired, stir in the water.

Per serving: 432 calories, 7.8 g. total fat (16% of calories), 1.4 g. saturated fat, 50 mg. cholesterol, 746 mg. sodium

---

Roasted Turkey Breast

*U*sing a commercial roasting bag, as in this recipe, keeps lean turkey breast moist and tender without adding any fat. It also decreases the cooking time and makes cleanup a snap.

MAKES 8 SERVINGS

1   **bone-in turkey breast (6–7 pounds)**
2   **tablespoons all-purpose flour**
1   **teaspoon Worcestershire sauce**
¼   **teaspoon salt (optional)**
⅛   **teaspoon ground black pepper**
1   **medium onion, halved**
1   **small stalk celery, cut into thirds**
1   **small carrot, halved**

Sprinkle the flour in an oven roasting bag according to the directions on the package; set aside.

In a cup, mix the Worcestershire sauce, salt (if using) and pepper.

Loosen the skin from the breast. Use your fingers to rub the Worcestershire mixture into the surface of the meat.

Place the onions, celery and carrots in the roasting bag. Top with the turkey. Close the bag with the twist tie provided, leaving enough air in the bag so that it can puff up around the turkey breast during roasting. Using a small, sharp knife, make 6 small cuts in the top of the bag, according to the directions on the package. Place the bag in a shallow roasting pan.

Roast at 350° for 18 to 20 minutes per pound (about 1¾ to 2¼ hours), or until the pop-up thermometer in the turkey breast pops up, indicating that the meat is done.

Remove from the oven and allow to stand on a wire rack for 20 minutes.

Remove the turkey from the bag. Remove and discard the skin and the vegetables. Use a sharp knife to slice the meat from the bones.

Per serving: 252 calories, 5 g. total fat (19% of calories), 1.6 g. saturated fat, 109 mg. cholesterol, 106 mg. sodium

---

Turkey with Cranberry Stuffing

*D*on't wait until Thanksgiving to enjoy a platter of sliced turkey with stuffing. You can make this quick and tasty version in a skillet anytime.

MAKES 4 SERVINGS

- 1 **pound turkey breast cutlets**
- 1 **large onion, chopped**
- 1 **large stalk celery, diced**
- 2 **tablespoons chopped fresh parsley**
- 1 **cup defatted reduced-sodium chicken broth**
- 4 **teaspoons nondiet tub-style margarine or butter**
- ½ **cup dried cranberries**
- ½ **teaspoon dried thyme**
- ¼ **teaspoon salt (optional)**
- ¼ **teaspoon ground black pepper**
- 2½ **cups seasoned commercial cube-style stuffing**

Place each turkey cutlet between 2 pieces of plastic wrap. Working from the center to the edges, lightly pound with the flat side of a meat mallet or the back of a large, heavy spoon to ⅛" thickness. Remove the turkey from the plastic and set aside.

In a large no-stick skillet, combine the onions, celery, parsley, 3 tablespoons of the broth and 2 teaspoons of the margarine or butter. Cook over medium heat, stirring frequently, for 6 to 7 minutes, or until the onions are tender.

Add the cranberries, thyme, salt (if using), pepper and remaining broth. Stir to mix well. Bring to a boil. Cook for 2 to 3 minutes, until the liquid has thickened slightly. Stir in the stuffing. Reduce the heat and cook for 2 minutes, stirring frequently. Transfer the stuffing to a platter, cover with foil and keep warm.

Wash and dry the skillet. Add the remaining 2 teaspoons margarine or butter and melt over medium heat. Add the turkey and cook for 2 minutes per side, or until cooked through; do not overcook. Transfer to the platter with the stuffing.

Per serving: 318 calories, 7.6 g. total fat (21% of calories), 1.2 g. saturated fat, 50 mg. cholesterol, 803 mg. sodium

---

Turkey Pot Roast Dinner

Now that boneless turkey breast halves are readily available in supermarkets, you can make a "pot roast" dinner quite quickly.

MAKES 6 SERVINGS

- 1⅓ cups defatted chicken broth
- 1 medium onion, chopped
- 2 tablespoons lemon juice
- 1 tablespoon olive oil
- 1 tablespoon finely chopped fresh ginger
- 1 tablespoon paprika
- 1 teaspoon ground coriander
- ¾ teaspoon ground allspice
- ½ teaspoon ground cardamom
- ¼ teaspoon salt
- ⅛ teaspoon ground black pepper
- 1 boneless turkey breast half (1¼ pounds), skin removed
- 5 large carrots, cut into 1″ pieces
- 5 large potatoes, peeled and cut into eighths
- 4 large onions, quartered

In a Dutch oven, stir together the broth, chopped onions, lemon juice, oil, ginger, paprika, coriander, allspice, cardamom, salt and pepper.

Add the turkey and bring to a boil over medium-high heat. Reduce the heat, cover and gently simmer for 8 minutes. Turn the turkey over and continue simmering, covered, for 8 minutes more.

Layer the carrots, potatoes and quartered onions around the turkey. Cover and simmer for 25 to 30 minutes, or until the vegetables and turkey are tender.

To serve, slice the turkey. Then arrange the turkey and vegetables on a deep serving platter. Spoon the broth mixture over the turkey and vegetables.

THINK AHEAD: To save even more time on a busy weekday evening, cook the turkey and vegetables ahead. Slice the turkey. Reheat in the microwave.

Per serving: 313 calories, 5.3 g. total fat (15% of calories), 1.2 g. saturated fat, 49 mg. cholesterol, 222 mg. sodium

Turkey Tortilla Roll-Ups

When you need dinner on the table in less than 15 minutes, serve these turkey roll-ups. To keep the preparation quick, use either leftover cooked turkey breast or turkey breast from the deli. Serve the tortillas topped with nonfat sour cream and additional salsa.

MAKES 10 SERVINGS

- 2 cups chopped broccoli, zucchini or cauliflower
- 1 medium onion, chopped
- 10 ounces cooked and chopped turkey breast
- 1½ cups reduced-sodium salsa
- ¾ cup (3 ounces) finely shredded fat-free Cheddar cheese
- ½ cup (2 ounces) shredded reduced-fat Cheddar cheese
- 10 flour tortillas (8″ diameter)

In a medium microwave-safe bowl, mix the broccoli, zucchini or cauliflower and the onions. Cover with a piece of wax paper. Microwave on high power for a total of 3 to 4 minutes, or until the vegetables are tender; stop and stir after 1½ minutes.

Stir in the turkey and the salsa. Set aside.

In a small bowl, toss together the fat-free cheese and reduced-fat cheese.

Place a tortilla on a flat work surface. Spoon about 3 tablespoons of the turkey mixture in the center, slightly off-center. Sprinkle with a scant 2 tablespoons of the cheese mixture. Then carefully roll up the tortilla and place it, seam side down, on a baking sheet. Repeat to use all the tortillas, turkey mixture and cheese.

Broil the tortillas 2″ from the heat for 3 to 4 minutes, or just until the cheese melts.

THINK AHEAD: These roll-ups store well and can be reheated in the microwave. To reheat, place one tortilla on a microwave-safe plate. Cover with a piece of wax paper and microwave on high power for 30 seconds, or until heated through.

Per serving: 402 calories, 8.7 g. total fat (19% of calories), 2.9 g. saturated fat, 62 mg. cholesterol, 612 mg. sodium

Hearty Beef & Pork Dinners

New-Fashioned Beef Stew

*T*his version has the same robust flavor as a long-simmered beef stew, but you make it in less time using the microwave.

MAKES 6 SERVINGS

- 2 cups finely chopped onions
- 1 large clove garlic, minced
- 1½ cups defatted chicken broth
- 1 pound beef top round steak, trimmed of all visible fat and cut diagonally into bite-size strips
- 2 tablespoons all-purpose flour
- ½ cup burgundy wine or nonalcoholic red wine
- 1 can (15 ounces) tomato sauce
- 1 tablespoon Dijon mustard
- 1½ teaspoons dried thyme
- 1 teaspoon dried marjoram
- 1 large bay leaf
- ¼ teaspoon ground black pepper
- 1 pound potatoes, cut into ¾" cubes
- 2 cups green beans cut into 1" pieces
- 2 large carrots, sliced
- ½ teaspoon salt (optional)

In a 3-quart microwave-safe casserole, combine the onions, garlic and 3 tablespoons of the broth. Cover and microwave on high power for a total of 8 to 9 minutes, or until the onions are tender; stop and stir after 4 minutes.

Spread the beef in a single layer in a shallow baking pan. Sprinkle with the flour and toss until coated. Broil 2" from the heat for a total of 5 to 7 minutes, or until the meat is browned on both sides; stir once or twice during this time.

Stir the wine, tomato sauce, mustard, thyme, marjoram, bay leaf, pepper and the remaining broth into the casserole. Mix well. Add the beef, potatoes, beans and carrots.

Cover and microwave for a total of 20 to 25 minutes, or until the vegetables are tender; stop and stir the mixture after 8, 12 and 15 minutes. Remove and discard the bay leaf. Stir in the salt (if using).

Per serving: 314 calories, 5.2 g. total fat (15% of calories), 1.7 g. saturated fat, 68 mg. cholesterol, 717 mg. sodium

---

≫ Tips from the Family Chef ≪

HEALTHY STEWS

*I*f you are in a stew over what to make for dinner, you are in the right place, according to Sharon Tyler Herbst, a California-based food consultant and author of seven books on food, including *The Food Lover's Tiptionary*.

Stews are easily prepared ahead of time and can be reheated in minutes. In fact, for maximum flavor, says Sharon, it really is best to make stew a day or two before eating it. That lets the flavors meld and heighten.

"A bonus is that any fat in the stew will float to the surface and solidify, making it easier to remove."

Here are some other stew-related tips that Sharon offers.

- Add vegetables to a stew toward the end of the cooking time so they retain their texture.
- To rescue a stew that's too garlicky, place a handful of parsley in a tea caddy or a piece of cheesecloth tied with a string. Add to the stew and simmer for ten minutes; remove.

- Use a puree of cooked vegetables (potatoes, carrots or onions, for example) as a low-fat thickener. Or stir in instant mashed potato flakes or soft bread crumbs; add a tablespoon or two at a time and cook for a minute before determining whether more is needed.

Round Steak
with Roasted Vegetables

$\mathcal{F}$or this quick pot-roast dinner, we cut the meat into thin strips and partially cook the vegetables in a microwave.

MAKES 6 SERVINGS

- 3 large potatoes, peeled and cut into 1¼" pieces
- 6 medium onions, quartered
- 2 medium carrots, cut into ½" slices
- 1 large turnip, peeled and cut into 1" cubes
- 2 cloves garlic, sliced
- 1 teaspoon dried thyme
- 1 teaspoon dried basil
- 1 pound boneless beef round steak, trimmed of all visible fat and thinly sliced on the diagonal into 3" strips
- ¼ teaspoon salt (optional)
- ⅛ teaspoon ground black pepper
- 2 tablespoons defatted beef broth
- 1 tablespoon canola oil

In a 3-quart microwave-safe casserole, stir together the potatoes, onions, carrots, turnips, garlic, ½ teaspoon of the thyme and ½ teaspoon of the basil.

Cover the casserole with wax paper. Microwave on high power for a total of 10 minutes; stop and stir after 5 minutes.

Spread the meat in a roasting pan. Sprinkle with the salt (if using), pepper and the remaining ½ teaspoon thyme and ½ teaspoon basil. Roast at 400° for 10 minutes; stir occasionally during roasting.

Stir the broth and oil into the vegetables. Then spread the vegetables on top of the meat and pour any liquid from the casserole over all.

Roast, stirring occasionally, for 35 to 40 minutes, or until the potatoes are tender and begin to brown. (If needed, add more broth during roasting.)

Per serving: 291 calories, 6.6 g. total fat (20% of calories), 1.3 g. saturated fat, 47 mg. cholesterol, 91 mg. sodium

Swiss-Style Steak and Potatoes

$\mathcal{P}$artially cooking the potatoes in a microwave lets you get a quick start on preparing this dish.

- 5 cups thinly sliced small red potatoes
- 1 large onion, chopped
- 1 small clove garlic, minced
- 1 pound beef top round steak, trimmed of all visible fat and diagonally cut into thin 1" strips
- 1 can (15 ounces) reduced-sodium tomato sauce
- ⅓ cup ketchup
- 1 tablespoon packed brown sugar
- 1 tablespoon cider vinegar
- ½ teaspoon dried thyme
- ¼ teaspoon salt (optional)
- ⅛ teaspoon ground black pepper
- 1 large bay leaf

In a 2½-quart microwave-safe casserole, combine the potatoes, onions and garlic. Cover and microwave on high power for a total of 5 to 6 minutes, or until the potatoes are partially cooked; stop and stir after 3 minutes.

Meanwhile, lightly coat a Dutch oven or large saucepan with no-stick spray. Add the beef. Sauté over medium heat until the strips are browned. Stir in the tomato sauce, ketchup, brown sugar, vinegar, thyme, salt (if using), pepper and bay leaf.

Stir in the potato mixture. Bring to a boil, then reduce the heat. Cover and gently simmer for 25 to 30 minutes, or until the beef is tender. Remove and discard the bay leaf.

Per serving: 381 calories, 5.5 g. total fat (13% of calories), 1.9 g. saturated fat, 52 mg. cholesterol, 240 mg. sodium

---

Tangy Slow-Cooked Beef

*G*rating the vegetables before cooking them gives the sauce thick body and rich flavor. To speed up this process, you can cut the vegetables into chunks and finely chop them in a food processor.

MAKES 6 SERVINGS

- 1 **can (15 ounces) reduced-sodium tomato sauce**
- 1 **large onion, grated**
- 1 **carrot, grated**
- 1 **stalk celery, grated**
- ⅓ **cup ketchup**
- 1 **tablespoon packed brown sugar**
- 1 **tablespoon cider vinegar**
- 1 **teaspoon dried thyme**
- ½ **teaspoon dry mustard**
- 1 **small clove garlic, minced**
- ⅛ **teaspoon ground black pepper**
- 2–3 **drops hot-pepper sauce**
- 1 **pound beef flank steak, trimmed of all visible fat**
- 10 **ounces yolk-free egg noodles**

In a 6-quart Crock-Pot or other slow-cooker, stir together the tomato sauce, onions, carrots, celery, ketchup, brown sugar, vinegar, thyme, mustard, garlic, black pepper and hot-pepper sauce.

Add the meat, then spoon some of the sauce mixture over it. Cover and cook on the high heat setting for 1 hour. Stir, then reduce the heat setting to low. Cook, covered, for 4 to 4½ hours, or until the meat is tender.

Transfer the meat to a cutting board. Using a sharp knife, cut the meat across the grain into thin slices.

Just before serving, cook the noodles in a large pot of boiling water for 5 minutes, or until just tender. Drain, rinse with hot water and drain again. Serve topped with the meat and sauce.

Per serving: 371 calories, 6.5 g. total fat (16% of calories), 2.5 g. saturated fat, 35 mg. cholesterol, 538 mg. sodium

---

Pepper Steak Stir-Fry and Rice

To ensure maximum tenderness of the meat, it's important to thinly slice it across the grain. To cut the meat easily, partially freeze it (30 to 45 minutes is usually sufficient).

Makes 4 servings

1¼ cups long-grain white rice
1 pound beef top round steak, trimmed of all visible fat and partially frozen
3 tablespoons ketchup
2½ tablespoons reduced-sodium soy sauce
1 large clove garlic, minced
3 teaspoons peanut oil
2 small sweet red or green peppers, cut into julienne strips
10 scallions, quartered lengthwise and cut into 1¼" pieces
½ cup defatted beef broth
¼ cup water
1 tablespoon cornstarch
1 teaspoon paprika
1 teaspoon chili powder

Cook the rice according to the package directions.

While the rice is cooking, cut the beef across the grain into very thin bite-size strips. Transfer to a small bowl. Add the ketchup, soy sauce and garlic. Stir until the meat is coated.

Warm 1 teaspoon of the oil in a large skillet over medium-high heat. Add half of the beef mixture. Cook and stir for 3 minutes; transfer the meat to a bowl. Repeat with the remaining meat; transfer to the bowl.

Heat the remaining 2 teaspoons oil in the same pan. Add the peppers and scallions. Sauté for 3 to 4 minutes, or until the scallions are almost tender.

In a small bowl, stir together the broth, water, cornstarch, paprika and chili powder until smooth. Slowly stir the mixture into the pan. Add the beef.

Stir-fry until the mixture begins to thicken. Serve over the rice.

Per serving: 339 calories, 7 g. total fat (19% of calories), 1.6 g. saturated fat, 66 mg. cholesterol, 581 mg. sodium

---

Round Steak Stir-Fry

Since round steak is very lean, it gives beef lovers the opportunity to indulge and still control their intake of fat and cholesterol. If desired, you can combine the beef and seasoning mixture ahead and let it marinate in the refrigerator for up to 24 hours.

MAKES 4 SERVINGS

1⅓ cups long-grain white rice
¼ cup orange juice
3 tablespoons Dijon mustard
2½ tablespoons reduced-sodium soy sauce
1 tablespoon finely chopped onions
1 teaspoon lemon juice
1 teaspoon curry powder
⅛ teaspoon ground black pepper
1 pound top round steak, trimmed of all fat
½ cup cold water
2½ teaspoons cornstarch
1 tablespoon peanut oil
2 cups small broccoli florets
2 cups small cauliflower florets
¼ cup diced sweet red peppers
2 tablespoons sliced scallions

Cook the rice according to the package directions.

Meanwhile, in a shallow baking dish large enough to hold the steak, stir together the orange juice, mustard, soy sauce, onions, lemon juice, curry powder and black pepper. Add the steak; turn to coat both sides. Set aside for 20 minutes.

Remove the steak from the marinade; reserve the marinade. Using a large sharp knife, cut the steak across the grain into very thin slices.

Add the water and cornstarch to the reserved marinade and stir to blend the mixture and dissolve the cornstarch.

Add the oil to a large no-stick skillet and place over medium-high heat until hot but not smoking. Add the broccoli, cauliflower, red peppers and scallions. Stir-fry for 2 minutes. Add the beef; stir-fry for 2 minutes longer.

Add the marinade. Cook and stir until the liquid thickens and the vegetables are crisp-tender. Serve over the rice.

Per serving: 400 calories, 7.2 g. total fat (16% of calories), 1.6 g. saturated fat, 49 mg. cholesterol, 567 mg. sodium

---

Quick Chili with Beans

*T*his recipe is ready quite quickly because it cooks in the microwave. Extending the meat with bulgur helps keep the chili low in fat. And because bulgur has a similar texture to the cooked ground beef and easily absorbs seasonings, your family won't known they're actually eating less meat than usual.

MAKES 6 SERVINGS

1¼	cups boiling water
½	cup bulgur
12	ounces ground beef round
2	cups finely chopped onions
½	large green pepper, chopped
2	cloves garlic, minced
3	cans (15 ounces each) no-salt-added kidney beans, rinsed and drained
2	cans (15 ounces each) reduced-sodium tomato sauce
1½	tablespoons chili powder
¼	teaspoon salt (optional)
¼	teaspoon ground black pepper
1	teaspoon sugar

In a small bowl, stir together the water and bulgur; set aside for 15 minutes.

Meanwhile, in a 3-quart microwave-safe casserole, stir together the beef, onions, green peppers and garlic. Cover and microwave on high power for a total of 5 to 7 minutes, or until the meat is browned; stop and stir the mixture every 2 minutes to break up the meat. Break up any remaining large pieces of meat.

(continued)

Drain the meat mixture in a strainer or colander, then transfer it to a large plate lined with paper towels. Blot the top of the meat mixture with additional paper towels. Return the mixture to the casserole.

Stir in the beans, tomato sauce, chili powder, salt (if using), black pepper and sugar.

Cover and microwave on high power for a total of 8 minutes; stop and stir after 4 minutes.

Drain the bulgur well in a strainer. Stir it into the meat mixture. Cover and microwave for a total of 8 minutes; stop and stir after 4 minutes.

Per serving: 438 calories, 8.3 g. total fat (17% of calories), 2.7 g. saturated fat, 35 mg. cholesterol, 102 mg. sodium

---

❧ Tips from the Family Chef ❧

SET THE MOOD

*A*lthough he is classically trained in French cuisine, Jay Schaeffer, chef of the Green Hills Inn near Reading, Pennsylvania, knows that a meal is composed of more than just food. So even when serving hurry-up meals at home, Jay and his wife, Sue, create an atmosphere that is pleasing to all the senses.

"It doesn't matter if we are having only hamburgers, we still set the table with cloth napkins," Jay says. "Just a little thing like that can change the whole environment of the meal." And they make sure to accompany the meal with soothing music and pleasant conversation.

Jay also makes the effort to attractively garnish the food. Even simple soups, chili and stews rate a twist of lemon or lime, a flower from the garden or something else that pleases the eye.

Slow-Simmered Tex-Mex Chili

*E*njoy having a hot meal waiting for you when you come home from work. To keep early morning meal preparation to a minimum, cook the meat mixture the night before and refrigerate it. Then, in the morning, just add it to the slow-cooker with the other ingredients.

MAKES 6 SERVINGS

1	pound ground beef round
1½	cups finely chopped onions
1	clove garlic, minced
1	can (15 ounces) reduced-sodium tomato sauce
1	cup reduced-sodium salsa
1½	tablespoons chili powder
1	tablespoon cider vinegar
½	tablespoon packed brown sugar
2	teaspoons Worcestershire sauce
¼	teaspoon ground black pepper
3	cans (15 ounces each) no-salt-added kidney beans, rinsed and drained
2	cups frozen whole kernel corn

Place the beef, onions and garlic in a large no-stick skillet. Cook over medium-high heat, breaking up the beef with a spoon, until the beef is browned and the vegetables are tender. Drain the mixture in a strainer or colander, then transfer it to a large plate lined with paper towels. Blot the top of the mixture with additional paper towels, then return it to the skillet.

In a 6-quart Crock-Pot or other slow-cooker, stir together the tomato sauce, salsa, chili powder, vinegar, brown sugar, Worcestershire sauce and pepper. Stir in the beef mixture, beans and corn. Cover and cook on the low heat setting for 7 to 9 hours.

THINK AHEAD: Cover and store any leftover chili in the refrigerator for up to 4 days for a speedy lunch or supper.

Per serving: 396 calories, 9.8 g. total fat (21% of calories), 3.1 g. saturated fat, 40 mg. cholesterol, 220 mg. sodium

---

SAFETY FIRST

Kids have a natural curiosity about cooking and can easily be encouraged to become directly involved with food preparation. Often they're much more inclined to eat healthier foods if they've helped make them.

What's more, it is rewarding to watch a youngster's imagination run wild in the kitchen, says Nancie McDermott, author of *The 5 in 10 Pasta and Noodle Cookbook*. But for safety's sake, there are some precautions that adults should take to keep youthful culinary adventures free of accidents.

Nancie, who teaches cooking classes for disadvantaged children in south-central Los Angeles, says her students enjoy chopping food but that some of them are too young to handle sharp knives. The solution in that case, says Nancie, is to have an adult chop hard ingredients, such as carrots, and to teach kids to chop softer foods using plastic knives with a serrated edge. This works with green peppers, onions, garlic, tomatoes, herbs and such. And kids love it.

Nancie has some other rules for kids in the kitchen.

- Don't put knives in a sink full of dishwater. Somebody else could reach in there and get cut. Always be aware of where sharp knives are, and when you are handling them, be aware of where other people are.
- When you are taking something hot out of the oven, make sure you warn people where you are going with it so that they don't get in your way.
- Concentrate on what you are doing. Turn off the oven and the stove burners as soon as you are finished with them.

Nancie also advises parents not to be too picky when they are presented with a kid-made meal. "Adults tend to be perfectionists when it comes to food," she says. But it doesn't matter if the meals don't look like the pictures in the cookbook. With a little practice, the food will be tasty and the kids will love it more because they made it, she says.

Polynesian Marinated Flank Steak

*P*ineapple juice adds a wonderful tropical flavor to flank steak in this recipe. It also helps to break down the tough fibers in the meat during the marinating process, resulting in a tender, juicy steak. Because the meat really benefits from marinating, be sure to allow 6 to 24 hours for the process.

MAKES 4 SERVINGS

- 1 **pound beef flank steak, trimmed of all visible fat**
- ½ **cup pineapple juice**
- 2 **tablespoons dry sherry or nonalcoholic wine**
- 2 **tablespoons reduced-sodium soy sauce**
- 1 **tablespoon cider vinegar**
- 2 **teaspoons packed brown sugar**
- ½ **teaspoon ground ginger**
- 2–3 **drops hot-pepper sauce**
- 1 **small onion, finely chopped**
- 1 **clove garlic, minced**

Place the steak in a large resealable storage bag.

In a small bowl, stir together the pineapple juice, sherry or wine, soy sauce, vinegar, brown sugar, ginger and hot-pepper sauce. Stir in the onions and garlic.

Pour the mixture over the meat. Seal the bag and marinate in the refrigerator for 6 to 24 hours, turning the bag occasionally.

Remove the steak from the bag; reserve the marinade. Place the steak on the rack of a broiling pan. Broil 3″ from the heat for 6 minutes. Turn the meat over and spoon several teaspoons of the reserved marinade over the meat; discard the remaining marinade.

Broil for 6 to 8 minutes more for medium doneness. Transfer the meat to a cutting board. Let stand for 10 minutes.

To serve, use a sharp knife to cut the meat across the grain into thin slices.

Per serving: 203 calories, 7.5 g. total fat (35% of calories), 3.3 g. saturated fat, 46 mg. cholesterol, 135 mg. sodium

---

Potatoes Topped with Italian Beef and Vegetables

*T*his is just the thing to have on hand when your family operates on different dinner schedules. You can cook the whole batch and keep it in the refrigerator to reheat in the microwave as needed. We use cauliflower and zucchini as our vegetable choices, but you could substitute other vegetables, such as broccoli, mushrooms, eggplant and Italian beans.

MAKES 4 SERVINGS

8	ounces ground beef round
1	large onion, finely chopped
1	large carrot, grated or finely shredded
1	clove garlic, minced
1	can (15 ounces) reduced-sodium tomato sauce
1	cup finely chopped cauliflower florets
1	cup chopped zucchini
2	teaspoons dried Italian seasoning
¼	teaspoon salt (optional)
¼	teaspoon ground black pepper
4	large baking potatoes (8 ounces each)
2	tablespoons grated Parmesan cheese

In a 3-quart microwave-safe casserole, stir together the beef, onions, carrots and garlic. Cover and microwave on high power for a total of 7 to 8 minutes, or until the meat is browned; stop and stir every 3 minutes to break up the meat. Break up any remaining large pieces of meat.

Drain the meat mixture in a strainer or colander, then transfer it to a large plate lined with paper towels. Blot the top of the meat mixture with additional paper towels. Return the mixture to the casserole.

Add the tomato sauce, cauliflower, zucchini, Italian seasoning, salt (if using) and pepper. Cover and microwave for a total of 4 to 5 minutes, or until heated through; stop and stir after 2 minutes.

Pierce each potato in several places with a fork. Arrange on a microwave-safe plate like the spokes of a wheel. Microwave on high power for a total of

15 minutes, or until the potatoes are easily pierced with a sharp knife; stop and turn the potatoes over after 10 minutes. Let stand for 5 minutes.

Cut a lengthwise slit in each potato, then gently push in on the ends of the potato to slightly open the slit. Fluff the potato pulp with a fork. Then spoon the beef mixture on top of each potato. Serve sprinkled with the cheese.

Per serving: 422 calories, 8.2 g. total fat (17% of calories), 3.4 g. saturated fat, 38 mg. cholesterol, 151 mg. sodium

Hamburger Stroganoff

If you loved Mom's hamburger stroganoff while growing up, you'll enjoy this updated version, too. We use fat-free sour cream and add a blend of vegetables to cut fat but not flavor.

MAKES 6 SERVINGS

1	pound ground beef round
2	cups chopped onions
8	ounces mushrooms, sliced
1	large clove garlic, minced
1½	cups defatted beef broth
3	tablespoons tomato paste
1	carrot, thinly sliced
1	cup finely chopped cauliflower florets
1½	teaspoons prepared horseradish
1	teaspoon dried thyme
½	teaspoon salt (optional)
¼	teaspoon ground black pepper
1	large bay leaf
12	ounces medium yolk-free egg noodles
¾	cup fat-free sour cream

Place the beef, onions, mushrooms and garlic in a large no-stick skillet. Cook over medium-high heat, breaking up the beef with a spoon, until the beef is browned and the vegetables are tender. Drain the mixture in a strainer or colander, then transfer it to a large plate lined with paper towels. Blot the top of the mixture with additional paper towels, then return it to the skillet.

Stir in the broth and tomato paste until well-combined. Add the carrots, cauliflower, horseradish, thyme, salt (if using), pepper and bay leaf. Stir until well-combined. Bring to a boil, then reduce the heat. Cover and simmer, stirring occasionally, for 20 minutes, or until the vegetables are tender.

Meanwhile, cook the noodles in a large pot of boiling water for 8 minutes, or until just tender. Drain and rinse with hot water. Drain again.

Remove and discard the bay leaf from the meat mixture. Reduce the heat to low. Stir in the sour cream. Cook gently for 2 to 3 minutes, or until heated through. (Do not boil.) Serve over the noodles.

Per serving: 414 calories, 9.9 g. total fat (21% of calories), 3.7 g. saturated fat, 47 mg. cholesterol, 255 mg. sodium

Beef and Noodle Casserole

You might call this lasagna casserole. It's made with small lasagna-shaped noodles called mafalda. If your store doesn't carry them, you can substitute twists, macaroni, ziti or other medium pasta shapes.

MAKES 6 SERVINGS

- 8 ounces mafalda
- 1 medium onion, chopped
- 12 ounces ground beef round
- 1 clove garlic, minced
- 2 cans (15 ounces each) reduced-sodium tomato sauce
- ½ cup chopped fresh parsley
- 2 tablespoons water

1 tablespoon tomato paste
1 tablespoon dried Italian seasoning
¼ teaspoon salt (optional)
    Pinch of ground black pepper
1¼ cups fat-free ricotta cheese
1 cup (4 ounces) finely shredded fat-free or reduced-fat mozzarella cheese
4 tablespoons grated Parmesan cheese

Cook the mafalda in a large pot of boiling water for 10 minutes, or until just tender. Drain, rinse with hot water and drain again.

Meanwhile, place the onions in a 3-quart microwave-safe casserole. Cover and microwave on high power for 3 to 4 minutes, or until tender. Stir in the beef and garlic. Cover and microwave for a total of 5 to 7 minutes, or until the meat is browned; stop and stir every 2 minutes to break up the meat. Break up any remaining large pieces of meat.

Drain the meat mixture in a strainer or colander, then transfer it to a large plate lined with paper towels. Blot the top of the meat mixture with additional paper towels. Return the mixture to the casserole.

Stir in the tomato sauce, parsley, water, tomato paste, Italian seasoning, salt (if using) and pepper. Cover and microwave for a total of 8 to 9 minutes, or until heated through; stop and stir after 4 minutes.

Using a ladle, remove 4 cups of the sauce mixture and set aside. Top the remaining sauce in the casserole with half of the mafalda. Add half of the ricotta and use the back of a large spoon to evenly spread the cheese. Sprinkle with the mozzarella and top with 2 cups of the reserved sauce.

Add the remaining mafalda and sprinkle with 2 tablespoons of the Parmesan. Cover with the remaining 2 cups sauce.

Cover and microwave for a total of 5 to 6 minutes; stop and rotate the casserole a quarter turn after 3 minutes.

Sprinkle with the remaining 2 tablespoons Parmesan. Microwave for 1 to 2 minutes more, or until heated through. Let stand for 5 minutes before serving.

Per serving: 383 calories, 8.8 g. total fat (20% of calories), 3.5 g. saturated fat, 49 mg. cholesterol, 281 mg. sodium

Quick Spaghetti Sauce with Pasta

Here's a homemade spaghetti sauce that cooks quickly and is chock-full of vegetables for a fiber-rich meal. To save time, chop and grate the vegetables in a food processor.

MAKES 6 SERVINGS

- 1 cup chopped onions
- 1 cup grated cabbage
- 1 large carrot, grated
- 8 ounces ground beef round
- 8 ounces coarsely chopped mushrooms
- 2 large cloves garlic, minced
- 2 cans (15 ounces each) reduced-sodium tomato sauce
- ¼ cup water
- 2 tablespoons tomato paste
- 1 tablespoon dried Italian seasoning
- ½ teaspoon salt (optional)
- ¼ teaspoon ground black pepper
- 2 large bay leaves
- 12 ounces spaghettini

In a 3-quart microwave-safe casserole, combine the onions, cabbage and carrots. Cover and microwave on high power for a total of 6 to 7 minutes; stop and stir after 3 minutes.

Stir in the beef, mushrooms and garlic. Cover and microwave for a total of 5 to 7 minutes, or until the meat is browned; stop and stir every 2 minutes to break up the meat. Break up any remaining large pieces of meat.

Drain the meat mixture in a strainer or colander, then transfer it to a large plate lined with paper towels. Blot the top of the meat mixture with additional paper towels. Return the mixture to the casserole.

Stir in the tomato sauce, water, tomato paste, Italian seasoning, salt (if using), pepper and bay leaves.

Cover and microwave for a total of 13 to 16 minutes, or until heated through; stop and stir the mixture every 4 minutes. Remove and discard the bay leaves.

Meanwhile, cook the spaghettini in a large pot of boiling water for 5 minutes, or until just tender. Drain, rinse with hot water and drain again. Serve topped with the sauce.

Per serving: 334 calories, 7 g. total fat (18% of calories), 1.9 g. saturated fat, 23 mg. cholesterol, 208 mg. sodium

---

It's So Easy... It's Kid Stuff

THE DISCOVERY OF PASTA

*M*arco Polo is credited with bringing pasta to the Western world, but Ian Forester said he was 8 years old when he and his father discovered how to make it.

"My dad loves to cook on weekends," says Ian, who is now 13. "One day I went into the kitchen and asked if there was anything I could do. My dad said he was going to make spaghetti, but he just noticed we were out of store-bought pasta. So I asked him how they make spaghetti. He said he didn't know, but we looked it up in a cookbook."

The book showed that pasta was simply flour, eggs and salt. So the two started mixing. It was easy. They kneaded the dough until it was smooth and shiny and then allowed it to rest awhile. Then Ian took an old rolling pin to the ball of dough.

"It was fun. I rolled it out until it was a thin, flat sheet. We didn't have a pasta machine, so my dad just took a knife and cut off thin pieces. We put it in boiling water, and we had pasta."

The next Father's Day, Ian's dad got a pasta machine, and the two established a weekend ritual of making pasta together.

Other things Ian learned from his father include remembering to curl his fingers under when holding things to slice with a knife. He's gotten so proficient that he makes up a lot of his own meals now. One of his favorite treats is his tuna and bean burrito. He makes it by mixing a can of tuna with a can of refried beans and spreading it on a soft taco shell. Then he folds it in half and quickly bakes it or pan-sautés it.

Taco Casserole

We took all the wonderful flavors found in tacos and put them into a one-dish entrée. It's special enough for a party or potluck affair, but it's easy enough for a weekday dinner.

MAKES 8 SERVINGS

- 8 ounces ground beef round
- 8 ounces ground turkey breast
- 1 large onion, finely chopped
- 1 clove garlic, minced
- 2 cans (15 ounces each) reduced-sodium tomato sauce
- 2 cans (15 ounces each) no-salt-added kidney beans, rinsed and drained
- 2 tablespoons canned diced green chili peppers
- 1 tablespoon chili powder
- 1 teaspoon ground cumin
- ¼ teaspoon salt (optional)
- ¼ teaspoon ground black pepper
- 1 package (9 ounces) corn tortillas (6″ diameter)
- 1 cup (4 ounces) finely shredded reduced-fat sharp Cheddar cheese
- 2½ cups shredded lettuce
- 2 large tomatoes, chopped

Lightly coat a 13″ × 9″ baking pan with no-stick spray and set aside.

Place the beef, turkey, onions and garlic in a large no-stick skillet. Cook over medium-high heat, breaking up the meat with a spoon, until the meat is browned and the vegetables are tender. Drain the mixture in a strainer or colander, then transfer it to a large plate lined with paper towels. Blot the top of the mixture with additional paper towels, then return it to the skillet.

Stir in the tomato sauce, beans, chili peppers, chili powder, cumin, salt (if using) and black pepper.

Spread half of the mixture in the prepared baking pan. Place the tortillas on top, overlapping them to cover the entire surface. Top with the remaining meat mixture.

Bake at 375° for 30 to 35 minutes, or until the sauce is bubbly. Sprinkle with the cheese and bake for 2 to 3 minutes more to melt the cheese. Serve topped with the lettuce and tomatoes.

Per serving: 290 calories, 5.6 g. total fat (17% of calories), 1.7 g. saturated fat, 30 mg. cholesterol, 536 mg. sodium

≫ Tips from the Family Chef ≪

WHEN SECOND BEST CAN DO

Fresh is always best. But there are times when you don't have fresh foods on hand, or you don't have time to prepare them. In that case, says Jeanne Jones, author of *Cook It Light*, look to your pantry for the next-best thing.

"If you come home from work and decide to make a bean dish, it's too late to soak the beans overnight. So use canned beans. They're an easy and acceptable alternative," says Jeanne. Just make sure you rinse them to help remove some of the sodium that canned beans contain.

Jeanne also keeps cans of broth on hand. She stores a few in the refrigerator—for a very healthy reason: "The fat congeals when it's cold and is easier to remove."

Fresh tomatoes are a delight when they are in season. But when they aren't, Jeanne reaches for canned tomatoes. "They were picked and processed at the height of the season," she says. "And in most sauces, canned tomatoes work just fine." To save money, she suggests buying the biggest size cans and dividing them into small amounts that you can freeze for use as needed.

Saucy Meatball Dinner

*T*o create these low-fat meatballs, we combined lean ground round with bulgur, which not only lowers the amount of fat but also helps keep the meatballs juicy.

MAKES 6 SERVINGS

Meatballs

- 1 cup boiling water
- ½ cup bulgur
- 1 egg white, lightly beaten
- 2 teaspoons chili powder
- ¾ teaspoon salt (optional)
- 1 clove garlic, minced
- ½ teaspoon dried thyme
- ¼ teaspoon ground black pepper
- 1 pound ground beef round
- 1 small onion, finely chopped

Saucy Vegetables and Rice

- 1 can (15 ounces) reduced-sodium tomato sauce
- ½ cup ketchup
- ½ cup defatted beef broth
- 2 teaspoons sugar
- 1 teaspoon Dijon mustard
- 2 teaspoons cider vinegar
- 1 large bay leaf
- 2 large carrots, thinly sliced
- 2 cups frozen cut green beans
- 2 cups thinly sliced cabbage
- 1 cup long-grain white rice

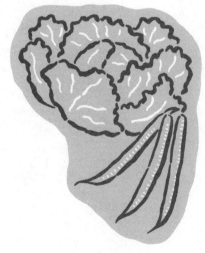

To make the meatballs: In a small bowl, stir together the water and bulgur; set aside for 15 minutes.

Coat a 15″ × 10″ baking pan with no-stick spray and set aside.

In a large bowl, stir together the egg white, chili powder, salt (if using), garlic, thyme and pepper. Add the beef and onions; mix until well-combined.

Drain the bulgur well in a strainer. Add the bulgur to the meat mixture and mix well. Form into 36 medium balls.

Place the meatballs in a single layer in the prepared pan. Bake at 325° for 10 to 12 minutes, or until the meatballs are browned on all sides.

To make the saucy vegetables and rice: While the bulgur is soaking, combine the tomato sauce, ketchup, broth, sugar, mustard, vinegar and bay leaf in a Dutch oven or large saucepan. Stir to mix well. Add the carrots, beans and cabbage. Cover and bring to a boil over medium-high heat. Reduce the heat to medium.

Using a slotted spoon, transfer the meatballs to the pan. Cover and simmer, stirring occasionally, for 20 to 25 minutes, or until the vegetables are tender.

While the vegetables are cooking, cook the rice according to the package directions.

Remove and discard the bay leaf from the vegetable mixture. Serve the meatballs and saucy vegetables over the rice.

THINK AHEAD: This is a good recipe to prepare in the evening for the next day's dinner. You can even cook the rice ahead. Refrigerate the meatballs and sauce right in their pan; at dinnertime, simply reheat them. Place the rice in a large microwave-safe bowl, add a few tablespoons of water, cover the bowl with vented plastic wrap and microwave on high power for 3 minutes, or until heated through.

Per serving: 394 calories, 10 g. total fat (23% of calories), 3.7 g. saturated fat, 47 mg. cholesterol, 458 mg. sodium

Tex-Mex Meatballs with Spicy Sauce

*T*hese zesty meatballs are made with half lean beef and half ground turkey breast, which keeps them low in fat. Serve them over rice or pasta.

MAKES 4 SERVINGS

- 2 egg whites, lightly beaten
- ¼ cup tomato paste
- ¼ cup canned diced green chili peppers
- 2 tablespoons Worcestershire sauce
- 1 tablespoon chili powder
- 1 teaspoon dried oregano
- ¼ teaspoon celery salt
- ¾ cup fresh bread crumbs
- ¼ cup finely chopped scallions
- 8 ounces ground beef round
- 8 ounces ground turkey breast
- 1 can (14½ ounces) plum tomatoes (with juice), cut up
- 3 tablespoons picante sauce
- 3 tablespoons finely chopped fresh cilantro

Coat a 15″ × 10″ baking pan with no-stick spray and set aside.

In a large bowl, stir together the egg whites, tomato paste, chili peppers, Worcestershire sauce, chili powder, oregano and celery salt. Then stir in the bread crumbs and scallions. Add the beef and turkey; mix well.

Form the mixture into 20 meatballs. Place the meatballs in a single layer in the prepared pan. Bake at 375° for 10 to 12 minutes, or until cooked through (test by cutting open a meatball). Transfer to a serving bowl and cover to keep warm.

While the meatballs are baking, combine the tomatoes (with juice), picante sauce and cilantro in a small saucepan. Heat through. Spoon over the meatballs.

Per serving: 205 calories, 5.8 g. total fat (26% of calories), 1.8 g. saturated fat, 63 mg. cholesterol, 539 mg. sodium

---

Mini Chili Meat Loaves

Mini meat loaves take about half as much time to bake as full-size ones.

MAKES 6 SERVINGS

Meat Loaves

- 1 cup quick-cooking rolled oats
- ⅔ cup ketchup
- ½ cup fat-free egg substitute
- ¼ cup finely chopped scallions
- 2½ tablespoons Worcestershire sauce
- 1½ tablespoons chili powder
- ¼ teaspoon celery salt
- ¼ teaspoon ground black pepper
- ⅛ teaspoon dried thyme
- 12 ounces ground beef round
- 8 ounces ground turkey breast

Sauce

- ⅓ cup ketchup
- 3 tablespoons water
- 2 teaspoons Worcestershire sauce

To make the meat loaves: Line a 15″ × 10″ baking pan with foil. Coat the foil with no-stick spray.

In a large bowl, combine the oats, ketchup, eggs, scallions, Worcestershire sauce, chili powder, celery salt, pepper and thyme. Add the beef and turkey and mix until combined. Shape into 6 oblong loaves (similar in shape to a potato).

Place the loaves on the prepared baking sheet, leaving space between them. Bake at 375° for 30 minutes.

To make the sauce: In a small bowl, stir together the ketchup, water and Worcestershire sauce. Brush the sauce over the meat loaves. Bake for 5 to 10 minutes, or until cooked through and evenly browned on top.

Per serving: 268 calories, 8.4 g. total fat (28% of calories), 2.9 g. saturated fat, 60 mg. cholesterol, 880 mg. sodium

---

Hungarian Goulash

*H*ere's another old-fashioned sour-cream dish that we've updated for today's interest in lower-fat foods.

MAKES 6 SERVINGS

12 ounces ground beef round
1 large onion, finely chopped
2 large stalks celery, sliced
1 large clove garlic, minced
1½ cups defatted beef broth
⅓ cup dry sherry or nonalcoholic wine
1 can (15 ounces) reduced-sodium tomato sauce
2 cups thinly sliced cabbage
2 large carrots, sliced
2 teaspoons paprika
1 teaspoon dried thyme
¼ teaspoon dry mustard
¼ teaspoon ground black pepper
1 large bay leaf
12 ounces thin yolk-free egg noodles
¾ cup fat-free sour cream

Place the beef, onions, celery and garlic in a large no-stick skillet. Cook over medium-high heat, breaking up the beef with a spoon, until the beef is browned and the vegetables are tender. Drain the mixture in a strainer or colander, then transfer it to a large plate lined with paper towels. Blot the top of the mixture with additional paper towels, then return it to the skillet.

Stir in the broth, sherry or wine and tomato sauce; mix well. Add the cabbage, carrots, paprika, thyme, mustard, pepper and bay leaf. Bring to a boil, then reduce the heat. Cover and simmer for 30 minutes, or until the vegetables are tender. Remove and discard the bay leaf.

Cook the noodles in a large pot of boiling water for 5 minutes, or until just tender. Drain and rinse with hot water. Drain again.

Reduce the heat under the skillet to low. Stir in the sour cream and gently heat through. (Do not boil.) Serve over the noodles.

Per serving: 410 calories, 7.8 g. total fat (17% of calories), 2.7 g. saturated fat, 35 mg. cholesterol, 182 mg. sodium

It's So Easy... It's Kid Stuff

HANDS-ON EXPERIENCE

One day I walked into a classroom full of very exuberant fifth-graders to put on a demonstration of fall vegetables," recalls Marian Morash, who has been cooking the produce grown on public television's *The Victory Garden* for more than 20 years.

"I took some boards, knives, sauté pans, hot plates and plenty of cabbage with me. When the kids found out they were going to be cooking cabbage, a universal cry of 'Awwwww' went up," she says. Undaunted by the hostile audience, Marian urged the kids themselves to help her.

"They loved slicing the cabbage," she says, noting that the youngsters were closely supervised by adults in the room. "Then they sautéed the cabbage in a little butter and curry powder."

Although this probably wouldn't be something a bunch of 11-year-olds would order at the burger joint, the dish was consumed eagerly by the kids, who were inspired to try something new because they made it.

"The most important thing a parent can do is get kids involved in the kitchen," Marian says. "Children love to chop and tear things. They get so involved with the food that they are eager to eat it. Have them grate some apples for pancakes in the morning. Let them wash the lettuce for a salad and dry it. More than anything else, let them taste as you go along. Ask them if they think it needs something more. Kids have a wonderful sense of taste."

Sweet-and-Sour Cabbage with Pork

*T*his German dish typically uses pork spare ribs, which are much higher in fat than the pork loin we use here as a replacement.

MAKES 4 SERVINGS

3½ cups peeled and thinly sliced potatoes

1 large onion, finely chopped

2 teaspoons olive oil

1 pound boneless pork loin, trimmed of all visible fat and cut into bite-size pieces

1 can (16 ounces) stewed tomatoes (with juice)

1 can (8 ounces) tomato sauce

2 tablespoons packed brown sugar

1 tablespoon cider vinegar

2 teaspoons caraway seeds

¼ teaspoon ground black pepper

1 bay leaf

4 cups shredded cabbage

In a medium microwave-safe bowl, combine the potatoes and onions. Cover with wax paper and microwave on high power for a total of 7 to 8 minutes, or until the potatoes are almost tender; stop and stir after 4 minutes.

Meanwhile, warm the oil in a Dutch oven or large saucepan over medium heat. Add the pork. Cook, stirring, until the pork is lightly browned. Add the tomatoes (with juice), tomato sauce, brown sugar, vinegar, caraway seeds, pepper and bay leaf. Mix well.

Stir in the potatoes and onions. Layer the cabbage on top. Bring to a boil. Cover and simmer for 15 minutes. Stir the cabbage into the sauce. Cover and cook for 15 minutes more. Remove and discard the bay leaf before serving.

Per serving: 356 calories, 10.2 g. total fat (25% of calories), 3 g. saturated fat, 51 mg. cholesterol, 676 mg. sodium

---

Pork and Sauerkraut Dinner

*S*auerkraut is high in sodium, so we compensated by using reduced-sodium tomato sauce in this dish. If you would like to reduce the sodium even further, use no-salt-added tomato sauce and be sure to rinse the sauerkraut well in a strainer.

MAKES 6 SERVINGS

- 1 package (16 ounces) refrigerated sauerkraut, drained
- 3 cups peeled and thinly sliced potatoes
- 12 ounces boneless pork loin, trimmed of all visible fat and cut into bite-size pieces
- 2 large onions, finely chopped
- 1½ teaspoons caraway seeds
- 1 teaspoon dried thyme
- ⅛ teaspoon ground black pepper
- 2 bay leaves
- 1¼ cups apple juice
- 2 tablespoons packed brown sugar
- 1 can (8 ounces) reduced-sodium tomato sauce

In a 6-quart Crock-Pot or other slow-cooker, stir together the sauerkraut, potatoes, pork, onions, caraway seeds, thyme, pepper and bay leaves.

In a small bowl, stir together the apple juice and brown sugar. Then pour the mixture over the sauerkraut mixture.

Cover and cook on the high heat setting for 1 hour. Stir the mixture and reduce the heat setting to low. Cover and cook for 6 to 7½ hours more.

Stir in the tomato sauce. Cover and cook for 5 minutes, or until hot. Remove and discard the bay leaves.

Per serving: 240 calories, 5.3 g. total fat (20% of calories), 1.8 g. saturated fat, 34 mg. cholesterol, 545 mg. sodium

---

Weekday Cassoulet

*T*his peasant-style French dish is usually made with several fatty meats and poultry. We keep the rich flavor of this classic but make it much leaner by using pork loin, chicken broth and an array of seasonings. We also use canned beans and otherwise simplify the procedure considerably so this cassoulet can be prepared on a weekday.

MAKES 6 SERVINGS

- 1 large onion, chopped
- 1 cup chopped cabbage
- 1 large stalk celery, finely chopped
- 1 large carrot, chopped
- 2 tablespoons dry sherry or nonalcoholic wine
- 2 cloves garlic, minced
- 2 teaspoons olive oil
- 1 pound boneless pork loin, trimmed of all visible fat and cut into bite-size pieces
- 2 cans (19 ounces each) cannellini beans, rinsed and drained
- 1 can (15 ounces) reduced-sodium tomato sauce
- 1 cup chopped zucchini
- ⅓ cup defatted reduced-sodium chicken broth
- 2 tablespoons finely chopped fresh parsley
- 2 teaspoons dried thyme
- 1 teaspoon sugar
- 1 teaspoon Dijon mustard
- ¼ teaspoon ground black pepper
- ¼ teaspoon ground allspice
- 3–4 drops hot-pepper sauce
- 1 large bay leaf

In a medium microwave-safe bowl, stir together the onions, cabbage, celery, carrots, sherry or wine and garlic. Cover with wax paper and microwave on high power for a total of 8 minutes, or until the vegetables are almost tender; stop and stir after 4 minutes.

Meanwhile, warm the oil in a Dutch oven or large saucepan over medium heat. Add the pork and cook, stirring, until lightly browned.

Stir in the cabbage mixture, beans, tomato sauce, zucchini, broth, parsley, thyme, sugar, mustard, black pepper, allspice, hot-pepper sauce and bay leaf. Bring to a boil. Cover and transfer to the oven.

Bake at 350° for 35 minutes. Remove and discard the bay leaf.

Per serving: 299 calories, 8.1 g. total fat (20% of calories), 1.9 g. saturated fat, 34 mg. cholesterol, 463 mg. sodium

Ham and Artichoke Quiche

a large pita bread makes an easy, reduced-fat pie crust for this creamy quiche. If your pita round is too large to easily fit in the bottom of the pie plate or quiche dish, trim it with a sharp knife.

MAKES 6 SERVINGS

1 cup canned artichoke hearts (packed in water), drained
1 large pita bread (8″ diameter)
1 medium onion, finely chopped
1 clove garlic, minced
1 container (16 ounces) 1% fat cottage cheese
½ cup fat-free egg substitute
6 ounces fully cooked reduced-sodium ham, trimmed of all visible fat
   and cut into bite-size pieces
1 teaspoon dried thyme
1 teaspoon dried basil
¼ teaspoon salt (optional)
¼ teaspoon ground black pepper
3–4 drops hot-pepper sauce
1 cup shredded reduced-fat Swiss or mozzarella cheese
2 tablespoons chopped scallions

Remove and discard the coarse outer leaves from the artichoke hearts. Coarsely chop the artichokes and transfer them to a small bowl.

Lightly coat a 10″ pie plate or quiche dish with no-stick spray. Place the pita in the dish.

In a small microwave-safe bowl, combine the onions and garlic. Cover with wax paper and microwave on high power for 1½ to 2 minutes, or until the onions are tender.

In a large bowl, stir together the cottage cheese and eggs. Then stir in the artichokes, onion mixture, ham, thyme, basil, salt (if using), black pepper and hot-pepper sauce. Stir in ¾ cup of the cheese. Spread the mixture on top of the pita; sprinkle the remaining ¼ cup cheese on top.

Bake at 350° for 45 to 50 minutes, or until the mixture is set and slightly browned on top. Cool the quiche on a wire rack for 5 minutes. Sprinkle with the scallions and cut into wedges to serve.

THINK AHEAD: Since this quiche takes awhile to bake, you could double up on oven time to get a jump on tomorrow's dinner. So bake some sweet potatoes, white potatoes or winter squash at the same time.

Per serving: 193 calories, 4.2 g. total fat (20% of calories), 2.2 g. saturated fat, 20 mg. cholesterol, 802 mg. sodium

---

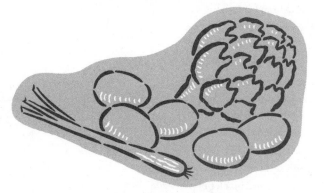

Fried Rice and Ham Skillet

Here's a dish that's more substantial than the fried rice offered in Chinese restaurants and a lot lower in fat.

MAKES 4 SERVINGS

- 1 tablespoon peanut oil
- 5 medium scallions, thinly sliced
- 2 medium stalks celery, diced
- ⅓ cup chopped sweet red peppers
- 3⅔ cups cooked rice
- 1 cup cubed fully cooked smoked ham
- 2½ tablespoons reduced-sodium soy sauce
- ¼ teaspoon curry powder
- ⅛ teaspoon ground black pepper
- ½ cup fat-free egg substitute

Warm the oil in a large no-stick skillet over medium-high heat. Add the scallions, celery and red peppers. Cook, stirring, for 5 minutes, or until the onions are tender.

Stir in the rice, ham, soy sauce, curry powder and black pepper. Cook, stirring, for 4 minutes, or until heated through.

Add the eggs. Cook, without stirring, for 2 to 3 minutes, or until the egg sets. Then, using a spatula, scrape the egg from the bottom of the skillet and stir it into the rice mixture until evenly incorporated.

Per serving: 332 calories, 4.9 g. total fat (13% of calories), 0.7 g. saturated fat, 0 mg. cholesterol, 743 mg. sodium

---

Harvest Fruit with Pork

Dried cranberries add a sweet-tangy flavor to this pork dish. Look for them in the produce section in your grocery store or in specialty food shops. If you can't find dried cranberries, replace them with dark raisins or currants.

MAKES 4 SERVINGS

1 pound boneless pork loin, trimmed of all visible fat and thinly sliced
¼ teaspoon salt (optional)
¼ teaspoon ground black pepper
2 teaspoons canola oil
1 large onion, chopped
3 large tart apples, cut into thin wedges
¾ cup dried cranberries
¾ cup cranberry juice
2 tablespoons packed brown sugar
1 tablespoon cider vinegar
1 tablespoon Worcestershire sauce
1⅓ cups long-grain white rice

Sprinkle the pork with the salt (if using) and pepper.

Warm the oil in a Dutch oven or large saucepan over medium heat. Add the pork and onions. Cook, stirring, until the pork is lightly browned.

Stir in the apples, cranberries, cranberry juice, brown sugar, vinegar and Worcestershire sauce. Bring to a boil. Reduce the heat, cover and simmer, stirring occasionally, for 30 to 35 minutes, or until the apples are just tender and the pork is cooked through.

Meanwhile, cook the rice according to the package directions. Serve the pork mixture over the rice.

Per serving: 526 calories, 10.5 g. total fat (18% of calories), 2.9 g. saturated fat, 51 mg. cholesterol, 84 mg. sodium

Slow-Cooked
Sweet-and-Sour Pork

*F*ruit and sweet potatoes team together to enhance the flavor of pork in this long-simmered dinner.

MAKES 4 SERVINGS

 1 large onion, finely chopped
 1 large sweet potato, peeled and cut into ¾″ cubes
 2 large stalks celery, chopped
1½ cups defatted chicken broth
 1 cup pitted small whole prunes
 ½ cup halved dried apricots
 2 tablespoons packed brown sugar
 1 teaspoon cider vinegar
 ½ teaspoon ground ginger
 ¼ teaspoon ground cloves
 1 pound pork loin, trimmed of all visible fat and cut into bite-size pieces
 1 teaspoon dried thyme
 ¼ teaspoon salt (optional)
 ¼ teaspoon ground black pepper
1⅓ cups long-grain white rice

In a 6-quart Crock-Pot or other slow-cooker, combine the onions, sweet potatoes, celery, broth, prunes, apricots, brown sugar, vinegar, ginger and cloves. Stir to mix well.

Sprinkle the pork with the thyme, salt (if using) and pepper. Place the pork on top of the fruit and vegetable mixture. Cover and cook on the high heat setting for 1 hour. Stir the pork into the fruit and vegetables. Reduce the heat to low. Cook for 5 to 6 hours, or until the pork and vegetables are tender.

Just before serving, cook the rice according to the package directions. Serve the pork mixture over the rice.

Per serving: 580 calories, 8.6 g. total fat (13% of calories), 2.8 g. saturated fat, 51 mg. cholesterol, 196 mg. sodium

---

Risotto with Ham and Vegetables

Here's an updated version of risotto that uses the microwave and takes about half the usual cooking time. Arborio rice is traditionally used in risotto because its high starch content contributes to the creaminess of this dish. If you don't have Arborio rice, you may substitute long-grain or medium-grain white rice. The texture will be a little different, but the dish will be just as delicious.

MAKES 4 SERVINGS

Risotto
- ¾ cup Arborio rice
- 2 teaspoons olive oil
- 2⅔ cups defatted chicken broth
- ¼ teaspoon ground black pepper

Ham and Vegetables
- 1 fully cooked reduced-sodium ham steak (6–8 ounces), trimmed of all visible fat and cut into bite-size pieces
- 2 teaspoons olive oil
- 1 medium onion, chopped
- 1 medium green pepper, chopped
- 3 tablespoons defatted chicken broth
- 1 clove garlic, minced
- 4 plum tomatoes, chopped
- 2 teaspoons dried Italian seasoning
- 2 tablespoons grated Parmesan cheese

To make the risotto: In a 2½-quart microwave-safe casserole, stir together the rice and oil. Microwave on high power for 1 minute. Stir in the broth and pepper. Cover and microwave for a total of 6 minutes; stop and stir after 3 minutes. Stir again.

Microwave, uncovered, for 11 to 12 minutes, or until the rice is tender and most of the liquid is absorbed. Let stand for 2 to 3 minutes.

To make the ham and vegetables: While the rice is cooking, coat a large no-stick skillet with no-stick spray. Add the ham. Cook, stirring, over medium heat for 2 to 3 minutes, or until heated through. Transfer the ham to a small bowl and set aside.

Heat the oil in the same skillet. Add the onions, peppers, broth and garlic. Cook, stirring, over medium heat for 5 minutes, or until the onions are tender. Stir in the ham, tomatoes and Italian seasoning. Cook, stirring occasionally, for 3 to 4 minutes, or until heated through.

Stir the vegetable mixture into the risotto. Sprinkle with the cheese.

Per serving: 293 calories, 8.7 g. total fat (26% of calories), 1.8 g. saturated fat, 12 mg. cholesterol, 536 mg. sodium

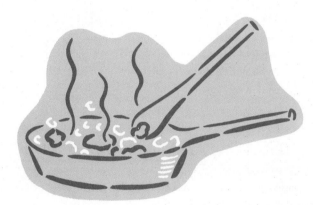

Italian-Style Pork Chops

*H*ere's a delicious alternative to plain pork chops that features an easy-to-make herbed tomato sauce. And for a different twist, we serve the chops over orzo—small rice-shaped pasta. If you like, you may substitute other types of small pasta.

MAKES 4 SERVINGS

- 4 boneless center loin pork chops (4 ounces each), trimmed of all visible fat
- 1 medium onion, chopped
- ¼ cup chopped sweet red peppers
- 1 large clove garlic, minced
- 1 can (16 ounces) stewed tomatoes (with juice)
- ½ teaspoon dried oregano
- ½ teaspoon dried marjoram
- ⅛ teaspoon dried thyme
- ⅛ teaspoon salt (optional)
- ⅛ teaspoon ground black pepper
- 1 cup orzo

Coat a large no-stick skillet with no-stick spray. Add the pork chops, onions, red peppers and garlic. Cook over medium-high heat for 2 minutes. Stir the vegetables and turn the chops. Cook for 2 minutes, or until the chops are lightly browned.

Add the tomatoes (with juice), oregano, marjoram, thyme, salt (if using) and black pepper. Cook over medium heat for 10 minutes, turning the chops over halfway during cooking.

While the chops are cooking, cook the orzo in a large pot of boiling water for 10 minutes, or until just tender. Drain in a colander. Rinse with hot water and drain again. Transfer to a serving bowl. Top with the chops and sauce.

Per serving: 272 calories, 8.5 g. total fat (28% of calories), 2.7 g. saturated fat, 51 mg. cholesterol, 267 mg. sodium

---

Skillet Pork Chops with Cabbage

*F*or an easy and hearty meal, serve this stir-fry pork-chop entrée with baked potatoes or sweet potatoes.

MAKES 4 SERVINGS

- 4 boneless center loin pork chops (4 ounces each), trimmed of all visible fat
- ½ teaspoon olive oil
- 1 medium onion, thinly sliced
- 1 large red sweet pepper, thinly sliced
- 2 cups coarsely shredded cabbage
- 1 medium tomato, chopped
- 6 tablespoons defatted chicken broth
- ¼ teaspoon paprika
- ¼ teaspoon chili powder
- ¼ teaspoon celery salt
- ¼ teaspoon salt (optional)
- ⅛ teaspoon ground black pepper

Coat a large no-stick skillet with no-stick spray. Add the pork chops. Cook over medium-high heat for 2 minutes per side, or until browned. Transfer the chops to a plate.

Heat the oil in the same skillet. Add the onions and red peppers. Cook, stirring, for 3 minutes. Stir in the cabbage, tomatoes, broth, paprika, chili powder, celery salt, salt (if using) and black pepper. Add the chops. Cook for 10 minutes, or until the chops are cooked through.

Per serving: 206 calories, 7.5 g. total fat (33% of calories), 2.4 g. saturated fat, 66 mg. cholesterol, 170 mg. sodium

Oven-Barbecued Pork Chops with Root Vegetables

Savor the taste of barbecued pork chops without fussing with a charcoal grill. Once the chops and vegetables are placed in the roasting pan, the work of this meal is completed.

MAKES 4 SERVINGS

⅔ cup ketchup

2 tablespoons water

1½ tablespoons brown sugar

1½ tablespoons cider vinegar

2 teaspoons canola oil

½ teaspoon chili powder

¼ teaspoon ground black pepper

Pinch of ground red pepper

3 large potatoes, cut into ¾″ cubes

3 large onions, cut into 1″ chunks

3 large carrots, thinly sliced

4 boneless pork loin chops (4 ounces each), trimmed of all visible fat

⅛ teaspoon salt (optional)

Generously spray a roasting pan or large shallow baking dish with no-stick spray.

In a small bowl, stir together the ketchup, water, brown sugar, vinegar, oil, chili powder, black pepper and red pepper.

In a large bowl, combine the potatoes, onions and carrots. Add two-thirds of the ketchup mixture. Toss until the vegetables are coated. Transfer the vegetables to the prepared pan.

Place the remaining ketchup mixture in the bowl. Add the pork chops and turn the chops until coated. Cover and refrigerate.

Bake the vegetables at 400° for 20 minutes. Then add the pork chops with the remaining sauce to the pan and toss until everything is well-mixed. Bake for 25 to

30 minutes, or until the vegetables are tender and the pork is cooked through; turn the chops over twice during baking. Sprinkle with the salt (if using).

Per serving: 401 calories, 10.2 g. total fat (22% of calories), 2.8 g. saturated fat, 51 mg. cholesterol, 612 mg. sodium

≫ Tips from the Family Chef ≪

MASTER THE ART OF CHOPPING

*W*hether you are preparing a simple snack or an elegant feast, it's almost certain that the food will have to be chopped. And, says Julia Child, if you want to take some of the work out of preparing food, you must become handy with the kitchen's most-used appliance—the knife.

"You can only begin to have some fun in the kitchen when you learn how to use a knife properly," says Julia, whose *French Chef* cookbooks and television shows have been classics for decades. Julia says that in the early days of her cooking education, she admired Dione Lucas's facility at fluting mushrooms. "I decided that if she could do it, I could do it. So I practiced for about a week before I finally got it right."

But you needn't concentrate on such fancy techniques. Just learning the basics will increase your efficiency in the kitchen—and cut the time you spend preparing meals. "Get a good book on kitchen techniques or go to a friend who knows how to handle a knife. And be sure to invest in good cutlery and keep it sharp," advises Julia.

Seafood for Everyone

Bayou Crispy Baked Fish

Red and black pepper make this oven-fried fish fairly spicy, though by Louisiana standards it doesn't qualify as hot. You can certainly adjust the piquancy by increasing, decreasing or even omitting the red pepper.

MAKES 4 SERVINGS

- ⅓ cup yellow cornmeal
- 1 teaspoon chili powder
- ½ teaspoon paprika
- ¼ teaspoon salt (optional)
- ¼ teaspoon garlic salt
- ¼ teaspoon onion powder
- ⅛ teaspoon ground black pepper
- ⅛ teaspoon red pepper
- 3 tablespoons fat-free egg substitute
- 3 tablespoons fat-free buttermilk
- 1 teaspoon canola oil
- 4 skinless grouper, cod or turbot fillets (5 ounces each and ¾" thick)

Line a 15" × 10" baking pan with foil. Generously spray the foil with no-stick spray.

In a shallow bowl, stir together the cornmeal, chili powder, paprika, salt (if using), garlic salt, onion powder, black pepper and red pepper.

In another shallow bowl, use a fork to stir together the eggs, buttermilk and oil.

Dip the fish into the egg mixture. Then roll the fish in the cornmeal mixture until evenly coated.

Place the fish in a single layer in the prepared baking pan. Bake at 425° for 9 to 12 minutes, or until the fish flakes easily when tested with a fork.

Per serving: 189 calories, 3.1 g. total fat (15% of calories), 0.5 g. saturated fat,
52 mg. cholesterol, 225 mg. sodium

Middle Eastern Cod
with Curried Vegetables

Fresh parsley, cilantro and lemon zest combine with curry to give this dish a slightly exotic flavor. Serve it with pita bread and a spinach salad tossed with a low-fat vinaigrette for a change-of-pace dinner.

MAKES 4 SERVINGS

1⅓ cups long-grain white rice
1½ teaspoons olive oil
1 teaspoon nondiet tub-style margarine or butter
2 medium onions, chopped
2 medium stalks celery, chopped
1 carrot, finely chopped
2 large cloves garlic, minced
½ cup defatted chicken broth
¼ cup chopped fresh parsley
¼ cup chopped fresh cilantro
1 tablespoon curry powder
1 teaspoon lemon juice
⅛ teaspoon grated lemon peel
¼ teaspoon salt (optional)
4 skinless cod fillets (4 ounces each and ¾" thick)

Cook the rice according to the package directions.

Heat the oil and margarine or butter in a large no-stick skillet over medium heat. Add the onions, celery, carrots and garlic. Cook, stirring, for 3 minutes. Stir in the broth, parsley, cilantro, curry powder, lemon juice, lemon peel and salt (if using). Bring to a simmer. Add the fish.

Cover and gently simmer for 6 to 9 minutes, or until the fish flakes easily when tested with a fork; as the fish cooks, occasionally baste it with the broth mixture. Serve the fish mixture over the rice.

Per serving: 283 calories, 4.2 g. total fat (13% of calories), 1.1 g. saturated fat, 48 mg. cholesterol, 145 mg. sodium

---

Herbed Scrod with Creamed Tomato Sauce

Here's a quick and easy fish entrée that you prepare in the microwave. You may replace the scrod with cod, haddock, turbot or other lean, mild white fish fillets.

MAKES 4 SERVINGS

½ cup 2% low-fat milk

¼ cup finely chopped fresh basil

3 tablespoons finely chopped fresh chives

¼ teaspoon salt

¼ teaspoon ground black pepper

1 large tomato, peeled, cored and chopped

1½ teaspoons nondiet tub-style margarine or butter

4 skinless scrod fillets (5 ounces each and ¾" thick)

In a 10" deep-dish glass pie plate, stir together the milk, basil, chives, salt and pepper. Microwave on high power for 3 minutes, or until the mixture comes to a boil.

Stir in the tomatoes and margarine or butter. Microwave for 2 minutes more.

Arrange the fish on top of the milk mixture; arrange the fillets in a spoke-like fashion with the thicker ends near the edge of the dish. Spoon some of the liquid over the fish.

Cover with wax paper and microwave for 2 minutes. Rearrange the fish, moving the pieces that flake easily with a fork toward the center of the dish.

Cover and microwave for 1 minute, or until all the fish flakes easily with a fork. Let stand, covered, for 3 minutes before serving.

Per serving: 141 calories, 3 g. total fat (12% of calories), 1.4 g. saturated fat, 62 mg. cholesterol, 245 mg. sodium

---

Haddock Stew with Dill

By using a small amount of 2 percent milk in this cream-style stew, we keep the feeling of richness without going overboard.

MAKES 4 SERVINGS

- ½ cup finely chopped onions
- 2 teaspoons nondiet tub-style margarine or butter
- 3 cups peeled potatoes cut in ½" cubes
- 1 medium carrot, chopped
- 1 cup 2% low-fat milk
- ¼ cup finely chopped fresh dill
- 2 tablespoons finely chopped fresh parsley
- ½ teaspoon dry mustard
- ⅛ teaspoon celery salt
- ⅛ teaspoon ground black pepper
- 1 pound skinless haddock fillet, cut into 2" pieces

Place the onions and margarine or butter in a 10" deep-dish glass pie plate. Microwave on high power for a total of 1½ to 2 minutes, or until the onions are tender; stir after 1 minute. Stir in the potatoes and carrots. Push the vegetables toward the edge of the plate; set aside.

In a 2-cup glass measure, stir together the milk, dill, parsley, mustard, celery salt and pepper. Cover with wax paper. Microwave for 2 minutes, or until hot. Stir well, then pour half of the mixture over the vegetables.

Cover the vegetables with wax paper. Microwave for 5 minutes. Stir the vegetables, then again push them toward the edge of the plate. Cover and microwave for 5 minutes.

Stir the vegetables and spread them evenly on the bottom of the plate. Arrange the fish on top, placing the thicker pieces near the edge of the plate. Pour the remaining milk mixture over the fish.

Loosely cover and microwave for 3½ to 4½ minutes, or until the fish flakes easily when tested with a fork. Serve immediately in soup plates or large bowls.

Per serving: 301 calories, 4.2 g. total fat (12% of calories), 2.1 g. saturated fat, 55 mg. cholesterol, 197 mg. sodium

Curried Haddock with Vegetables

*T*he light curry sauce served over the fish and vegetables give this one-dish meal an Indian twist. Serve this dish by itself or team it with brown rice.

MAKES 6 SERVINGS

2   large potatoes, cut into 1″ cubes
4   carrots, thinly sliced
½   tablespoon nondiet tub-style margarine or butter
1   medium onion, thinly sliced
2   tablespoons curry powder
½   cup water
½   cup dry sherry or nonalcoholic wine
1½ pounds skinless haddock fillets, cut into 2″ pieces
1   cup frozen peas
1   teaspoon dried basil
½   teaspoon sugar
½   teaspoon salt (optional)
½   cup 1% low-fat milk
4   teaspoons cornstarch

In a large saucepan with a tight-fitting lid, bring 1″ of water to a boil. Place the potatoes and carrots in a steamer basket and set the basket in the saucepan, making sure the basket sits above the water. Cover the saucepan and steam for 10 to 12 minutes, or until the vegetables are tender.

Melt the margarine or butter in a large no-stick skillet over medium heat. Add the onions. Cook, stirring, for 3 minutes. Add the curry powder; cook, stirring, for 30 seconds.

Stir in the water and sherry or wine. Bring to a boil. Add the fish, then reduce the heat. Cover and simmer for 3 to 4 minutes, or until the fish flakes easily when tested with a fork. Using a slotted spoon, transfer the fish to a serving platter; cover and keep warm.

Add the peas, basil, sugar and salt (if using) to the cooking liquid and return it to a simmer. Meanwhile, stir together the milk and cornstarch.

Slowly stir the milk mixture into the cooking liquid. Cook, stirring, over medium heat until the mixture begins to thicken and comes to a boil. Add the potatoes and carrots. Heat through.

To serve, use a slotted spoon to remove the vegetables and arrange them around the fish on the platter. Then pour the sauce over the fish and serve immediately.

Per serving: 280 calories, 2.5 g. total fat (8% of calories), 0.9 g. saturated fat, 70 mg. cholesterol, 146 mg. sodium

---

Baked Rockfish with Spinach and Feta

*R*ockfish is also known as Pacific perch. It has a delicate nutty, sweet flavor that complements the herbs and salty feta cheese in this dish. If rockfish is unavailable at your market, use red snapper, Atlantic perch or flounder. You can replace the fresh spinach with a ten-ounce package of frozen chopped spinach. Cook it according to the package directions, then drain it well by squeezing out the excess liquid.

MAKES 4 SERVINGS

1	pound spinach, stems removed
4	tablespoons water
2	teaspoons olive oil
1	medium onion, finely chopped
2	tablespoons pitted and chopped black olives (optional)
1	clove garlic, minced
½	teaspoon dried oregano
½	teaspoon dried basil
4	skinless rockfish fillets (6 ounces each and ½"–¾" thick)
2	tablespoons lemon juice
½	teaspoon ground black pepper
¼	cup (1 ounce) crumbled feta cheese

Coat a baking dish large enough to hold the fish in a single layer with no-stick spray.

Place half of the spinach and 2 tablespoons of the water in a large no-stick skillet. Cover and cook over medium heat until wilted. Transfer to a colander. Repeat with the remaining spinach and water. Drain well and squeeze the spinach to remove the excess moisture. Coarsely chop the spinach.

Wash and dry the skillet. Add the oil, onions, olives (if using) and garlic. Cook, stirring, over medium heat for 2 minutes. Stir in the spinach, oregano and basil. Cook, stirring, for 1 minute more.

Place the fillets, skinned-side down, in the prepared baking dish. Sprinkle with the lemon juice and pepper. Top the fillets with the spinach mixture, then sprinkle with the cheese.

Bake at 425° for 12 to 15 minutes, or until the fish flakes easily when tested with a fork.

Per serving: 258 calories, 8.6 g. total fat (30% of calories), 3.3 g. saturated fat, 72 mg. cholesterol, 342 mg. sodium

---

Cajun-Style Red Snapper

*F*or a Louisiana dinner, serve okra and cornbread as accompaniments to these spicy, flavorful fish fillets. For variety, replace the snapper with catfish.

MAKES 4 SERVINGS

- ¼ cup paprika
- 1 tablespoon sugar
- 1 teaspoon dried oregano
- 1 teaspoon dried basil
- 1 teaspoon dried thyme
- 1 teaspoon dried rosemary, crushed
- ½ teaspoon salt
- ¼ teaspoon ground red pepper
- 4 skinless red snapper fillets (6 ounces each and ½"–¾" thick)
- 1 tablespoon olive oil
- 1 large clove garlic, halved
- ¼ cup lemon juice

In a small bowl, stir together the paprika, sugar, oregano, basil, thyme, rosemary, salt and pepper. Transfer the mixture onto a flat plate.

Pat the fish dry with paper towels. Dredge the fillets in the paprika mixture to coat both sides. Place on another plate, cover with plastic wrap and chill in the refrigerator for at least 10 minutes.

Warm the oil in a large no-stick skillet over medium heat until hot but not smoking. Add the garlic. Cook, stirring, for 45 seconds, or until lightly browned. Remove and discard the garlic.

Add the fish to the skillet in a single layer. Cook for 3 minutes. Turn the fillets over, then add the lemon juice. Cook for 4 minutes, or until the fish flakes easily when tested with a fork.

Per serving: 239 calories, 6.6 g. total fat (25% of calories), 1 g. saturated fat, 62 mg. cholesterol, 344 mg. sodium

---

Salmon Risotto

*F*or this version of risotto, we've combined salmon with the rice. We're sure you'll love how the flavor of the fish combines with the nuttiness of the rice. For other rich-tasting combinations, substitute crab, chopped shrimp or chopped chicken breast for the salmon.

MAKES 4 SERVINGS

Risotto
- ¾ cup Arborio rice
- 2 teaspoons nondiet tub-style margarine or butter
- 2⅔ cups defatted reduced-sodium chicken broth
- ¼ teaspoon ground black pepper

Salmon and Sauce
- 12 ounces skinless salmon fillets (½"–1" thick), cut into 2" pieces
- 2 teaspoons nondiet tub-style margarine or butter
- 1 cup chopped onions
- 3 tablespoons defatted reduced-sodium chicken broth
- 1 clove garlic, minced
- 1 tablespoon all-purpose flour
- 1½ cups 1% low-fat milk
- 2 teaspoons lemon juice
- 1 teaspoon dried dill
- ½ teaspoon dry mustard
- ⅛ teaspoon ground black pepper
- 2 tablespoons grated Parmesan cheese

To make the risotto: In a 2½-quart microwave-safe casserole, combine the rice and margarine or butter. Microwave on high power for 1 minute. Stir well.

Stir in the broth and pepper. Cover and microwave for a total of 6 minutes; stop and stir well after 3 minutes. Stir again.

Uncover the casserole and microwave for 11 to 12 minutes, or until most of the liquid has been absorbed and the rice is tender. Let stand for 2 to 3 minutes.

To make the salmon and sauce: While the rice is cooking, coat a large no-stick skillet with no-stick spray. Add the salmon. Cook, stirring, over medium-high heat for 4 to 8 minutes, or until the salmon flakes easily. Transfer the salmon to a medium bowl and set aside.

Rinse and dry the skillet. Add the margarine or butter, onions, broth and garlic. Cook, stirring, over medium heat for 5 minutes, or until the onions are tender.

Stir in the flour, making a smooth paste. Then slowly stir in the milk until the mixture is smooth. Stir in the lemon juice, dill, mustard and pepper. Cook, stirring, until the mixture begins to thicken and comes to a boil. Cook, stirring, for 1 minute more. Reduce the heat to low.

Flake the salmon and add it to the sauce mixture. Heat through.

Stir the salmon mixture into the risotto. Sprinkle with the cheese.

Per serving: 326 calories, 8.9 g. total fat (25% of calories), 1.7 g. saturated fat, 20 mg. cholesterol, 390 mg. sodium

---

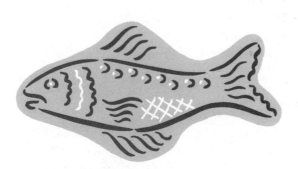

Salmon Loaf

Salmon loaf is a classic recipe that's easy to prepare and popular with families. It's also an excellent way to use canned salmon, which is a very good source of calcium because of the small, soft, edible bones it contains.

MAKES 4 SERVINGS

- 2 cans (7½ ounces each) pink salmon
- 1 medium onion, finely chopped
- 1 large stalk celery, chopped
- 1 tablespoon nondiet tub-style margarine or butter
- ½ cup quick-cooking rolled oats
- ¼ cup fat-free egg substitute
- ½ teaspoon dried thyme
- ½ teaspoon dried basil
- ¼ teaspoon dry mustard
- ⅛ teaspoon ground celery seeds
- ⅛ teaspoon ground black pepper
- ¼ teaspoon salt (optional)

Drain the salmon, reserving 3 tablespoons of the liquid and placing the liquid in a medium bowl.

Remove and discard the skin from the salmon. Transfer the salmon to the bowl with the liquid. Use a fork to flake the salmon and crush the bones.

In a 2-cup glass measure, stir together the onions, celery and margarine or butter. Cover with wax paper. Microwave on high power for 2 minutes.

Add the onion mixture to the salmon. Stir in the oats, eggs, thyme, basil, mustard, celery seeds, pepper and salt (if using). Mix well.

Lightly spray an 8" × 4" glass loaf pan with no-stick spray. Transfer the salmon mixture to the dish. Lightly pat evenly in the dish. Bake at 350° for 35 minutes.

Place the pan on a wire rack and let stand for 5 minutes. Cut the loaf into 1" slices and use a wide-blade spatula to remove the slices from the dish.

Per serving: 224 calories, 8.1 g. total fat (33% of calories), 2 g. saturated fat, 41 mg. cholesterol, 581 mg. sodium

---

Asian Steamed Salmon

*S*teaming is a healthy and tasty way to prepare fresh salmon as well as other varieties of fish. The steam keeps the fish wonderfully moist without adding any fat.

MAKES 4 SERVINGS

1 **salmon fillet (1¼ pounds and ½″–¾″ thick), cut into 4 pieces**
2 **teaspoons reduced-sodium soy sauce**
3 **tablespoons finely chopped scallions**
2 **teaspoons minced fresh ginger**
⅛ **teaspoon ground black pepper**

In a large saucepan with a tight-fitting lid, bring ¾″ of water to a boil.

Coat a steamer basket with no-stick spray. Place the salmon, skin side down, in the basket and brush the top surface with 1 teaspoon of the soy sauce. Sprinkle with 1½ tablespoons of the scallions.

Carefully set the basket in the saucepan, making sure the basket sits above the water. Cover and steam for 4 to 7 minutes, or until the salmon flakes easily when tested with a fork.

Transfer the salmon, skin-side down, to a serving platter or individual plates. Drizzle with the remaining 1 teaspoon soy sauce. Then sprinkle with the ginger, pepper and remaining 1½ tablespoons scallions.

Per serving: 160 calories, 4.9 g. total fat (29% of calories), 1.2 g. saturated fat, 63 mg. cholesterol, 153 mg. sodium

---

Potatoes Topped with Tuna and Broccoli

*T*his is a perfect dish to serve on busy nights. The potatoes take only minutes to bake in the microwave. And the sauce is easy to prepare.

MAKES 4 SERVINGS

     4 large potatoes (8 ounces each)
     3 cups small broccoli florets
     1 cup water
     1 tablespoon nondiet tub-style margarine or butter
     1 medium onion, chopped
     2 tablespoons defatted chicken broth
  1½ tablespoons all-purpose flour
  1¾ cups 1% low-fat milk
     1 teaspoon dried thyme
     ½ teaspoon salt (optional)
     ½ teaspoon dried basil
     ¼ teaspoon dry mustard
     ⅛ teaspoon ground celery seeds
     ⅛ teaspoon ground black pepper
     ½ cup (2 ounces) finely shredded reduced-fat sharp Cheddar cheese
     ½ cup (2 ounces) finely shredded fat-free Cheddar cheese
     1 can (6½ ounces) water-packed tuna, drained and flaked

Pierce each potato in several places with a fork. Arrange on a microwave-safe plate like the spokes of a wheel. Microwave on high power for a total of 15 minutes, or until the potatoes are easily pierced with a sharp knife; stop and turn the potatoes over after 10 minutes. Let stand for 5 minutes.

While the potatoes are cooking, combine the broccoli and water in a medium saucepan. Bring to a boil over high heat, then reduce the heat to medium. Cover and simmer for 3 to 5 minutes, or until the broccoli is crisp-tender. Drain well and set aside.

Dry the saucepan. Add the margarine or butter, onions and broth. Cook, stirring, over medium heat for 5 minutes, or until the onions are tender.

Stir in the flour, making a smooth paste. Then slowly stir in the milk until the mixture is smooth. Stir in the thyme, salt (if using), basil, mustard, celery seeds and pepper. Cook, stirring, until the mixture begins to thicken and just comes to a boil. Cook, stirring, for 1 minute more. Reduce the heat to low.

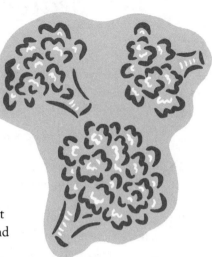

Stir in the reduced-fat cheese and fat-free cheese. Cook, stirring, until melted (the fat-free cheese may not melt completely). Then stir in the broccoli and tuna and heat through.

To serve, make a lengthwise slit in each potato. Then gently push in on the ends of the potatoes to slightly open the slits. Fluff the potato pulp with a fork. Place each potato on a dinner plate. Spoon some of the tuna mixture on top of each potato.

THINK AHEAD: You can prepare the sauce ahead and reheat it at dinnertime. Transfer it to a large microwave-safe bowl, cover with plastic wrap and refrigerate. To reheat, turn back a corner of the plastic wrap. Microwave on 50% power for a total of 5 minutes; stop and stir after 2 minutes. If the sauce is not heated through, continue microwaving at 1-minute intervals. You can also reheat previously baked or microwaved potatoes until hot or you can steam them until heated through while the sauce warms.

Per serving: 443 calories, 7.5 g. total fat (15% of calories), 2.2 g. saturated fat, 23 mg. cholesterol, 460 mg. sodium

---

Seafood Stew

*H*addock, red snapper and perch are all good fish choices for this stew. If you want, you can use some of each. They're all low in fat and have firm flesh so that they won't easily fall apart during simmering.

MAKES 8 SERVINGS

8	littleneck clams, scrubbed
1	cup dry white wine or nonalcoholic white wine
5	cups water
4	large tomatoes, coarsely chopped
3	stalks celery, chopped
2	large potatoes, peeled and cut into 1″ cubes
2	onions, coarsely chopped
2	tablespoons finely chopped fresh parsley
1	teaspoon salt (optional)
1	teaspoon dried oregano
1	teaspoon ground red pepper
½	teaspoon sugar
1	large clove garlic, minced
1	bay leaf
1	cup tomato paste
1½	pounds skinless fish fillets, cut into 1″ cubes
4	ounces medium shrimp, shelled, deveined and halved lengthwise

In a large saucepan, combine the clams, wine and 1 cup of the water. Bring to a boil over high heat, then reduce the heat. Cover and gently simmer for 5 minutes, or until the clams open. Using a slotted spoon, remove the clams. Discard any unopened clams.

Add the tomatoes, celery, potatoes, onions, parsley, salt (if using), oregano, pepper, sugar, garlic, bay leaf and the remaining 4 cups water to the pan. Bring to a boil, then reduce the heat to medium-low. Cook for 12 to 15 minutes, or until the potatoes are tender.

Stir in the tomato paste until no lumps remain. Add the fish and shrimp. Cook over medium heat for 3 to 5 minutes, or until the fish flakes easily when tested with a fork and the shrimp turn pink. Add the clams and heat through. Use a spoon to remove any foam from the top of the soup before serving.

Per serving: 202 calories, 1.6 g. total fat (7% of calories), 0.3 g. saturated fat, 68 mg. cholesterol, 363 mg. sodium

It's So Easy... It's Kid Stuff

FISH FOR DINNER

*F*ish is an ideal food for kids to prepare, says John Schumacher, the chef/owner at Schumacher's New Prague Hotel in Minnesota. He especially recommends his fish Voltoua, a dish that's so tasty that even the most finicky eaters love it.

"It is very easy to prepare and very heart-healthy," John says. "You start with a tablespoon of olive oil, two large diced onions, some yellow peppers and large mushrooms." Sauté the vegetables in the oil until the onions start to caramelize. Then add a can of whole plum tomatoes and ½ cup each of water and tomato puree. Season the mixture with salt, pepper, thyme and paprika. Boil for 10 minutes.

Meanwhile, cut enough fish into 1″ chunks to make 4 cups. "You can use any firm-fleshed fish, like cod, pike, scrod, grouper, halibut or lake trout," he says. Place the fish in a casserole, pour the vegetables and liquid over it, cover and bake in a hot oven for about 30 minutes. Serve garnished with low-fat sour cream and parsley.

Layered Fish Stew

*I*n this slightly different stew, the fish is layered on top of vegetables and cooked by steam. Our cooking times are based on ¾"-thick fillets. If your fillets are thinner or thicker, adjust the cooking time accordingly.

MAKES 4 SERVINGS

- 3 cups cubed potatoes
- 2 carrots, sliced
- 1 large onion, finely chopped
- 1 large tomato, chopped
- 2 cups small cauliflower florets
- ⅓ cup chopped fresh parsley
- 1 teaspoon dried thyme
- 1 teaspoon dried basil
- 2 cloves garlic, minced
- ¾ teaspoon salt (optional)
- ¼ teaspoon ground black pepper
- ¾ cup defatted chicken broth
- 1 pound skinless turbot or haddock fillets (¾" thick)
- 2 teaspoons lemon juice
- 2 teaspoons olive oil

Coat a Dutch oven or large saucepan with no-stick spray. Layer in the potatoes, carrots, onions, tomatoes and cauliflower, using all of each. Sprinkle with the parsley, thyme, basil, garlic, salt (if using) and pepper.

Pour the broth over the vegetables. Bring to a boil over high heat, then reduce the heat to medium. Cover and simmer for 12 minutes. Place the fish on top of the vegetables in a single layer. Drizzle with the lemon juice and olive oil.

Cover and simmer for 12 minutes. Uncover and continue cooking for 12 minutes more, or until the potatoes are tender and the fish flakes easily.

To serve, transfer the fish to a shallow serving platter. Arrange the vegetables around the fish and pour the liquid over all.

Per serving: 285 calories, 6.4 g. total fat (20% of calories), 0.8 g. saturated fat, 55 mg. cholesterol, 273 mg. sodium

---

Quick and Easy Paella

*T*his version of the traditional Spanish paella is a lot easier to prepare than usual and a lot lower in fat. Serve it with crusty bread and a tossed romaine and tomato salad.

- 12 mussels, scrubbed
- 1 teaspoon olive oil
- 1 large onion, chopped
- 5 cups water
- 1¾ cups long-grain white rice
- 8 ounces reduced-fat turkey sausage, sliced
- ¼ teaspoon saffron threads, crumbled
- 4 ounces medium shrimp, shelled, deveined and halved lengthwise
- 2 cups frozen peas
- ½ teaspoon ground red pepper
- 12 littleneck clams, scrubbed

Prepare the mussels by pulling out the beards that are visible between the shells. Set the mussels aside.

Warm the oil in a medium saucepan over medium heat. Add the onions. Cook, stirring, for 2 minutes. Add the water, rice, sausage and saffron. Bring to a boil, then reduce the heat. Cover and simmer for 12 minutes, or until the rice is partially tender and there is still plenty of liquid remaining.

Stir in the shrimp, peas and pepper. Transfer the mixture to a large shallow casserole or baking dish. Arrange the clams and mussels around the edge of the dish. Tightly cover with foil.

Bake at 375° for 30 minutes, or until the clams and mussels open and the rice is tender. Remove and discard any unopened clams and mussels.

Per serving: 362 calories, 6.6 g. total fat (17% of calories), 1.1 g. saturated fat, 62 mg. cholesterol, 336 mg. sodium

---

Clams with Linguine and Fresh Tomato Sauce

*M*any recipes for clam sauce are high in fat. This one isn't.

MAKES 4 SERVINGS

10	ounces linguine
1	tablespoon olive oil
1	large onion, chopped
2	cloves garlic, minced
4	tomatoes, chopped
2	teaspoons dried basil
1	teaspoon dried Italian seasoning
¼	teaspoon ground black pepper
1½	cups defatted reduced-sodium chicken broth
24	small littleneck clams, scrubbed
1½	cups water
1	tablespoon cornstarch
1	tablespoon finely chopped fresh parsley

Cook the linguine in a large pot of boiling water according to the package directions. Drain, rinse with hot water and drain again. Transfer to a large bowl, cover and keep warm.

While the linguine is cooking, heat the oil in a large skillet over medium heat. Add the onions and garlic. Cook, stirring, for 2 minutes. Add the tomatoes, basil, Italian seasoning and pepper. Cook, stirring, for 3 to 4 minutes.

Stir in the broth. Bring to a boil. Add the clams, then reduce the heat. Cover and gently simmer about 5 minutes, or until the clams open.

Using tongs, transfer the clams to a medium bowl. Discard any unopened clams. Cover the open clams and keep warm.

Add 1 cup of the water to the tomato mixture. In a custard cup, stir together the cornstarch and the remaining ½ cup water. Stir into the pan. Cook, stirring, over medium heat until the tomato mixture comes to a boil and thickens.

Pour the tomato mixture over the linguine; toss well. Sprinkle with the parsley and top with the clams.

Per serving: 427 calories, 6.4 g. total fat (13% of calories), 0.8 g. saturated fat, 18 mg. cholesterol, 59 mg. sodium

---

⋙ Tips from the Family Chef ⋘

A QUICK PASTA SAUCE

Giuliano Hazan's favorite quick and healthy meal is pasta with a sauce. That's not surprising, since his mother, Marcella Hazan, taught him the secrets of Italian cooking.

You can make a very good sauce from some lightly sautéed, then simmered, vegetables. Giuliano says a favorite of his uses onions, eggplant, zucchini, red peppers and tomatoes. He sautés the onions in a little oil until they are soft. Then he adds the other vegetables and cooks the mixture until the vegetables are tender. A few seasonings complete the sauce, which he serves with fusilli or any other hefty pasta shape.

"I follow this with a nice salad, and the whole meal takes less than 45 minutes," says Giuliano, who is a chef and author of *The Classic Pasta Cookbook.*

"When I was growing up, I used to like to sit in the kitchen and watch my mother cook," he says. From Marcella, Giuliano learned to have on hand the basics of cooking: olive oil, tomatoes and a variety of pasta shapes. With just those few staples and fresh vegetables, you can always prepare quick and delicious meals.

Sautéed Shrimp with Artichokes, Olives and Pasta

*A*rtichokes and olives complement the mild flavor of shrimp and enhance this simple tomato sauce. Add crusty bread and a salad for a complete meal.

MAKES 4 SERVINGS

- 1 **large onion, chopped**
- 1 **clove garlic, minced**
- 2 **tablespoons dry sherry or nonalcoholic wine**
- 2 **tablespoons + ⅓ cup defatted chicken broth**
- 1 **can (16 ounces) stewed tomatoes (with juices)**
- 1 **jar (14¾ ounces) artichoke hearts (packed in water), drained**
- 5 **large pimento-stuffed green olives, sliced**
- 2 **teaspoons dried Italian seasoning**
- ¼ **teaspoon ground black pepper**
- 1 **pound medium shrimp, shelled and deveined**
- 3 **cups fusilli**

Coat a large no-stick skillet with no-stick spray. Add the onions, garlic, sherry or wine and 2 tablespoons of the broth. Cook, stirring, over medium heat for 5 minutes, or until the onions are tender.

Add the tomatoes (with juices), artichokes, olives, Italian seasoning, pepper and the remaining ⅔ cup broth. Bring to a boil, then reduce the heat. Cover and simmer for 10 minutes. Add the shrimp and simmer, uncovered, for 3 minutes, or until the shrimp turn pink.

While the sauce is cooking, cook the fusilli in a large pot of boiling water according to the package directions. Drain, rinse with hot water and drain again. Serve the shrimp mixture over the fusilli.

Per serving: 435 calories, 3 g. total fat (6% of calories), 0.5 g. saturated fat, 174 mg. cholesterol, 785 mg. sodium

---

Shrimp Fajitas

*T*he easiest way to serve fajitas is to bring the skillet right to the table (use a trivet or heavy pot holders under it) along with the warmed tortillas. Have the lettuce, tomatoes and scallions in bowls. Then let people assemble their own fajitas. If desired, have salsa, shredded cheese or nonfat sour cream on hand for diners to include in or on top of their fajitas.

MAKES 6 SERVINGS

- 12 flour tortillas (8″ diameter)
- 1 tablespoon olive oil
- 2 medium onions, thinly sliced
- 1 sweet red pepper, thinly sliced
- 1 yellow pepper, thinly sliced
- 1 pound medium shrimp, shelled, deveined and halved lengthwise
- 2 tablespoons defatted reduced-sodium chicken broth
- 2 teaspoons dried Italian seasoning
- 1 teaspoon chili powder
- ½ teaspoon ground cumin
- ¼ teaspoon ground red pepper
- 2 cups shredded romaine lettuce
- 2 large tomatoes, chopped
- 1 bunch scallions, chopped

Stack the tortillas and wrap them in a piece of foil. Place on a baking sheet and bake at 350° about 10 minutes, or just until heated.

Meanwhile, warm the oil in a large skillet over medium heat. Add the onions, red peppers and yellow peppers. Cook, stirring, for 6 minutes. Add the shrimp, broth, Italian seasoning, chili powder, cumin and ground red pepper. Stir until combined. Cover and cook for 3 minutes, or until the shrimp turn pink.

Fill the tortillas with the shrimp mixture and top with the lettuce, tomatoes and scallions. Roll to enclose the filling.

Per serving: 350 calories, 8.2 g. total fat (21% of calories), 1.2 g. saturated fat, 116 mg. cholesterol, 474 mg. sodium

---

Italian Shrimp and Spaghetti Dinner

*T*his easy Italian entrée features plump shrimp in a homemade tomato sauce. It tastes best when fresh shrimp are used, but you may substitute frozen ones. We wouldn't recommend canned shrimp because they're high in sodium and tend to have a tinny taste.

MAKES 4 SERVINGS

- 8 ounces spaghetti
- 2 teaspoons olive oil
- 1 medium onion, chopped
- 1 large green pepper, chopped
- 1 clove garlic, minced
- 3 tablespoons defatted chicken broth
- 2 cups small cauliflower florets
- 1 can (16 ounces) stewed tomatoes (with juice)
- ½ cup dry sherry or nonalcoholic wine
- 1 teaspoon dried basil
- 1 teaspoon dried thyme
- ½ teaspoon dried marjoram
- ⅛ teaspoon ground black pepper
- 1 bay leaf
- ¼ cup water
- 2 teaspoons cornstarch
- 1 pound medium shrimp, shelled and deveined

Cook the spaghetti in a large pot of boiling water according to the package directions. Drain, rinse with hot water and drain again. Cover and keep warm.

While the spaghetti is cooking, heat the oil in a large no-stick skillet over medium heat. Add the onions, green peppers, garlic and broth. Cook, stirring, for 5 minutes, or until the onions are tender.

Stir in the cauliflower, tomatoes (with juice), sherry or wine, basil, thyme, marjoram, black pepper and bay leaf. Mix well. Bring to a boil, then reduce the heat. Cover and simmer for 5 minutes, or until the cauliflower is slightly tender.

In a custard cup, mix the water and cornstarch. Add to the pan. Cook, stirring, for 1 minute. Add the shrimp and simmer for 3 minutes, or until the shrimp turn pink. Remove and discard the bay leaf. Serve over the spaghetti.

Per serving: 439 calories, 4.7 g. total fat (10% of calories), 0.8 g. saturated fat, 174 mg. cholesterol, 496 mg. sodium

≫ Tips from the Family Chef ≪

GRILLED SHRIMP

The Driver's Seat restaurant in Southampton is a Long Island staple thanks to its outdoor ambiance in the summer, its warm, cozy atmosphere in the winter and the American seafood specialties featured on the menu.

But while owner-chef John Barnhill enjoys preparing food for his customers, he also likes to entertain at home. And when he does, he wants to enjoy the company of his guests. So on those occasions, he likes to keep the food preparation quick and simple.

"Pasta is always good for entertaining. So is soup," John says. "I also use the grill a lot because things cook so quickly on it." One of his specialties is grilled shrimp.

John starts by marinating the shrimp in a mixture of balsamic vinegar, olive oil, honey, soy sauce and garlic for about ten minutes. Then he threads them onto skewers and cooks them over a hot fire for the few minutes it takes for them to be done.

"Serve the shrimp over some rice and you have a quick meal that can feed quite a few people without much trouble," he says.

Lean Shrimp Scampi

*J*ust a small amount of butter adds a delectable buttery flavor to this shrimp dish without an excess of fat or calories. Serve the shrimp over rice pilaf or angel hair pasta for an elegant, special entrée.

MAKES 4 SERVINGS

½	tablespoon nondiet tub-style margarine or butter
1	large shallot, chopped
4	cloves garlic, minced
1	cup dry white wine or nonalcoholic white wine
¼	cup water
1	tablespoon finely chopped fresh parsley
¼	teaspoon salt (optional)
¼	teaspoon dried basil
⅛	teaspoon ground red pepper
1	pound medium shrimp, shelled, deveined and halved lengthwise
1½	tablespoons lemon juice
1	tablespoon cornstarch

Melt the margarine or butter in a large no-stick skillet over medium-low heat. Add the shallots and garlic. Cook, stirring, for 2 minutes.

Stir in the wine and water; bring to a boil over high heat. Reduce the heat to medium. Stir in the parsley, salt (if using), basil and pepper. Add the shrimp.

In a custard cup, stir together the lemon juice and cornstarch. Stir into the pan. Cook, stirring, for 3 minutes, or until the liquid thickens and the shrimp turn pink.

Per serving: 156 calories, 2.4 g. total fat (14% of calories), 1.1 g. saturated fat, 174 mg. cholesterol, 218 mg. sodium

---

Maryland Crab Cakes

These tasty crab cakes are baked rather than deep-fried, so they're a lot lower in fat and calories than traditional ones. Serve them plain or with cocktail sauce. Or make sandwiches using buns, tomato slices and lettuce or low-fat cole slaw. To make sure your crab cakes are light in texture, use very fine bread crumbs. Start with French bread, tear it into pieces and grind them in a food processor until quite small. Place in a sieve and shake all the tiny pieces through.

MAKES 6 SERVINGS

- ¾ cup fat-free plain yogurt
- 1 tablespoon Dijon mustard
- 1 tablespoon lemon juice
- 2 teaspoons reduced-fat mayonnaise
- 1 teaspoon dried seafood seasoning
- ¼ teaspoon ground red pepper
- 1 tablespoon finely chopped fresh parsley
- 1 teaspoon Worcestershire sauce
- ¾ cup fresh bread crumbs
- 1 pound lump crab meat, broken into bite-size pieces
- 2 egg whites

Coat a baking sheet with no-stick spray and set aside.

In a large bowl, stir together the yogurt, mustard, lemon juice, mayonnaise, seafood seasoning, pepper, parsley and Worcestershire sauce. Add the bread crumbs and stir until well-combined.

Add the crab. Gently stir until combined, being careful to keep the lumps of crab intact.

In a small bowl, use a whisk or an electric mixer to beat the egg whites until they form soft peaks. Fold the egg whites into the crab mixture.

Form into 6 patties and place them on the prepared baking sheet. Bake at 375° for 12 to 15 minutes, or until lightly browned.

Per serving: 70 calories, 2 g. total fat (27% of calories), 0.3 g. saturated fat, 11 mg. cholesterol, 321 mg. sodium

---

Dill Crab and Pasta Salad

$\mathcal{F}$or a lovely summer entrée, serve this refreshing salad on a bed of lettuce with red and yellow cherry tomatoes. For variety, you can transform this into a tuna salad by replacing the crab with a 12¼-ounce can of water-packed tuna. Take your pick of pasta shapes; radiatore, ruffles, rotelli and small shells work well.

MAKES 8 SERVINGS

16	ounces small pasta
2	cups frozen peas
1½	cups fat-free or reduced-fat plain yogurt
¼	cup reduced-fat mayonnaise
2	tablespoons finely chopped fresh dill
2	tablespoons red wine vinegar
1	tablespoon lemon juice
1	teaspoon dry mustard
1	teaspoon dried seafood seasoning
½	teaspoon sugar
⅛	teaspoon ground red pepper
1	pound lump crab meat, broken into bite-size pieces
2	large carrots, shredded

Cook the pasta in a large pot of boiling water according to the package directions; about 1 minute before draining, add the peas. Drain, rinse with cold water and drain again.

In a large bowl, stir together the yogurt, mayonnaise, dill, vinegar, lemon juice, mustard, seafood seasoning, sugar and pepper.

Add the pasta, crab and carrots. Gently toss until coated. Cover and chill in the refrigerator for 20 minutes to blend the flavors.

Per serving: 270 calories, 3.9 g. total fat (13% of calories), 0.5 g. saturated fat, 10 mg. cholesterol, 241 mg. sodium

20-Minute Scallop and Sweet Pepper Stir-Fry

Scallops are quick to fix—just be sure not to overcook them or they'll turn tough and chewy.

MAKES 4 SERVINGS

- 1⅓ cup long-grain white rice
- 1 teaspoon minced fresh ginger
- 2 tablespoons reduced-sodium soy sauce
- 1 pound bay scallops or halved sea scallops
- ⅓ cup defatted chicken broth
- 1 tablespoon rice wine vinegar
- 1 tablespoon cornstarch
- ½ teaspoon sugar
- ½ teaspoon oriental sesame oil
- 1½ teaspoons peanut oil
- 1 cup sweet red peppers cut into 1″ pieces
- ½ cup scallions cut into 1″ pieces
- 1 large clove garlic, minced

Cook the rice according to the package directions.

While the rice is cooking, stir together the ginger and 1 tablespoon of the soy sauce in a medium bowl. Add the scallops and toss until well-coated.

In a custard cup, stir together the broth, vinegar, cornstarch, sugar, sesame oil and the remaining 1 tablespoon soy sauce until the cornstarch dissolves.

Place the peanut oil in a large no-stick skillet over medium-high heat until hot but not smoking. Add the peppers, scallions and garlic. Stir-fry for 4 minutes, or until the scallions are just tender.

Add the scallop mixture. Stir-fry for 30 seconds. Add the broth mixture. Cook, stirring, for 1 minute, or until the mixture thickens and the scallops are opaque. (Do not overcook.) Serve over the rice.

Per serving: 293 calories, 3.7 g.total fat (12% of calories), 0.5 g. saturated fat, 38 mg. cholesterol, 504 mg. sodium

---

Oriental Scallop
and Sweet Vegetable Kabobs

*F*or this recipe, we use sea scallops, which are larger than bay scallops and easier to thread onto skewers. Try to get the size that comes 20 to 28 per pound. If your scallops are larger (meaning you get fewer per pound), cut them in half before marinating them.

MAKES 4 SERVINGS

Scallops
- ½ cup rice wine vinegar
- ½ cup orange juice
- 2 teaspoons grated fresh ginger
- ½ teaspoon oriental sesame oil
- ½ teaspoon reduced-sodium soy sauce
- 1½ pounds sea scallops

Glaze
- ½ cup ketchup
- ¼ cup packed brown sugar
- 2 tablespoons rice wine vinegar
- 1 tablespoon minced garlic
- 1 tablespoon grated fresh ginger
- 2 teaspoons oriental sesame oil
- 1 teaspoon reduced-sodium soy sauce

Kabobs
- 1 sweet red pepper, cut into 1½" pieces
- 1 green pepper, cut into 1½" pieces
- 1 large onion, cut into 1½" cubes
- 16 medium mushrooms

To make the scallops: In a large bowl, stir together the vinegar, orange juice, ginger, oil and soy sauce. Add the scallops and toss until coated. Cover and marinate in the refrigerator for 15 to 30 minutes.

To make the glaze: In a small saucepan, stir together the ketchup, brown sugar, vinegar, garlic, ginger, oil and soy sauce. Cook, stirring, over medium heat for 5 minutes.

To make the kabobs: While the scallops are marinating, soak 8 long (10″) bamboo skewers in water for at least 15 minutes.

Drain the scallops. Discard the marinade. Alternately thread the scallops, red peppers, green peppers, onions and mushrooms onto the skewers, leaving a small space between the pieces.

Place the kabobs on a baking sheet and brush with the glaze. Bake at 375° for 4 minutes. Turn the kabobs over and brush with more of the glaze. Bake for 4 minutes, or until the scallops are opaque.

Per serving: 158 calories, 2.4 g. total fat (13% of calories), 0.2 g. saturated fat, 36 mg. cholesterol, 412 mg. sodium

---

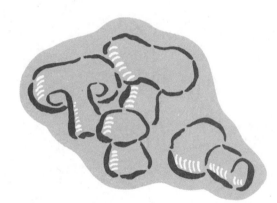

No Meat Tonight

Summertime Vegetable Stew

*W*hen fresh beans and corn are in season, this simple stew is the ticket to an easy, delicious meal.

- 1½ tablespoons olive oil
- 1 medium onion, chopped
- 2 medium potatoes, diced
- 2 large ripe tomatoes, chopped
- ½ cup reduced-sodium vegetable or defatted chicken broth
- 2 large cloves garlic, thinly sliced
- 1 tablespoon chopped fresh oregano
- 8 ounces green beans, trimmed
- 1 cup fresh or frozen whole kernel corn
- 2 tablespoons finely chopped fresh basil
- ¾ teaspoon salt (optional)
- ¼ teaspoon ground black pepper

Warm the oil in a large no-stick skillet over medium heat. Add the onions. Cook, stirring, for 3 minutes. Stir in the potatoes. Cover and cook for 3 to 4 minutes, stirring occasionally.

Stir in the tomatoes, broth, garlic and oregano. Cover and cook for 5 minutes, stirring occasionally. Stir in the beans. Cover and cook for 5 minutes.

Stir in the corn, basil, salt (if using) and pepper. Cover and cook for 5 minutes, or until the potatoes and beans are tender. Cool slightly before serving.

THINK AHEAD: This stew actually tastes best if made a day ahead so that the flavors have time to blend. If you do make it ahead, remove it from the refrigerator about 30 minutes before serving since it's especially good served at room temperature.

Per serving: 228 calories, 5.4 g. total fat (20% of calories), 0.6 g. saturated fat, 0 mg. cholesterol, 22 mg. sodium

---

Lentil Stew

To give this vegetarian stew an extra flavor punch, add some ground dried chili peppers or hot-pepper flakes.

MAKES 6 SERVINGS

- 7 cups water
- 1 pound lentils, sorted and rinsed
- 1 bay leaf
- ½ teaspoon salt (optional)
- 1 large potato, cubed
- 1 large carrot, thinly sliced
- 1 medium onion, chopped
- 1 small green pepper, chopped
- ¼ cup tomato paste
- 4 cloves garlic, minced
- 1 teaspoon dried savory
- ¼ cup chopped fresh parsley

In a large saucepan, combine the water, lentils, bay leaf and salt (if using). Bring to a boil over high heat, then reduce the heat to medium, cover and gently simmer for 10 minutes.

Stir in the potatoes, carrots, onions, peppers, tomato paste, garlic and savory. Mix well. Cover and gently simmer, stirring occasionally, for 30 minutes, or until the lentils are tender.

Stir in the parsley. Remove and discard the bay leaf.

Per serving: 302 calories, 1 g. total fat (3% of calories), 0.1 g. saturated fat, 0 mg. cholesterol, 96 mg. sodium

---

Cheese, Zucchini and Carrot Casserole

$\mathcal{T}$his vegetable casserole uses the microwave to speed up the cooking of the zucchini and carrots; then it's finished in the oven for an old-fashioned, homey look and taste.

MAKES 4 SERVINGS

- 1 large onion, finely chopped
- 1 stalk celery, finely chopped
- 1 teaspoon olive oil
- 1 clove garlic, minced
- 2 cups diced zucchini
- 1 large carrot, chopped
- 1 teaspoon dried thyme
- 1 teaspoon dried basil
- ½ teaspoon salt (optional)
- ¼ teaspoon dry mustard
- 2–3 drops hot-pepper sauce
- 4 cups whole-wheat bread cubes
- 1 cup (4 ounces) finely shredded fat-free Cheddar cheese
- 1 cup (4 ounces) finely shredded reduced-fat Cheddar cheese

In a 2½-quart oven-safe, microwave-safe casserole, stir together the onions, celery, oil and garlic. Cover and microwave on high power for a total of 6 minutes; stop and stir after 3 minutes.

Stir in the zucchini, carrots, thyme, basil, salt (if using), mustard and hot-pepper sauce. Cover and microwave for a total of 7 minutes, or until the vegetables are crisp-tender; stop and stir after 3 minutes.

Stir in the bread cubes, fat-free cheese and ¾ cup of the reduced-fat cheese.

Bake at 400° for 15 minutes, or until the cheese is melted. Sprinkle with the remaining ¼ cup reduced-fat cheese. Bake for 2 to 3 minutes, or until the cheese on top is melted.

THINK AHEAD: To reheat leftovers for lunch or dinner the next day, place a portion on a microwave-safe plate, cover with wax paper and microwave until heated through.

Per serving: 239 calories, 6.6 g. total fat (25% of calories), 2.4 g. saturated fat,
20 mg. cholesterol, 760 mg. sodium

It's So Easy ... It's Kid Stuff

MICROWAVE SAFETY

*I*n many ways, using a microwave is safer than using a regular oven. But before you let your kids tackle microwaving, teach them about safety.

Barbara Kafka is the author of several cookbooks on microwaving, and she has these tips. First, teach your kids that the food coming out of a microwave is hot, even if the container doesn't seem hot. And stress patience. Children often run the risk of undercooking some foods that should be cooked longer.

Other rules kids should abide by, says Barbara:

- Always prick the plastic covers and wrappers after cooking to let steam escape from foods before unwrapping them.

- Always use potholders.
- When opening a bag of popcorn, keep it away from your face because steam can burn your hands and face.

Most important, remember that even though microwaving tends to be safer than using a stove or oven, children should still be supervised in the kitchen.

Oriental Mixed-Vegetable Stir-Fry

*T*his no-meat stir-fry is both pleasing to the eye and filling for the hungry appetite. Serve it over cooked rice or lo mein noodles.

MAKES 4 SERVINGS

2 teaspoons peanut oil
⅔ cup thinly sliced red onions
4 teaspoons grated fresh ginger
2 large cloves garlic, minced
1 large carrot, thinly cut on the diagonal
1 cup thinly sliced sweet red peppers
1 cup asparagus or green beans cut into 1″ pieces
6 cups coarsely shredded savoy cabbage
3 ounces oyster or domestic mushrooms, thinly sliced
2 tablespoons rice wine vinegar
1 tablespoon reduced-sodium soy sauce
1 teaspoon sugar
1 teaspoon oriental sesame oil
4 ounces mung bean sprouts
Hot-pepper sauce (optional)

Warm the peanut oil in a large no-stick skillet over medium heat. Add the onions, ginger and garlic. Cook, stirring, for 4 minutes.

Stir in the carrots, peppers and asparagus or beans. Cover and cook over medium-low heat for 3 minutes. Stir in the cabbage and mushrooms. Cover and cook for 4 minutes.

In a custard cup, stir together the vinegar, soy sauce, sugar and sesame oil. Add to the skillet; mix well. Cover and cook for 2 to 3 minutes, or until the vegetables are crisp-tender. Stir in the bean sprouts and heat through. Serve with the hot-pepper sauce (if using).

Per serving: 131 calories, 4.1 g. total fat (25% of calories), 0.5 g. saturated fat, 0 mg. cholesterol, 176 mg. sodium

---

THE CHINESE ADVANTAGE

When it comes to quick and healthy cooking, the Chinese wrote the book, says author Nina Simonds. Nina studied cooking in Asia for 20 years and has written four books that neatly simplify classical Chinese cooking for people who don't have handy access to exotic ingredients.

"The idea behind Chinese cooking is to prepare what is fresh and readily available," she says. You can whip up a quick meal by steaming some vegetables—any vegetables found in a regular supermarket—and tossing them with a Chinese-style sauce. Here are some of Nina's favorite quick sauces.

- *Sesame-vinegar sauce:* Combine soy sauce and vinegar with a bit of sesame oil and a pinch of sugar.

- *Garlic sauce:* Mix minced garlic with soy sauce and a pinch of sugar.

- *Spicy peanut butter sauce:* In a food processor, blend peanut butter, ginger, garlic, Worcestershire sauce, crushed red pepper and a little water.

In addition to perking up hot vegetables, Nina says, the sauces can act as a pickling agent in the refrigerator overnight and give leftover vegetables a zesty new life.

Vegetable Frittata

Combining only one whole egg per serving with extra egg whites cuts the amount of fat and cholesterol in this frittata without affecting its taste or texture.

⅔ cup coarsely chopped onions
⅔ cup coarsely chopped zucchini
⅔ cup coarsely chopped sweet red peppers
4 eggs
6 egg whites
2 teaspoons water
2 tablespoons finely chopped fresh basil
½ teaspoon salt
  Pinch of ground black pepper

Combine the onions, zucchini and red peppers in a 2-cup glass measure. Microwave on high power for 3 minutes, or until the vegetables are softened.

Place a large broiler-safe no-stick skillet over medium-high heat for 2 minutes. Add the vegetables. Cook, stirring occasionally, for 5 minutes, or until lightly browned.

While the vegetables are cooking, lightly beat together the eggs, egg whites, water, basil, salt and black pepper in a medium bowl. Add to the pan and swirl to evenly distribute the mixture. Cook over medium heat for 5 minutes, gently lifting the egg mixture from the sides of the pan with a spatula as it becomes set. Cook until the eggs are set on the bottom but still moist on the top. Remove from the heat.

Wrap the handle of the skillet with 2 layers of heavy foil. Broil 4″ from the heat for 1 minute, or until the top is golden.

Use a spatula to loosen the frittata from the skillet and slide it onto a serving plate. Cut into wedges to serve.

Per serving: 129 calories, 5.1 g. total fat (37% of calories), 1.5 g. saturated fat, 213 mg. cholesterol, 414 mg. sodium

---

Southwestern Frittata

$\mathcal{T}$his colorful frittata can turn a brunch or light dinner into a fiesta. Serve it with frozen no-fat-added hash browns and assorted fresh fruit, such as melon cubes, strawberries and blueberries.

MAKES 4 SERVINGS

2   teaspoons butter
⅔   cup chopped red onions
⅔   cup chopped sweet red peppers
1   cup fresh or frozen whole kernel corn
1   jalapeño pepper, seeded and finely chopped
      (wear disposable gloves when handling)
4   eggs
6   egg whites
⅓   cup finely chopped fresh cilantro
½   teaspoon salt (optional)
     Pinch of ground black pepper

Coat a large no-stick skillet with no-stick spray. Add the butter and melt over medium heat. Add the onions and red peppers; cook, stirring, for 3 minutes. Add the corn and jalapeño peppers; cook, stirring, for 3 minutes.

In a small bowl, lightly beat together the eggs, egg whites, cilantro, salt (if using) and black pepper. Add to the pan and swirl to evenly distribute the mixture. Cook for 5 minutes, gently lifting the egg mixture from the sides of the pan with a spatula as it becomes set. Cook until the eggs are set on the bottom but still moist on the top. Remove from the heat.

Wrap the handle of the skillet with 2 layers of heavy foil. Broil 4″ from the heat for 1 minute, or until the top is golden.

Use a spatula to loosen the frittata from the skillet and slide it onto a serving plate. Cut into wedges to serve.

THINK AHEAD: Frittatas are good hot, cold and at room temperature. Take leftovers along to work for an easy lunch.

Per serving: 180 calories, 6.8 g. total fat (35% of calories), 2.4 g. saturated fat,
216 mg. cholesterol, 380 mg. sodium

New Mexican Egg and Chili Bake

*T*hink of this egg dish as a cross between a frittata and a taco. It's got the characteristic flavors of a taco but is served as a casserole. Dish it up as is or top it with additional picante or taco sauce.

MAKES 6 SERVINGS

1½   teaspoons canola oil
1   cup finely chopped onions
⅔   cup chopped mushrooms
¼   cup finely chopped celery
⅔   cup skim milk
3   egg whites
1   can (4 ounces) diced green chili peppers, drained
3½   tablespoons picante or taco sauce
1   tablespoon chili powder
1   cup (4 ounces) finely shredded reduced-fat Cheddar cheese
1⅓   cups dry bread cubes
1⅓   cups rinsed and drained canned kidney beans

Coat an 11″ × 7″ baking dish with no-stick spray and set aside.

Warm the oil in a large no-stick skillet over medium heat. Add the onions, mushrooms and celery. Cook, stirring, for 3 minutes. Stir in the milk. Cook, stirring, until very hot but not boiling. Remove from the heat.

In a large bowl, use a fork to lightly beat the egg whites. Stir in the chili peppers, picante or taco sauce and chili powder. Then stir in all but 2 tablespoons of the cheese.

Use a fork to beat the hot milk mixture, a little at a time, into the cheese mixture.

Spread the bread cubes evenly in the prepared baking dish. Top with the beans, then carefully pour the milk mixture over the beans. Sprinkle with the remaining 2 tablespoons cheese.

Bake at 350° for 25 to 30 minutes, or until the mixture is set in the center when the baking dish is slightly jiggled.

Cool on a wire rack for 5 minutes. Cut into pieces to serve.

Per serving: 185 calories, 7.5 g. total fat (35% of calories), 3.7 g. saturated fat, 20 mg. cholesterol, 746 mg. sodium

---

It's So Easy ... It's Kid Stuff

SOUTHWESTERN AND EASY

*W*e do all sorts of things with tortillas, and they just lend themselves to quick meals for kids," says Barbara Pool Fenzl, the owner of Les Gourmettes Cooking School in Phoenix and a guru of the Southwestern style of cooking.

Once you have the ingredients on hand, Southwestern cookery is easy, healthy and quick. And because the variations are nearly endless, they lend themselves to a youngster's imagination.

Kids can fill tortillas with a host of healthy foods, top them with some salsa and bake them in an oven. Certainly, says Barbara, we're all familiar with tacos. Try them sometime with fish for a deliciously different variation.

Another quick and tasty Southwestern dish the kids can whip up is huevos rancheros—scrambled eggs on a tortilla topped with salsa. Or they can put together a nutritious salad with black beans, salad greens and a colorful variety of green and yellow peppers, all topped off with fresh lime juice, Barbara says.

Nachos are a favorite with youngsters and can be made in a hurry. Simply cover a layer of corn chips with some grated low-fat Monterey Jack or Cheddar cheese and place under the broiler for a few minutes to melt the cheese. Serve with salsa.

Crustless Onion-Mushroom Quiche

Bread crumbs replace the typical fat-laden crust in this quiche. And they save the time and effort needed to make pastry dough.

MAKES 6 SERVINGS

1⅓ cups dry bread crumbs
2 teaspoons canola oil
1½ cups sliced mushrooms
⅔ cup thinly sliced scallions
⅔ cup finely chopped onions
1 cup skim milk
2 egg whites
1 egg
¼ teaspoon ground black pepper
⅛ teaspoon salt (optional)
⅛ teaspoon ground nutmeg
1¼ cups (5 ounces) finely shredded reduced-fat Swiss cheese

Coat a 9" pie plate with no-stick spray and spread the bread crumbs evenly in the bottom of the pie plate.

Warm the oil in a large no-stick skillet over medium heat. Add the mushrooms, scallions and onions. Cook, stirring, for 5 minutes, or until the scallions are tender.

Stir in the milk. Cook, stirring, until very hot but not boiling. Remove from the heat.

In a large bowl, use a fork to beat together the egg whites, egg, pepper, salt (if using) and nutmeg until well-combined. Stir in 1 cup of the cheese.

Use the fork to beat the egg mixture, a little at a time, into the mushroom mixture. Pour into the pie plate. Sprinkle with the remaining ¼ cup cheese.

Bake at 350° for 25 to 30 minutes, or until the quiche is set in the center when the pie plate is slightly jiggled.

Cool the quiche on a wire rack for 5 minutes. Then cut into wedges to serve.

Per serving: 222 calories, 7.8 g. total fat (32% of calories), 3.1 g. saturated fat, 53 mg. cholesterol, 274 mg. sodium

---

Polenta with Tomato and Mushroom Sauce

*Y*ou can make this dish with regular white button mushrooms, but for variety, substitute crimini, shiitake or other more exotic varieties.

MAKES 4 SERVINGS

- 1 can (28 ounces) tomatoes (with juices), cut up
- 1 small onion, chopped
- 1 small carrot, finely shredded
- ½ teaspoon dried basil
- 1 clove garlic, minced
- 4 ounces mushrooms, sliced
- 1½ cups yellow cornmeal
- 4 cups water
- 2 teaspoons olive oil (optional)
- ½ teaspoon salt (optional)

In a medium saucepan, stir together the tomatoes (with juices), onions, carrots, basil and garlic. Bring to a boil over medium-high heat. Reduce the heat, cover and simmer for 15 minutes. Remove from the heat and let stand for 5 minutes.

Working in batches, puree the tomato mixture in a blender. Return the mixture to the saucepan. Stir in the mushrooms. Cover and cook over medium heat for 10 minutes, or until the mushrooms are tender.

While the sauce is cooking, stir together the cornmeal, water, oil (if using) and salt (if using) in a 2½-quart microwave-safe casserole.

Microwave on high power for a total of 9 minutes; stop and stir every 3 minutes with a wire whisk. Whisk again until the mixture is smooth. Cover and microwave for 6 minutes more. Let stand, covered, for 3 minutes.

Divide the cornmeal among serving plates and top with the mushroom mixture.

Per serving: 230 calories, 2.2 g. total fat (9% of calories), 0.2 g. saturated fat, 0 mg. cholesterol, 346 mg. sodium

Penne with Broccoli and Peppers

To keep this simple entrée quick, prepare the vegetable mixture while the pasta is cooking. And to easily round out the meal, serve it with crusty Italian bread. For variety, use half a red pepper and half a yellow one.

MAKES 4 SERVINGS

8	ounces penne
12	ounces broccoli stalks, sliced lengthwise and cut into 1½" pieces
1	tablespoon olive oil
1	sweet red pepper, thinly sliced
3	large cloves garlic, slivered
½	cup vegetable or defatted chicken broth
1¼	teaspoons Dijon mustard
½	teaspoon salt (optional)
	Pinch of ground black pepper
2	teaspoons balsamic vinegar
	Finely shredded fresh Parmesan cheese (optional)

Cook the penne in a large pot of boiling water according to the package directions. Drain, rinse with hot water and drain again. Keep warm.

While the penne is cooking, cook the broccoli in a small amount of boiling water for 6 minutes, or until crisp-tender. Drain.

Warm the oil in a large no-stick skillet over medium heat. Add the red peppers. Cook, stirring, for 2 minutes. Add the garlic and cook for 2 minutes.

Stir in the broth and broccoli. Cook for 3 minutes. Stir in the mustard, salt (if using) and black pepper.

Add the penne. Toss until combined. Drizzle with the vinegar and toss again. Sprinkle with the cheese (if using).

Per serving: 262 calories, 5.5 g. total fat (18% of calories), 0.7 g. saturated fat, 0 mg. cholesterol, 90 mg. sodium

---

Springtime Linguine with Asparagus

*H*ere is a quick and tasty way to prepare asparagus when it is in season.

MAKES 4 SERVINGS

    1 bunch scallions
   12 ounces asparagus
   12 ounces fresh linguine
    4 teaspoons olive oil
    3 cloves garlic, minced
    6 ounces mushrooms, thinly sliced
    4 teaspoons all-purpose flour
 1⅓ cups hot vegetable or defatted chicken broth
 1¼ teaspoons reduced-sodium soy sauce
    4 teaspoons grated Parmesan cheese
  ¼ teaspoon red-pepper flakes (optional)
  ¼ teaspoon ground black pepper

Cut the tops from the scallions, leaving 3″ bottoms. Thinly slice the tops.

Break off and discard the tough bottoms of the asparagus stems. Then cut each stalk into 3 or 4 pieces. Cook the asparagus in a small amount of boiling water for 4 to 5 minutes, or until crisp-tender. Drain.

Cook the linguine in a large pot of boiling water according to the package directions. Drain, rinse with hot water and drain again. Cover and keep warm.

Warm the oil in a large no-stick skillet over medium heat. Add the garlic. Cook, stirring, for 30 seconds. Add the mushrooms and stir for 1 minute. Cover and cook for 3 minutes.

Reduce the heat to medium-low. Stir in the flour. Cook, stirring, for 2 minutes. Slowly stir in the broth and soy sauce.

Add the scallion bottoms, sliced scallions, asparagus, linguine, cheese, pepper flakes (if using) and black pepper. Toss until well-combined.

Per serving: 392 calories, 8.3 g. total fat (19% of calories), 1.3 g. saturated fat,
2 mg. cholesterol, 227 mg. sodium

Orzo and Spinach Casserole

Orzo is small, rice-shaped pasta that cooks quickly. Serve the casserole with carrot sticks or sliced tomatoes for a no-fuss dinner. The easiest way to thaw the spinach is in the microwave; follow the package directions.

MAKES 4 SERVINGS

8   ounces orzo
3   teaspoons olive oil
8   scallions, sliced
2   large cloves garlic, minced
1   egg
2   egg whites
1   cup reduced-fat cottage cheese
2   tablespoons grated Parmesan cheese
¼   teaspoon salt (optional)
¼   teaspoon ground black pepper
⅛   teaspoon ground nutmeg
2   packages (10 ounces each) frozen chopped spinach, thawed, drained and squeezed dry
⅓   cup dry bread crumbs

Coat a shallow 2-quart casserole with no-stick spray.

Cook the orzo in a large pot of boiling water according to the package directions. Drain, rinse with hot water and drain again. Place in a large bowl and drizzle with 1 teaspoon of the oil. Toss to mix.

Warm the remaining 2 teaspoons oil in a large no-stick skillet over medium heat. Add the scallions and sauté for 4 minutes. Add the garlic and cook for 1 minute. Add to the orzo.

In a medium bowl, lightly beat together the egg, egg whites, cottage cheese, Parmesan, salt (if using), pepper and nutmeg. Add the spinach and mix well. Add to the orzo and mix well.

Transfer the mixture to the prepared casserole. Sprinkle with the bread crumbs. Bake at 350° for 30 to 35 minutes, or until heated through.

THINK AHEAD: You can assemble the casserole the night before and bake it just before serving.

Per serving: 406 calories, 8.4 g. total fat (19% of calories), 2 g. saturated fat, 58 mg. cholesterol, 494 mg. sodium

---

≫ Tips from the Family Chef ≪

AN INDISPENSABLE STAPLE

I always keep certain staples in the house, but the most important one is extra-virgin olive oil," says Julia della Croce, a frequent guest on radio and television talk shows and author of *The Vegetarian Table: Italy* and other highly acclaimed books on Italian cuisine.

It's excellent as a flavoring agent, especially for steamed vegetables, says Julia. "I use it on green beans, cauliflower, kale, spinach and other greens. With broccoli, I add a sprinkle of lemon juice to the oil at the table. Another favorite of mine is to dress cooked beets with extra-virgin oil and a touch of orange juice."

Extra-virgin olive oil also figures prominently in Julia's puttanesca sauce, a quick summer mixture that is made cold and heated only by the hot pasta on which it is served. "I combine the oil with chopped fresh tomatoes, some basil or mint and maybe some chopped black olives and diced mozzarella." What could be easier?

Tomato Macaroni and Cheese

*B*oth kids and adults will like this low-fat variation of macaroni and cheese. We replaced most of the standard cheese with just a small amount of regular Cheddar and some reduced-fat cottage cheese. Then we added tomato sauce to boost the flavor and color.

MAKES 4 SERVINGS

- 8 ounces elbow macaroni
- 1 cup tomato sauce
- ¼ cup finely chopped onions
- 1 large clove garlic, minced
- 1 cup 2% low-fat milk
- ½ cup reduced-fat cottage cheese
  Pinch of ground black pepper
- ½ cup (2 ounces) finely shredded Cheddar cheese

Cook the macaroni in a large pot of boiling water according to the package directions. Drain, rinse with hot water and drain again. Transfer to a large bowl.

Meanwhile, in a small saucepan, stir together the tomato sauce, onions and garlic. Cook over medium-low heat, stirring occasionally, for 10 minutes, or until the onions are tender. Pour over the macaroni and toss until coated.

In a small bowl, stir together the milk, cottage cheese and pepper. Add to the macaroni mixture and stir well.

Transfer half of the macaroni mixture to a 1½-quart casserole. Sprinkle with ¼ cup of the Cheddar. Top with the remaining macaroni mixture and the remaining ¼ cup Cheddar.

Bake at 350° for 30 minutes.

Per serving: 344 calories, 7.4 g. total fat (19% of calories), 4 g. saturated fat, 22 mg. cholesterol, 608 mg. sodium

---

Ricotta-Stuffed Shells

Stuffed shells are always popular and make a filling meal. To cut back on the sodium content of this dish, use reduced-sodium tomato sauce.

MAKES 4 SERVINGS

- 20 jumbo pasta shells
- 2 cups tomato sauce
- ¼ cup finely chopped onions
- 4 cloves garlic, minced
- ½ teaspoon dried basil
- 1 container (16 ounces) reduced-fat ricotta cheese
- ¼ teaspoon ground black pepper
- ⅛ teaspoon ground nutmeg
- 2 packages (10 ounces each) frozen chopped spinach, thawed, drained and squeezed dry

Coat a 13″ × 9″ baking dish with no-stick spray and set aside.

Cook the shells in a large pot of boiling water according to the package directions. Drain, rinse with cold water and drain again.

While the shells are cooking, stir together the tomato sauce, onions, garlic and basil in a small saucepan. Bring to a simmer over medium heat, then reduce the heat to low.

In a medium bowl, stir together the cheese, pepper and nutmeg. Add the spinach and mix well. Spoon about 3 tablespoons of the mixture into each shell.

Spread a few spoonfuls of tomato sauce in the bottom of the prepared baking dish. Add the shells, setting them upright. Spoon on the remaining sauce.

Bake at 350° for 25 minutes, or until the sauce is bubbly and the shells are heated through.

THINK AHEAD: These shells freeze well, so you can easily double the recipe and save the extras for future meals. If desired, make up individual servings by dividing the shells and sauce among small casseroles. Cover well and freeze. To use, bake until heated through.

Per serving: 326 calories, 4.9 g. total fat (13% of calories), 0.2 g. saturated fat, 16 mg. cholesterol, 961 mg. sodium

Vegetarian Chili

To add the texture of meat to this meatless chili, we use tofu that was previously frozen. Freezing tofu alters its texture and makes it chewy like meat. Serve this chili with assorted low-fat toppings, such as chopped scallions, reduced-fat sour cream, shredded reduced-fat Cheddar cheese and sliced jalapeño peppers. If you like, you can serve the chili over rice.

MAKES 6 SERVINGS

- 1   tablespoon olive oil
- 1   large onion, diced
- 1   large stalk celery, chopped
- 1   sweet red pepper, chopped
- 1   pound firm tofu, frozen, thawed and crumbled
- 5   cloves garlic, minced
- 1   tablespoon chili powder
- 2   cans (15 ounces each) no-salt-added kidney beans, rinsed and drained
- 1   can (28 ounces) no-salt-added tomatoes (with juice), cut up
- 1   can (4 ounces) diced green chili peppers, drained
- ½   teaspoon salt (optional)
- ¼   cup chopped fresh parsley

Warm the oil in a large skillet over medium heat. Add the onions, celery and red peppers. Cook, stirring, for 3 minutes. Add the tofu, garlic and chili powder. Cook, stirring, for 5 minutes.

Add the beans, tomatoes (with juice), chili peppers and salt (if using). Cover and simmer for 15 minutes. Stir in the parsley.

THINK AHEAD: Freeze the tofu overnight for use the next day. First drain it, then cut the large block into thick slices. Place in a single layer on a small tray lined with wax paper. Cover with plastic wrap. Remove from the freezer in the morning and let thaw until ready to use. Crumble before using.

Per serving: 345 calories, 10.2 g. total fat (25% of calories), 1.3 g. saturated fat, 0 mg. cholesterol, 278 mg. sodium

COLORS COUNT

*I*f you teach your youngsters to think of food in terms of color—the more colorful the better—they will automatically start eating healthier meals, according to Pat Baird, a registered dietitian and author of *The Pyramid Cookbook*.

"I often tell people to cook by color and to include a variety of vegetables that are red, green, yellow and orange," she says. "If you eat a wide variety of colors, you will be getting a large variety of the nutrients you need."

She says orange doesn't restrict you to oranges. There's cantaloupe, apricots, papayas, mangoes, winter squash and orange peppers also. Younger children can make a game out of listing how many different foods of various colors they can name and find in the produce section.

Another way to get kids involved in healthier eating is by making nutritious foods easily available. The combination of the freezer and the microwave oven is invaluable for this.

"What I tend to do is make large batches of beans, lentils and brown rice and freeze them in plastic bags," Pat says. "Then whoever wants a meal can pop a bag in the microwave and serve the food with salsa and leftover chicken. Or they can add fresh tomatoes and make a pita sandwich."

Frozen vegetables are another favorite in Pat's kitchen. They're especially nice because they come in such a variety of combinations. Toss them into soups, stir-fries and casseroles, she says. Or thaw the vegetables and serve them cold with a low-fat salad dressing.

Fiesta Bean Tostadas with Corn Relish

Beans cook fast in a pressure cooker, so you can use dry beans if you prefer them over canned ones and still assemble dinner quickly.

MAKES 6 SERVINGS

1	pound dried pinto beans, sorted, rinsed and soaked overnight
¾	cup chopped onions
3	large cloves garlic, minced
1	teaspoon ground cumin
1	teaspoon dried oregano
12	corn tortillas (6″ diameter)
1½	cups fresh or frozen whole kernel corn
1	tablespoon water
⅛	teaspoon salt
1	green pepper, coarsely chopped
¼	cup thinly sliced scallions
1	jalapeño pepper, seeded and finely chopped (wear disposable gloves when handling)
1	teaspoon lime juice
¼	teaspoon ground black pepper
¾	cup shredded reduced-fat Cheddar cheese
3	cups shredded leaf lettuce

Drain the beans and place them in a pressure cooker. Add enough cold water to cover the beans by 1″. Follow the manufacturer's directions to cover the pot and cook the beans for 9 minutes.

Remove the pressure cooker from the heat. Let stand for 5 minutes. Set the cooker under cold running water for several minutes to reduce pressure rapidly. Loosen and remove the lid following the manufacturer's directions.

Stir in the onions, garlic, cumin and oregano. Cook, uncovered, over low heat for 15 minutes, stirring occasionally.

Meanwhile, wrap the tortillas in a piece of foil. Place on a baking sheet and bake at 350° for 10 minutes to heat through.

While the tortillas are heating, place the corn in a medium microwave-safe bowl. Add the water and salt. Cover with wax paper. Microwave on high power for 1 to 2 minutes, or until tender. Drain. Stir in the green peppers, scallions, jalapeño peppers, lime juice and black pepper.

To serve, place the tortillas on individual plates. Divide the bean mixture among them, spreading it to the edges. Sprinkle with the cheese and lettuce. Top with the corn relish.

THINK AHEAD: This recipe makes a lot, so you can get a second dinner or some lunches from it. The best way to deal with leftovers is to refrigerate the individual components (beans, corn relish and toppings) separately and assemble the tostadas just before eating.

If you don't have a pressure cooker, cook the beans in a large saucepan with plenty of water to cover for 1¼ to 1¾ hours, or until tender. Drain and continue with the recipe.

Per serving: 464 calories, 6.6 g. total fat (13% of calories), 3 g. saturated fat, 12 mg. cholesterol, 234 mg. sodium

---

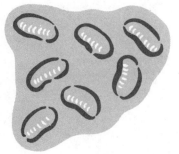

Easy Side Dishes

Stuffed Artichokes

*F*resh artichokes are a delicious treat when they are in season, and stuffing them is a satisfying, low-fat alternative to dipping them in butter, mayonnaise or olive oil.

MAKES 4 SERVINGS

  1 **lemon, halved**
  4 **large artichokes**
1½ **cups fresh bread crumbs**
  2 **cloves garlic, minced**
¼ **cup minced fresh parsley**
¼ **cup water**
  4 **teaspoons lemon juice**
  4 **teaspoons olive oil**
¼ **teaspoon ground black pepper**

Squeeze half of the lemon into a large bowl of cold water.

Cut the base of 1 artichoke so that it sits upright without tilting. Rub all the cut surfaces with the remaining lemon half as you work. Snap off the lower outer leaves and cut the thorny tips in the center about 1½" from the tops. Trim the thorns from the remaining leaves with scissors. Remove some center leaves with a small, sharp knife. Remove the chokes with a melon baller or a grapefruit spoon. Discard all the trimmings. Place the artichoke in the bowl of water.

Repeat with the remaining 3 artichokes.

In a medium bowl, combine the bread crumbs, garlic and parsley. Add the water, lemon juice, oil and pepper. Mix well.

Remove the artichokes from the water. Drain well and pat them dry. Gently spread the artichoke leaves out from the center and stuff the bread crumb mixture between the leaves. Loosely pack some of the stuffing in the center.

Place 2 of the artichokes in a medium microwave-safe dish that is deep enough to hold them upright. Add about ½ cup water.

Cover and microwave on high power for 10 minutes, or until the outer leaves are tender (test by pulling off an outer leaf to see if it is soft). Set aside for 5 minutes. Repeat with the remaining 2 artichokes.

Serve hot or at room temperature.

Per serving: 152 calories, 5.4 g. total fat (29% of calories), 0.8 g. saturated fat, 0 mg. cholesterol, 203 mg. sodium

---

⫸ Tips from the Family Chef ⫷

INSTANT SOUTHERN CHARM

Cooking in a Southern kitchen that has been in continuous operation since 1835, Donna Gill, chef of the Science Hill Inn in Shelbyville, Kentucky, has some great traditions to carry on.

But because traditional Southern cooking is heavy on the fat, Donna has come up with some quick tricks that not only lighten up meals but also add some hospitable Southern charm.

Donna says her venture into more healthful foods has led her to the pomegranate, that beautiful fruit with the juicy ruby-red seeds.

"I'll start with a Bibb lettuce salad, add a few walnuts and a simple vinaigrette dressing. Then I'll garnish it with pomegranate seeds," she says. "They add a tartness that really perks up the salad." And they add instant visual appeal to an otherwise ordinary salad.

Oven-Roasted Asparagus

*H*ere's an unusual way to cook fresh asparagus. If you use thin asparagus, shorten the cooking time, and if you use big, fat stalks, it might take a few minutes more. If you don't want to use the wine, use water in its place.

MAKES 4 SERVINGS

- 1 pound asparagus
- 2 cloves garlic, slivered
- 2 tablespoons water
- 2 tablespoons dry white wine or nonalcoholic white wine
- 2 teaspoons lemon juice
- 1 teaspoon olive oil
- ¼ teaspoon salt
- ⅛ teaspoon ground black pepper

Break off the tough ends from the asparagus spears. With a vegetable peeler, peel the bottom half of the asparagus stalks.

Scatter the garlic in a 13″ × 9″ baking dish. Arrange the asparagus in a single layer.

In a small bowl, combine the water, wine, lemon juice, oil, salt and pepper. Pour over the asparagus.

Bake at 400° for 10 minutes. Turn the asparagus over and roast for 8 to 10 minutes more, or until the asparagus are tender but slightly crisp and the liquid is almost gone.

Per serving: 39 calories, 1.5 g. total fat (29% of calories), 0.2 g. saturated fat, 0 mg. cholesterol, 111 mg. sodium

---

Oriental Green Beans with Sesame Seeds

These beans go particularly well with Asian menus, and the sesame seeds add a pleasant crunch to the dish. Although the recipe calls for fresh beans, you can substitute a 10-ounce package of frozen cut green beans. In that case, cook the beans just until thawed, then drain and proceed as directed.

Makes 4 servings

1½ teaspoons sesame seeds
1 pound green beans, cut into 2″ lengths
1⅓ cups water
1 teaspoon peanut oil
1 scallion, chopped
1 tablespoon cider vinegar
2 teaspoons packed brown sugar
1 tablespoon reduced-sodium soy sauce

Place the sesame seeds in a large no-stick skillet. Cook, stirring, over medium-high heat for 2 to 3 minutes, or until fragrant and lightly browned. Set aside in a small bowl.

In the same skillet, combine the beans and water. Bring to a boil over medium-high heat. Reduce the heat to low and simmer for 5 to 8 minutes, or until the beans are almost tender when pierced with a fork. Drain off the water.

Add the oil and scallions; cook, stirring, for 1 minute. Add the vinegar, brown sugar and soy sauce; cook, stirring, for 2 minutes, or until the beans are coated with the liquid. Sprinkle with the sesame seeds.

Per serving: 49 calories, 1.8 g. total fat (29% of calories), 0.3 g. saturated fat, 0 mg. cholesterol, 144 mg. sodium

---

Green Beans
with Water Chestnuts

*O*riental seasonings and water chestnuts add pizzazz to these green beans. The hoisin sauce called for is used frequently in Chinese cookery and can be purchased at specialty markets and large grocery stores.

MAKES 4 SERVINGS

1	pound green beans, halved
2	cups water
2	teaspoons oriental sesame oil
3	tablespoons defatted chicken broth
1	onion, chopped
2	tablespoons reduced-sodium soy sauce
½	large sweet red pepper, chopped
1	teaspoon hoisin sauce
1	can (8 ounces) sliced water chestnuts, cut into thin strips
2–3	drops hot chili oil

In a medium saucepan, combine the beans and water. Bring to a boil over high heat. Reduce the heat to low. Cover and simmer for 5 minutes, or until the beans are crisp-tender. Drain the beans in a colander and set aside.

Combine the sesame oil, broth, onions and 1 tablespoon of the soy sauce in a large no-stick skillet. Cook, stirring, over medium heat for 4 to 5 minutes. Stir in the peppers, hoisin sauce and the remaining 1 tablespoon soy sauce. Cook for 2 minutes more, stirring frequently. Add the beans, water chestnuts and chili oil. Cook, stirring, 1 to 2 minutes more.

Per serving: 113 calories, 2.7 g. total fat (20% of calories), 0.5 g. saturated fat, 0 mg. cholesterol, 306 mg. sodium

---

Red Beets with Orange Sauce

Beets and orange make a winning combination. This is especially good in the spring when tender young beets are available.

MAKES 4 SERVINGS

- 4 medium beets
- ⅓ cup orange juice
- 1 teaspoon grated orange peel
- 1 teaspoon olive oil
- 1 clove garlic, minced
- ⅛ teaspoon salt (optional)
- ⅛ teaspoon ground pepper

Scrub the beets. Trim, leaving ¾″ of the stems and roots in place. Place in a medium saucepan with enough water to cover. Cover and bring to a boil over high heat. Reduce the heat to a simmer and cook for 45 minutes, or until crisp-tender.

Rinse the beets under cold running water. Rub them between your hands, and the skins and stems should slip right off. Slice the beets and arrange them on a serving dish.

In a small bowl, mix the orange juice, orange peel, oil, garlic, salt (if using) and pepper. Pour over the beets. Serve hot or at room temperature.

THINK AHEAD: Because beets take awhile to cook, you can do them ahead. Peel the cooked beets but leave them whole; place in a bowl, cover and refrigerate. Just before serving, slice the beets and reheat them in a microwave for about 1 minute. Add the sauce.

This orange sauce is also good on fresh asparagus. You can make a double batch to serve on asparagus another night.

Per serving: 75 calories, 1.3 g. total fat (15% of calories), 0.2 g. saturated fat, 0 mg. cholesterol, 155 mg. sodium

---

Broccoli with Mushrooms

*Y*ou can use most any variety of fresh mushrooms for this dish. Among the many choices are button mushrooms, chanterelles and shiitakes.

MAKES 4 SERVINGS

1½	teaspoons olive oil
1½	cups thinly sliced mushrooms
2	cloves garlic, minced
½	cup defatted chicken broth
1	tablespoon dry white wine or nonalcoholic white wine (optional)
⅛	teaspoon ground black pepper
3½	cups broccoli florets

Warm the oil in a large no-stick skillet over medium-high heat. Add the mushrooms. Cook, stirring, for 4 minutes, or until the mushrooms are lightly browned. Add the garlic. Cook for 1 minute.

Stir in the broth, wine (if using) and pepper. Add the broccoli. Bring to a simmer. Cook, stirring occasionally, for 4 to 5 minutes, or until the broccoli is crisp-tender.

Per serving: 47 calories, 2.1 g. total fat (35% of calories), 0.3 g. saturated fat, 0 mg. cholesterol, 50 mg. sodium

---

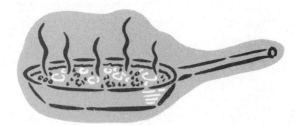

GRILLED MUSHROOMS

*J*oe's Restaurant in Reading, Pennsylvania, is a venerable establishment built on the mystique of the wild mushroom. But third-generation proprietor and chef Jack Czarnecki says it is only recently that he has taken the mushroom out of the usual pools of butter and heavy cream that tend to accompany it and brought it into a more natural state in his cooking.

Mushrooms cook up fast and are a good companion for a grilled dish. They can even be an entrée on their own.

"I've been grilling marinated mushrooms," Jack says, noting that adding herbs to the marinade imparts a lively flavor.

At home, Jack is fond of grilling up portobello mushrooms, those very large, brown, meaty mushrooms that are becoming available in supermarkets. He says, however, that large white mushrooms work just fine also.

"I cut off the stems and marinate the caps for three or four minutes in a mixture that is two-thirds vinegar and one-third olive oil." He varies the mixture by adding savory, thyme, sage or other herbs.

"Then I put the mushrooms on the fire," he says. "It's just great for a summer grill." Jack warns that because grills vary in heat intensity, the mushrooms have to be watched closely so they do not dry out. "You want them to be cooked but still moist."

Broccoli with Garlic Vinaigrette and Croutons

*T*his is a quick way to jazz up broccoli, and it's good served hot or at room temperature. The garlic croutons are a nice garnish.

MAKES 4 SERVINGS

- 1 pound broccoli
- 2 tablespoons water
- 2 teaspoons olive oil
- 2 teaspoons lemon juice
- 1 clove garlic, minced
- ⅛ teaspoon ground black pepper
- 2 slices whole-wheat bread
- 1 clove garlic, halved

Trim the tough ends from the broccoli and discard them. Cut the florets into spears and the stems into 3″ pieces. Place in a large, shallow microwave-safe dish. Add the water.

Cover and microwave on high power for a total of 5 to 6 minutes, or until the broccoli is crisp-tender; stop and stir after 2 minutes. Drain, leaving a few teaspoons of water in the dish.

In a small bowl, mix the oil, lemon juice, garlic and pepper. Pour over the broccoli while it is still hot. Toss well and set aside for 5 minutes.

Toast the bread and allow it to cool. Rub both sides of each piece with the garlic. Cut the bread into ¼″ cubes. Sprinkle on the broccoli just before serving.

Per serving: 87 calories, 3.2 g. total fat (29% of calories), 0.5 g. saturated fat, 0 mg. cholesterol, 96 mg. sodium

---

Broccoli-Tomato Skillet

*T*his quick-cooking combination of broccoli and stewed tomatoes makes a nice side dish with an Italian meal or with roasted chicken.

Makes 4 servings

- 1 medium onion, finely chopped
- 2 teaspoons olive oil
- 1 clove garlic, minced
- 1 can (14½ ounces) reduced-sodium stewed tomatoes (with juice)
- ¼ teaspoon dried thyme
- ¼ teaspoon dried basil
- ⅛ teaspoon salt
  Pinch of ground black pepper
- 3 cups small broccoli florets

In a large no-stick skillet, combine the onions, oil and garlic. Cook over medium heat, stirring frequently, for 5 to 6 minutes, or until the onions are tender. Add the tomatoes (with juice), thyme, basil, salt and pepper. Stir to mix well. Add the broccoli and bring to a boil.

Reduce the heat to low and simmer, stirring frequently, for 5 to 7 minutes, or until the broccoli is just tender.

Per serving: 72 calories, 2.8 g. total fat (31% of calories), 0.4 g. saturated fat, 0 mg. cholesterol, 99 mg. sodium

---

Indian Broccoli and Cauliflower

*T*his is a fragrant and zesty dish, particularly if you use the mustard seeds. If you like your vegetables milder, simply omit the seeds.

- 1 **can (14½ ounces) plum tomatoes, drained**
- 1 **teaspoon finely chopped fresh ginger**
- 1 **teaspoon ground coriander**
- ¾ **teaspoon sugar**
- ½ **teaspoon curry powder**
- ⅛ **teaspoon mustard seeds (optional)**
- ⅛ **teaspoon salt**
- 4 **cups mixed small broccoli and cauliflower florets**
- 1 **teaspoon nondiet tub-style margarine or butter**

In a large no-stick skillet, combine the tomatoes, ginger, coriander, sugar, curry powder, mustard seeds (if using) and salt. Bring to a boil over medium-high heat, breaking up the tomatoes with a spoon. Cook, stirring occasionally, for 5 minutes.

Add the broccoli and cauliflower. Reduce the heat to low and simmer, stirring occasionally, for 6 to 8 minutes, or until most of the excess liquid has evaporated and the broccoli and cauliflower are tender. Stir in the margarine or butter.

Per serving: 74 calories, 1.9 g. total fat (20% of calories), 0.8 g. saturated fat, 0 mg. cholesterol, 339 mg. sodium

---

DEALING WITH VEGETABLES

*A*ccording to Chinese chef and TV host Martin Yan, whose nationally televised show and San Francisco–based cooking school both proclaim "Yan Can Cook," there are two ways to get kids to eat more vegetables: "Dress them up or hide them."

"Kids get turned off to vegetables when they are overcooked," Martin says. So steam or stir-fry your vegetables lightly to retain their color. Youngsters seem to respond to colorful vegetable dishes.

But if they still push their plates away after eating only the meat and potatoes, try sneaking the vegetables into the entrée.

"Normally, when you have a piece of meat by itself and vegetables on the side, kids will eat the meat first," Martin says. "My tip is to cook the vegetables into the meat or the sauce. If you are making spaghetti, incorporate the vegetables into the meatballs—add some spinach or cabbage, for instance. And there is no reason why you can't put some in the sauce. Even when you make a pizza, add more vegetables on the top," he says.

Moroccan Cauliflower

*T*his is a good side dish for meat or poultry. You can turn it into a vegetarian main dish by serving it over couscous or rice. If you don't like your food too spicy, start with a small amount of ground red pepper and adjust the hotness according to your taste.

MAKES 6 SERVINGS

2 pounds cauliflower, trimmed and cut into large florets
4 cups water
1 can (28 ounces) tomatoes, chopped
2 cups sliced red onions
6 cloves garlic, minced
1 teaspoon dried marjoram
½ teaspoon ground cumin
½ teaspoon salt (optional)
1 teaspoon olive oil (optional)
½ teaspoon ground red pepper
2 teaspoons lemon juice
2 tablespoons minced fresh parsley

Combine the cauliflower and water in a Dutch oven or large saucepan. Cover and bring to a boil over medium-high heat. Reduce heat to medium and cook for 6 minutes.

Add the tomatoes, onions, garlic, marjoram, cumin, salt (if using), oil (if using) and pepper. Stir well, cover and bring to a simmer. Partially cover and cook, stirring occasionally, for 20 minutes. (As the cauliflower cooks, it will break into smaller pieces.) Stir in the lemon juice and parsley.

Per serving: 87 calories, 0.7 g. total fat (7% of calories), 0.1 g. saturated fat, 0 cholesterol, 227 mg. sodium

---

Herbed Cauliflower

*I*n this easy dish, the combination of dill, chives and chicken broth brings out the delicate taste of the cauliflower. Fresh dill and chives will give you much better results than the dried types.

MAKES 4 SERVINGS

- ⅔ cup defatted chicken broth
- 3 tablespoons chopped fresh dill
- 1 tablespoon chopped fresh chives
- Pinch of ground black pepper
- 3 cups small cauliflower florets
- ½ teaspoon nondiet tub-style margarine or butter

In a large no-stick skillet, combine the broth, dill, chives and pepper. Bring to a boil over medium-high heat and boil vigorously for 1 minute. Stir in the cauliflower. Reduce the heat to low and simmer, stirring occasionally, for 4 to 5 minutes, or until the cauliflower is crisp-tender. Stir in the margarine or butter.

Per serving: 27 calories, 0.8 g. total fat (22% of calories), 0.3 g. saturated fat, 0 mg. cholesterol, 69 mg. sodium

---

Zesty Sweet-and-Sour Cabbage

Try this pleasantly tangy cabbage with stuffed pork chops or a simple chicken or turkey entrée. Since cabbage is full of vitamins, quick to fix and inexpensive, it makes sense to serve it often. Tarragon is very appealing in this dish, but you could substitute another herb if you prefer.

MAKES 4 SERVINGS

2	teaspoons olive oil
4	scallions, chopped
1	carrot, finely shredded
¼	cup chopped celery
1	apple, chopped
⅓	cup dry white wine or nonalcoholic white wine
1½	tablespoons white wine vinegar
1½	teaspoons sugar
1	teaspoon tarragon leaves
1	teaspoon prepared mustard
⅛	teaspoon ground black pepper
5	cups coarsely shredded cabbage
¼	teaspoon salt (optional)

In a large no-stick skillet, combine the oil, scallions, carrots and celery. Cook, stirring, over medium-high heat for 3 to 4 minutes, or until the scallions are limp. Add the apples, wine, vinegar, sugar, tarragon, mustard and pepper. Cook, stirring occasionally, for 3 to 4 minutes, or until the liquid is reduced to about half. Add the cabbage and cook for 3 to 4 minutes, or until the cabbage is crisp-tender. Stir in the salt (if using).

Per serving: 98 calories, 2.6 g. total fat (23% of calories), 0.3 g. saturated fat, 0 mg. cholesterol, 50 mg. sodium

---

Sautéed Cabbage with Caraway

*T*ry this simple, savory side dish with mashed potatoes and grilled chicken. You can use either regular cabbage or the savoy variety, which has looser leaves and is more wrinkled.

MAKES 4 SERVINGS

    1 teaspoon nondiet tub-style margarine or butter
    1 teaspoon olive oil
    1 small onion, thinly sliced
    1 pound cabbage, thinly sliced and cut into 2″ strips
    1 teaspoon ground caraway seeds
    ½ cup defatted chicken broth
    ¾ teaspoon salt (optional)
    ¼ teaspoon ground black pepper
    1 teaspoon balsamic vinegar

Combine the margarine or butter, oil and onions in a large no-stick skillet. Cook, stirring, over medium heat for 2 minutes. Add the cabbage a handful at a time, stirring after each addition. Sprinkle with the caraway seeds and stir well. Cover and cook, stirring occasionally, for 15 minutes, or until the cabbage begins to brown.

Stir in the broth, salt (if using) and pepper. Cover and cook for 5 minutes. Sprinkle with the vinegar.

Per serving: 63 calories, 2.4 g. total fat (30% of calories), 0.8 g. saturated fat, 0 mg. cholesterol, 86 mg. sodium

---

Chinese Eggplant

*E*ven people who think they don't care for eggplant like this rich-tasting dish. It goes well with any Chinese main course.

MAKES 4 SERVINGS

4½ cups peeled and coarsely cubed eggplant
1 tablespoon + ⅓ cup water
6 scallions, thinly sliced
1½ teaspoons peanut oil
1 clove garlic, minced
3½ tablespoons hoisin sauce
1 tablespoon reduced-sodium soy sauce
2 teaspoons cider vinegar
2 teaspoons packed brown sugar
1½ teaspoons grated fresh ginger
1 teaspoon cornstarch

Place the eggplant in a large microwave-safe pie plate. Sprinkle with 1 tablespoon of the water. Cover with wax paper and microwave on high power for a total of 4 minutes, or until the pieces are crisp-tender; stop and stir after 2 minutes. Drain well.

Combine the scallions, oil and garlic in a large no-stick skillet. Cook, stirring, over medium-high heat for 4 minutes, or until the scallions are limp. Add the eggplant. Cook, stirring occasionally, for 3 minutes.

In a small bowl, stir together the hoisin sauce, soy sauce, vinegar, brown sugar, ginger, cornstarch and remaining ⅓ cup water until well-blended. Add to the skillet and cook for 2 to 3 minutes, or until the sauce thickens and the eggplant is tender.

Per serving: 74 calories, 1.9 g. total fat (21% of calories) 0.3 g. saturated fat, 0 mg. cholesterol, 330 mg. sodium

---

Baked Eggplant Slices

*E*ggplant slices serve as a sort of crust for this pizzalike side dish. Baking eggplant without added oil gives it a meaty and chewy texture that even kids will like.

MAKES 4 SERVINGS

1 eggplant (about 1½ pounds), peeled and sliced ⅜" thick
½ cup tomato sauce
1 clove garlic, minced
¼ teaspoon dried basil
½ cup shredded reduced-fat mozzarella cheese

Coat a baking sheet with no-stick olive oil spray. Place the eggplant slices on the sheet and spray them lightly. Bake at 375° for 12 minutes.

In a small saucepan, combine the tomato sauce, garlic and basil. Simmer for 5 minutes.

Remove the eggplant from the oven and turn the slices over. Spoon enough sauce over each slice to cover it. Sprinkle with the cheese. Bake for 10 to 12 minutes, or until the eggplant is tender when pierced with a fork and the cheese has melted.

Per serving: 72 calories, 2.5 g. total fat (29% of calories), 1.5 g. saturated fat, 8 mg. cholesterol, 254 mg. sodium

Stir-Fry of Snow Peas and Radishes

*T*he fresh-vegetable crunch of this stir-fry really appeals to children. If you want, add a little shredded carrot at the end for some extra color and some grated fresh ginger for a more grown-up flavor.

MAKES 4 SERVINGS

- 1 teaspoon peanut oil
- 2 tablespoons minced shallots
- 8 ounces snow peas, trimmed and strings removed
- 1 bunch radishes, thinly sliced
- 2 teaspoons reduced-sodium soy sauce
- 2 teaspoons rice wine vinegar
- ½ teaspoon sugar

Warm the oil in a large no-stick skillet over medium heat. Add the shallots and cook, stirring, for 1 minute. Add the snow peas; cook for 1 minute.

Reduce the heat to medium-low. Cover the pan and cook, stirring occasionally, for 2 minutes. Add the radishes, soy sauce, vinegar and sugar. Cover and cook for 2 minutes, until the vegetables are crisp-tender.

THINK AHEAD: If you're cooking for an older crowd, add 2 teaspoons fresh grated ginger while you cook the shallots. Or toss in some cucumber. Thinly slice it and add with the radishes.

Per serving: 42 calories, 1.3 g. total fat (27% of calories), 0.2 g. saturated fat, 0 mg. cholesterol, 93 mg. sodium

---

Peas with Mushrooms and Scallions

*T*his is a good dish to make when fresh peas are in season. When they're not available, substitute frozen baby peas.

Makes 6 servings

- 1 tablespoon olive oil
- 2 large shallots, minced
- 8 ounces mushrooms, sliced
- 3 cups peas
- 1 tablespoon water
- ½ teaspoon dried marjoram
- ¼ teaspoon salt
- ⅛ teaspoon ground black pepper
- 1 teaspoon balsamic vinegar

Warm the oil in a large no-stick skillet over medium heat. Add the shallots. Cook, stirring, for 2 minutes. Stir in the mushrooms. Cover and cook for 3 minutes. Add the peas, water and marjoram. Cover and cook over medium-low heat for 5 minutes, or until the peas are tender.

Stir in the salt, pepper and vinegar.

Per serving: 95 calories, 3.2 g. total fat (28% of calories), 0.3 g. saturated fat, 0 mg. cholesterol, 160 mg. sodium

---

Summer Squash Bake

*H*ere's a good way to use up extra zucchini and yellow summer squash.

MAKES 6 SERVINGS

2½ teaspoons olive oil
1¼ cups coarsely chopped mushrooms
 1 small onion, chopped
 ½ cup chopped sweet red peppers
 2 large cloves garlic, minced
 1 cup fresh bread crumbs
 2 cups cubed zucchini
 2 cups cubed yellow summer squash
 1 can (14½ ounces) Italian-style tomatoes,
    drained and chopped
 3 tablespoons tomato paste
 ½ teaspoon sugar
 ½ teaspoon chili powder
 ½ teaspoon paprika
 ½ teaspoon dried marjoram
 ¼ teaspoon salt (optional)
 ⅛ teaspoon ground black pepper

Warm the oil in a large no-stick skillet over medium heat. Add the mush-rooms, onions, red peppers and garlic. Cook, stirring, for 4 minutes, or until the onions begin to brown.

Stir in the bread crumbs. Cook, stirring, for 5 minutes, or until the bread crumbs are lightly browned and crisp.

Stir in the zucchini and yellow squash. Cook, stirring occasionally, for 2 minutes. Transfer to a medium bowl.

In the same skillet, stir together the tomatoes, tomato paste, sugar, chili powder, paprika, marjoram, salt (if using) and black pepper. Cook, stirring, over medium heat until the mixture just begins to boil. Add the zucchini mixture and stir well.

Coat a 2-quart casserole with no-stick spray. Bake at 375° for 20 to 25 minutes, or until the squash is tender.

THINK AHEAD: This casserole keeps well. In fact, you can bake it up to 4 days in advance. Cool it, then cover and refrigerate. To serve, reheat the casserole in a 350° oven.

Per serving: 132 calories, 2.3 g. total fat (21% of calories), 0.5 g. saturated fat, 0 mg. cholesterol, 304 mg. sodium

---

It's So Easy... It's Kid Stuff

FUN AND FLAVOR UNDER WRAPS

*Y*our youngsters can have fun creating their own lunchtime meals using wrappings such as tortillas and wonton wrappers, says Nicole Routhier, author of *Cooking under Wraps*.

"Wrapping is the perfect way you can get kids involved in creating their own dishes," Nicole says. "It is something that kids like to do."

She notes that wrappings are a convenient and often healthy way of preparing foods in many cultures in Southeast Asia and South America.

One of the easiest concoctions she has come up with is a variation on the grilled cheese sandwich. "You use flour tortillas and layer them with cheese and thin slices of fresh apples or pears," says Nicole. Your youngsters might want to try adding some seasoning, such as pepper or something more daring like coriander. Then you put another tortilla on top and secure the sandwich with toothpicks. Brush the top and bottom with oil or melted butter and grill the sandwich in a pan. The result is a crispy, flavorful and healthy treat for lunch or a snack. Be sure to remove the toothpicks before serving the sandwich.

Nicole says wonton wrappers also open up youngsters' imaginations. You can prepare a filling of ground chicken, minced onions, soy sauce and a little sesame oil. Let the kids put a small amount in the center of each wonton wrapper and pinch it closed like a little purse. "Then you can steam the wontons, which is a real healthy way of cooking them, or poach them in broth for a light soup. If you like, you can also pan-fry them in a little oil."

Italian Stewed Peppers

*T*here are many variations of this savory pepper side dish in Italy. Some are made with just peppers and onions; others add tomatoes and herbs, as we do here. You can use any color peppers you want. For a really colorful dish, mix one each of red, green, orange and yellow. To elevate this accompaniment to a lunch entrée, add crusty bread and cheese.

MAKES 4 SERVINGS

1½	teaspoons olive oil
1	large onion, thinly sliced
4	large peppers, thinly sliced
1	tomato, diced
3	cloves garlic, slivered
½	teaspoon dried oregano
½	teaspoon salt (optional)
¼	teaspoon ground black pepper

Coat a large no-stick skillet with no-stick spray. Add the oil and onions. Cook, stirring, over medium heat for 1 minute. Stir in the peppers. Cover and cook, stirring occasionally, for 5 minutes.

Stir in the tomatoes and garlic. Cover, reduce the heat to medium-low and cook for 10 minutes. Add the oregano, salt (if using) and black pepper. Cook for 3 to 5 minutes, or until the vegetables are crisp-tender.

THINK AHEAD: This dish is good cold and at room temperature as well as hot, so you can prepare it ahead.

Per serving: 80 calories, 2.6 g. total fat (27% of calories), 0.4 g. saturated fat, 0 mg. cholesterol, 8 mg. sodium

---

Wilted Spinach with Pine Nuts and Currants

This Mediterranean way to prepare spinach is popular all over Europe. No wonder—it's simple and versatile. In addition to serving it as a side dish, you can have it for a first course or even a salad. If you don't have fresh spinach, substitute two boxes of frozen whole-leaf spinach; cook it and drain it well.

MAKES 6 SERVINGS

1	tablespoon pine nuts
2	pounds spinach, washed and trimmed
¼	cup water
3	tablespoons lemon juice
2	teaspoons olive oil
1	clove garlic, minced
1	tablespoon currants

Place the pine nuts in a small skillet. Shake over medium heat for 5 minutes, or until lightly toasted.

In a Dutch oven, combine the spinach and water. Cover and cook over medium-high heat for 3 to 5 minutes, or until the spinach is completely wilted. Drain.

Add the lemon juice, oil, garlic and currants; toss well to mix. Sprinkle with the pine nuts.

Per serving: 43 calories, 1.8 g. total fat (31% of calories), 0.2 g. saturated fat, 0 mg. cholesterol, 81 mg. sodium

---

Stuffed Zucchini

*F*or variety, replace the zucchini with yellow summer squash (or use some of both). To serve as a vegetarian main dish, allow one zucchini per person.

MAKES 8 SERVINGS

- 4 zucchini (6–8 ounces each)
- 2 teaspoons olive oil
- ½ cup sliced onions
- 4 ounces mushrooms, diced
- ¼ teaspoon dried thyme
- 3 tablespoons fat-free buttermilk
- ¼ teaspoon salt (optional)
- ⅛ teaspoon ground black pepper
- 2 drops hot-pepper sauce
- 2 slices whole-grain bread, toasted and cut into ¼″ cubes
- 1 egg white, lightly beaten
- 1 tablespoon grated Parmesan cheese
- ⅓ cup water

Scrub the zucchini and cut off the ends; halve lengthwise. Arrange, cut side up, on a large microwave-safe plate in a spoke pattern. Microwave on high for a total of 5 minutes, or until the zucchini is just tender; stop and turn the zucchini over after 2 minutes. Let stand for 5 minutes. Use a grapefruit spoon to scoop out the pulp, leaving a sturdy shell.

Chop the zucchini pulp and place in a large no-stick skillet. Add the oil and onions. Cook, stirring, over medium heat for 5 minutes. Add the mushrooms and thyme; cook for 3 minutes.

Remove from the heat. Stir in the buttermilk, salt (if using), black pepper and hot-pepper sauce. Mix well. Add the bread cubes and egg white; toss well. (The mixture should be moist but not soupy; add an extra tablespoon of buttermilk, if necessary.)

Spoon the mixture into the zucchini shells. Place in a 13″ × 9″ baking dish. Sprinkle with the cheese. Pour the water into the pan.

Bake at 375° for 20 minutes, or until the zucchini is cooked through and golden brown.

THINK AHEAD: To save time you can stuff the zucchini in advance and refrigerate them until dinner. Bake for about 35 minutes.

Per serving: 62 calories, 2.3 g. total fat (33% of calories), 0.5 g. saturated fat, 27 mg. cholesterol, 71 mg. sodium

---

≫ *Tips from the Family Chef* ≪

FRESH TOMATO SAUCE IN NO TIME

*R*emember how Grandmother used to simmer her spaghetti sauce all day long?

Well, forget it, says Loretta Paganini, owner of the Loretta Paganini School of Cooking in Chesterland, Ohio. "Cooking tomatoes for a long time brings out the acid in them. You can have a better tomato sauce ready in 15 to 20 minutes."

First, sauté some onions and add a grated carrot. The carrot, Loretta says, cuts the acidity of the tomatoes and adds flavor.

Then add about a pound of chopped plum tomatoes, a little salt and pepper and some fresh basil. Cook that while you make a salad and boil the water for the pasta. Add some bread and you can have a meal ready in less than half an hour.

Stewed Tomatoes

*T*hese stewed tomatoes are full of flavor. Serve them as a side dish on their own or spoon them over mashed or baked potatoes.

Makes 4 servings

- 1 tablespoon olive oil
- 1 small onion, diced
- 1 stalk celery, diced
- 1 small sweet red pepper, diced
- 2 cloves garlic, minced
- 1 can (28 ounces) reduced-sodium tomatoes, chopped
- ½ cup water
- 1 teaspoon dried basil
- ¼ teaspoon salt (optional)
- ¼ teaspoon ground black pepper
- 1 teaspoon packed brown sugar
- 1 teaspoon paprika

Warm the oil in a large no-stick skillet over medium heat. Add the onions, celery and red peppers. Sauté for 5 minutes. Stir in the garlic and cook for 1 minute. Add the tomatoes, water, basil, salt (if using) and black pepper. Stir well and cook for 10 minutes.

Stir in the brown sugar and paprika. Simmer for 10 minutes.

Think ahead: Make a double batch and serve the leftovers later in the week with chicken, meat loaf or baked eggplant slices.

Per serving: 132 calories, 3.5 g. total fat (24% of calories), 0.5 g. saturated fat,
0 mg. cholesterol, 68 mg. sodium

Baked Butternut Squash

*T*his savory baked squash literally melts in your mouth. For variety, use blue hubbard, delicata or another winter squash.

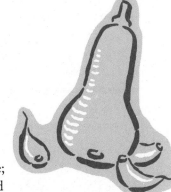

 1   butternut squash (about 1½ pounds)
 1   onion, thinly sliced
1½   tablespoons reduced-sodium soy sauce
 1   tablespoon olive oil
 6   cloves garlic, minced
 ½   teaspoon dried thyme
 ½   teaspoon salt (optional)
 ¼   teaspoon ground black pepper
 ¾   cup hot water

Coat a 13″ × 9″ baking dish with no-stick spray and set aside.

Peel the squash and cut it in half lengthwise; remove the seeds and strings. Shred using a food processor or box grater. Place in a large bowl.

Add the onions, soy sauce, oil, garlic, thyme, salt (if using) and pepper to the bowl. Transfer the mixture to the prepared pan and pour the water in the pan.

Bake at 450° for 20 minutes. Stir the squash well. Reduce the heat to 350° and bake for a total of 30 minutes; stir after 15 minutes. The squash should be soft and golden brown around the edges.

Per serving: 108 calories, 3.6 g. total fat (27% of calories), 0.4 g. saturated fat, 0 mg. cholesterol, 206 mg. sodium

---

Potato Pancakes

*P*otato pancakes are traditionally served during Hanukkah, but they make an interesting and tasty accompaniment to any dinner in place of plain potatoes or rice. They're especially good with a beef or pork roast. You could make a vegetarian dinner out of them by accompanying them with applesauce and fat-free sour cream.

MAKES 4 SERVINGS

2 **cups peeled and shredded baking potatoes**
1 **small onion, finely shredded**
1 **tablespoon fat-free egg substitute**
2 **tablespoons all-purpose flour**
¼ **teaspoon salt (optional)**
   Pinch of ground black pepper
2 **teaspoons canola oil**

Coat a large baking sheet with no-stick spray and set aside.

Place the potatoes in a colander and rinse with cold water. Use the back of a large spoon to press out the excess moisture.

Transfer the potatoes to a medium bowl. Stir in the onions, eggs, flour, salt (if using) and pepper.

Warm the oil in a large no-stick skillet over medium-high heat. Spoon about ⅓ cup of the potato mixture into the skillet for each pancake. Use the back of the measuring cup to spread the mixture into a flat pancake. Cook for 3 to 4 minutes per side, or until browned.

Transfer the pancakes to the baking sheet. Bake at 350° for 20 minutes, or until cooked through.

Per serving: 116 calories, 2.4 g. total fat (19% of calories), 0.3 g. saturated fat,
0 mg. cholesterol, 10 mg. sodium

Mashed Potatoes and Turnips

Here's a dynamic vegetable duo you're sure to enjoy. Mashed turnips give the ordinary whipped spud a delicious new twist. You won't even miss the gravy.

MAKES 6 SERVINGS

- ¾ pound turnips, peeled and cut into 1″ pieces
- 1½ cups water
- 1½ pounds potatoes, peeled and cut into 1″ pieces
- 2 cloves garlic, halved lengthwise
- 2 tablespoons nondiet tub-style margarine or butter
- ¼ cup 1% low-fat milk
- ¾ teaspoon salt (optional)
- ¼ teaspoon ground black pepper
- ¼ cup finely chopped fresh chives

In a medium microwave-safe dish, combine the turnips and ½ cup of the water. Cover and microwave on high power for a total of 8 minutes, or until tender; stop and stir after 5 minutes.

In another medium microwave-safe dish, combine the potatoes, garlic and remaining 1 cup water. Cover and microwave for a total of 10 minutes, or until tender; stop and stir after 5 minutes.

Add 1 tablespoon of the margarine or butter to the turnips and mash them with a potato masher. Add the remaining 1 tablespoon margarine or butter to the potatoes and mash them. Add the turnips, milk, salt (if using) and pepper to the potatoes. Mix well. Sprinkle with the chives.

Per serving: 146 calories, 4.1 g. total fat (24% of calories), 2.5 g. saturated fat, 1 mg. cholesterol, 76 mg. sodium

Oven-Roasted Potatoes with Leeks and Red Peppers

Here's a nice way to dress up potatoes. For a similar but different dish on other nights, use green, yellow or orange peppers, replace the leeks with onions and use thyme instead of rosemary.

MAKES 8 SERVINGS

- 6 sprigs fresh rosemary
- 2 pounds potatoes, halved lengthwise and thinly sliced
- ½ teaspoon salt
- ¼ teaspoon ground black pepper
- 1 large sweet red pepper, thinly sliced
- 2 large leeks, thinly sliced
- 2 tablespoons olive oil

Coat a 13" × 9" baking dish with no-stick spray. Place 3 sprigs of the rosemary in the dish. Add half of the potatoes in a thick layer. Sprinkle with half of the salt and black pepper. Top with the red peppers, then the leeks.

Top with the remaining 3 rosemary sprigs and the rest of the potatoes. Sprinkle with the remaining salt and black pepper. Drizzle with the oil. Cover with foil.

Bake at 425° for 25 minutes. Remove the foil, toss the vegetables to mix them and bake, uncovered, for 25 minutes, or until the vegetables are tender and browned on the edges.

Per serving: 165 calories, 3.7 g. total fat (19% of calories), 0.5 saturated fat,
0 mg. cholesterol, 148 mg. sodium

Stuffed Potatoes

Wonderfully rich and tangy, these stuffed potatoes are quite low in fat.

MAKES 10 SERVINGS

- 5 baking potatoes (8 ounces each)
- 1 cup (4 ounces) shredded reduced-fat Cheddar cheese
- 1 cup fat-free ricotta cheese
- ¾ cup fat-free buttermilk
- 2 tablespoons chopped fresh chives
- ⅛ teaspoon salt (optional)
- ⅛ teaspoon ground black pepper

Bake the potatoes at 400° for 1 hour, or until tender. Set aside for 5 minutes. Cut each potato in half lengthwise. Use a small spoon to scoop out the pulp, leaving a ¼″ shell. Transfer the pulp to a large bowl and mash with a potato masher.

Stir in the Cheddar until partially melted. Add the ricotta, buttermilk, chives, salt (if using) and pepper. Mix well. Add more buttermilk if the mixture is too stiff.

Spoon the potato mixture into the skins. Place on a baking sheet. Broil 5″ from the heat for 4 to 6 minutes, or until the potato mixture begins to brown.

THINK AHEAD: This makes a lot, so you can have leftovers for lunch or other dinners. Reheat one serving at a time in the microwave until warmed through.

If you're baking potatoes earlier in the week, make extras to use in this dish. The pulp is easiest to mash if it's warm. So if you have the time, make the filling and stuff the potatoes then. Cover and refrigerate. To serve, bake the potatoes at 350° for about 20 minutes to heat them through, then broil briefly to brown the tops.

Per serving: 151 calories, 2.1 g. total fat (12% of calories), 1.1 g. saturated fat, 8 mg. cholesterol, 126 mg. sodium

---

Sweet Potato Fritters

Sweet potatoes are high in beta-carotene, so it's good to have many ways to serve them. These fritters are easy to make and are a delightful change from plain baked sweets.

MAKES 8 SERVINGS

2 large sweet potatoes (1 pound each)
2 teaspoons nondiet tub-style margarine or butter
1 medium onion, minced
1 clove garlic, minced
1⅓ cups fresh bread crumbs
1 egg white
2 tablespoons orange juice
1 teaspoon reduced-sodium soy sauce
1 teaspoon packed brown sugar
¼ teaspoon ground ginger
Pinch of ground cloves
¼ teaspoon salt (optional)
⅛ teaspoon ground black pepper

Scrub the sweet potatoes and pierce the skin several times with the tines of a fork. Place on a microwave-safe plate, arranging them in a spoke fashion. Microwave on high power for a total of 10 minutes, or until tender; stop and turn the sweet potatoes over after 5 minutes. Cool slightly.

Cut the sweet potatoes in half lengthwise and scoop out all the pulp; discard the skin. Transfer the pulp to a medium bowl and mash with a fork. Stir in the margarine or butter.

In a 1-cup glass measure, combine the onions and garlic. Cover with wax paper and microwave for 1½ to 2 minutes, or until softened. Add to the bowl. Stir in the bread crumbs, egg white, orange juice, soy sauce, brown sugar, ginger, cloves, salt (if using) and pepper. Mix well.

Form into 8 patties.

Coat a large no-stick skillet with no-stick spray. Add the patties and cook over medium heat for 3 to 4 minutes per side, or until they are nicely browned.

THINK AHEAD: Leftover fritters keep well and taste great when reheated. To reheat, wrap in wax paper and microwave on high power for 20 seconds.

Per serving: 128 calories, 0.9 g. total fat (6% of calories), 0.2 g. saturated fat, 0 mg. cholesterol, 88 mg. sodium

---

≫ Tips from the Family Chef ≪

STRIVE FOR SIMPLICITY

*A*s the executive chef overseeing food preparation in the seven restaurants and two hotels that constitute Virginia's Colonial Williamsburg, Pierre Monet faces a multitude of problems every day. That's why he strives for simplicity in his own kitchen.

"The simple foods are the best," Pierre says, explaining that foods naturally rich in flavor don't require fancy preparation techniques. Steaming vegetables, for instance, cooks them quickly while preserving their flavor and valuable nutrients.

"You can make a variation of Vichy carrots easily by slicing the carrots, cooking them in a little bit of water and seasoning them with lemon juice and parsley," he says.

If you'd like a poached egg for breakfast but know you won't have time to fuss with it in the morning, prepare it the night before. Cook the egg in unsalted water until done, then use a slotted spoon to dunk it in ice water. That instantly stops the cooking process. Put the egg, still in the water, in the refrigerator. In the morning, you can quickly reheat it by dunking it in boiling water.

When you make stock, freeze a portion of it in ice cube trays. Then put the cubes in a sealed plastic bag in the freezer for quick and handy flavor enhancers.

Sweet Potato Casserole

*U*sing the microwave to cook the sweet potatoes helps cut down on preparation time. Kids especially enjoy this casserole, which contains crushed pineapple and raisins.

MAKES 6 SERVINGS

2 large sweet potatoes (1 pound each)
1 can (15½ ounces) crushed pineapple (packed in juice), drained
3 tablespoons packed brown sugar
2 tablespoons nondiet tub-style margarine or butter
½ cup raisins
1 teaspoon vanilla
¼ teaspoon ground cinnamon
¼ teaspoon salt (optional)
⅛ teaspoon ground cloves

Scrub the sweet potatoes and pierce the skin several times with the tines of a fork. Place on a microwave-safe plate, arranging them in a spoke fashion. Microwave on high power for a total of 10 minutes, or until tender; stop and turn the sweet potatoes over after 5 minutes. Cool slightly.

Cut the sweet potatoes in half lengthwise and scoop out all the pulp; discard the skin. Transfer the pulp to a large bowl and mash with a fork. Stir in the pineapple, brown sugar, margarine or butter, raisins, vanilla, cinnamon, salt (if using) and cloves; mix well.

Transfer to a microwave-safe 2½-quart casserole. Cover and microwave for 4 to 6 minutes, or until the sweet potato mixture is heated through.

Per serving: 236 calories, 2.7 g. total fat (10% of calories), 0.5 g. saturated fat,
0 mg. cholesterol, 70 mg. sodium

Winter Vegetable Stew

$\mathcal{T}$his is a hearty accompaniment for simple baked chicken, roast turkey or lean roast pork. The recipe calls for rutabaga, but if you don't care for it, use an extra celery stalk instead.

MAKES 6 SERVINGS

1 tablespoon nondiet tub-style margarine or butter
2 medium onions, quartered
1 stalk celery, thinly sliced
3 carrots, thinly sliced
1 small rutabaga, cut into ½″ chunks
1⅓ cups defatted chicken broth
3 potatoes, cubed
¾ teaspoon dried marjoram
¾ teaspoon dry mustard
¼ teaspoon dried tarragon
⅛ teaspoon curry powder
⅛ teaspoon ground black pepper
⅔ cup 2% low-fat milk
¼ teaspoon salt (optional)

In a Dutch oven or large saucepan, combine the margarine or butter, onions and celery. Cook, stirring, over medium-high heat for 4 minutes, or until the onions are limp. Stir in the carrots and rutabagas; cook for 3 minutes. Add the broth, potatoes, marjoram, mustard, tarragon, curry powder and pepper; bring the mixture to a boil.

Reduce the heat to low and simmer for 15 minutes, or until most of the liquid evaporates; stir the mixture occasionally to prevent the vegetables from sticking. Add the milk and salt (if using). Cook for 5 minutes, or until the vegetables are tender.

Per serving: 129 calories, 2.9 g. total fat (19% of calories), 0.5 g. saturated fat, 2 mg. cholesterol, 111 mg. sodium

---

Vegetable Kabobs

*T*he oriental-style marinade included in this recipe also goes well with shrimp and sea scallops.

Makes 6 servings

- 3 tablespoons rice wine vinegar
- 1½ tablespoons water
- 1 tablespoon grated fresh ginger
- 1 tablespoon reduced-sodium soy sauce
- 1 clove garlic, minced
- 1½ teaspoons peanut oil
- 1 teaspoon oriental sesame oil
- ½ teaspoon crushed red-pepper flakes (optional)
- 1 small zucchini, halved lengthwise and sliced ⅜″ thick
- 1 small yellow summer squash, halved lengthwise and sliced ⅜″ thick
- 1 small eggplant, cut into ¾″ cubes
- 3 small onions, quartered
- 1 sweet red or green pepper, cut into 1″ pieces
- 12 mushrooms
- 12 cherry tomatoes

In a small bowl, mix the vinegar, water, ginger, soy sauce, garlic, peanut oil, sesame oil and pepper flakes (if using).

Soak 12 (8″) bamboo skewers in water for at least 15 minutes. Alternately thread the zucchini, squash, eggplant, onions, red or green peppers, mushrooms and cherry tomatoes onto the skewers, leaving a small space between the pieces. (Alternate the colors and shapes so that the kabobs look appetizing. Leave an inch free on each end for easy handling.)

Place the kabobs in a large, shallow dish in a single layer. Pour the marinade over the kabobs. Cover and marinate at room temperature for at least 30 minutes.

Remove the kabobs from the dish, reserving the marinade.

To prepare the grill for cooking, spray the unheated grill rack with no-stick spray. Then light the grill according to the manufacturer's directions. Place the rack on the grill.

Place the kabobs on the rack over medium-high heat. Grill, turning the kabobs occasionally, for 15 to 20 minutes, or until the vegetables are crisp-tender; brush with the marinade occasionally.

Per serving: 60 calories, 2.2 g. total fat (30% of calories), 0.4 g. saturated fat, 0 mg. cholesterol, 94 mg. sodium

Grilled Vegetables

Grilling is such a simple way to prepare vegetables and brings out their best flavors. In addition to the vegetables used here, mushrooms, leeks and asparagus can be grilled successfully. You can also prepare these vegetables indoors under the broiler. Cook them 4 to 6 inches from the heat for 5 to 8 minutes.

MAKES 6 SERVINGS

2 **small zucchini, sliced diagonally ¼" thick**
2 **small yellow summer squash, sliced diagonally ¼" thick**
2 **small eggplant, sliced diagonally ¼" thick**
1 **large sweet red pepper, halved lengthwise and seeded**
2 **medium red onions, sliced crosswise ⅜" thick**
¼ **teaspoon ground black pepper**
   Pinch of salt

Coat an unheated grill rack with olive oil no-stick spray. Arrange the zucchini, yellow squash, eggplant, red peppers and onions on the rack and coat lightly with the spray. Place the rack over medium-hot coals, arranging it so the vegetables are 6" from the coals. Grill for 4 to 6 minutes on each side, or until the vegetables turn golden brown. Sprinkle with the black pepper and salt.

Per serving: 49 calories, 0.4 g. total fat (7% of calories), 0.1 g. saturated fat, 0 mg. cholesterol, 5 mg. sodium

Vegetable Pudding

*T*his soft, savory pudding makes a good accompaniment for baked chicken or fish. But it's also good as a vegetarian main dish accompanied by a salad. For variety, you can replace the corn and zucchini with mushrooms and spinach or other vegetables.

MAKES 6 SERVINGS

- 1 tablespoon nondiet tub-style margarine or butter
- 1 medium onion, diced
- 1 medium zucchini, halved lengthwise and thinly sliced
- 1½ cups frozen whole kernel corn, thawed
- 2 eggs
- 1 egg white
- 1½ cups skim milk
- 3½ tablespoons all-purpose flour
- 1 teaspoon dried basil
- ½ teaspoon salt
- ¼ teaspoon ground black pepper
- 3 drops hot-pepper sauce
- ⅓ cup grated Parmesan cheese

Coat a 1½-quart casserole with no-stick spray and set aside.

Melt the margarine or butter in a large no-stick skillet over medium heat. Add the onions. Cook, stirring, for 2 to 3 minutes, or until tender. Add the zucchini and cook, stirring occasionally, for 5 minutes. Add the corn and cook for 2 to 3 minutes.

In a large bowl, whisk the eggs and egg white until blended. Whisk in the milk, flour, basil, salt, black pepper and hot-pepper sauce. Add the vegetables and cheese. Mix well.

Pour into the prepared casserole and bake at 375° for 25 minutes, or until the top turns a golden brown and the pudding is set. Let stand for 5 minutes before serving.

Per serving: 156 calories, 5.6 g. total fat (31% of calories), 2.9 g. saturated fat, 81 mg. cholesterol, 347 mg. sodium

---

Southwestern Vegetable Sauté

*U*sually served as a side dish, this can also be used as a filling for flour tortillas to produce a main course. This is a good dish to make when summer produce is at its peak. If you like spicy food, add the jalapeño pepper; if you are making this for children, leave it out.

MAKES 4 SERVINGS

  1 **tablespoon olive oil**
  ¾ **cup chopped onions**
  ½ **sweet red pepper, chopped**
  1 **small zucchini, halved lengthwise and thinly sliced**
  2 **cups fresh or frozen whole kernel corn**
  1 **can (4 ounces) diced green chili peppers, drained**
  1 **jalapeño pepper, seeded and finely chopped**
     (wear disposable gloves when handling)
  2 **tablespoons chopped fresh cilantro**
  ½ **teaspoon salt (optional)**
  ¼ **teaspoon ground black pepper**

Warm the oil in a large no-stick skillet over medium heat. Add the onions, red peppers and zucchini. Cook, stirring, for 5 minutes, or until tender. Add the corn, chili peppers and jalapeño peppers. Cover and cook over medium-low heat, stirring occasionally, for 5 minutes.

Stir in the cilantro, salt (if using) and black pepper.

Per serving: 140 calories, 3.7 g. total fat (21% of calories), 0.5 g. saturated fat, 0 mg. cholesterol, 10 mg. sodium

---

Spicy Mixed-Vegetable Stir-Fry

You can vary the vegetables according to what your family likes or what you have on hand. If you don't have hot chili oil, substitute a pinch of ground red pepper or hot-pepper flakes.

MAKES 4 SERVINGS

2 tablespoons reduced-sodium soy sauce
1 tablespoon hoisin sauce
1 teaspoon cornstarch
½ teaspoon minced fresh ginger
3–5 drops hot chili oil
½ cup water
1½ teaspoons peanut oil
1½ cups cauliflower florets
1½ cups broccoli florets
1 cup halved mushrooms
3 scallions, cut into 1″ pieces
1 cup snow peas, trimmed and strings removed

In a small bowl, stir together the soy sauce, hoisin sauce, cornstarch, ginger, chili oil and ¼ cup of the water. Set aside.

Warm the peanut oil in a large no-stick skillet over medium-high heat. Add the cauliflower, broccoli, mushrooms and scallions; stir-fry for 2 minutes. Stir in the remaining ¼ cup water; stir-fry for 2 minutes.

Add the snow peas; stir-fry for 30 seconds. Stir in the soy sauce mixture. Cook, stirring, over medium heat until the sauce thickens and comes to a boil.

Per serving: 66 calories, 2 g. total fat (25% of calories), 0.3 g. saturated fat,
0 mg. cholesterol, 337 mg. sodium

Roasted Italian Vegetables

*T*his delicious, fuss-free vegetable medley goes very well with many pasta dishes.

  2 **onions, cut into 1″ chunks**
  3 **teaspoons olive oil**
2½ **cups halved mushrooms**
1½ **cups mixed zucchini and yellow summer squash**
       cut into 1¼″ chunks
1½ **cups peeled and cubed eggplant**
 ½ **cup chopped tomatoes**
  2 **cloves garlic, minced**
 ½ **teaspoon dried marjoram**
 ⅛ **teaspoon ground black pepper**
 ¼ **teaspoon salt (optional)**

Coat a very large shallow baking pan with no-stick spray.

In a large bowl combine the onions and 1 teaspoon of the oil. Spread evenly in the pan and bake at 400° for 10 minutes.

In the same bowl, mix the mushrooms, zucchini and yellow squash, eggplant, tomatoes, garlic, marjoram, pepper and the remaining 2 teaspoons oil. Add to the baking pan and stir to mix with the onions.

Bake, stirring occasionally, for 20 to 25 minutes, or until the vegetables are lightly browned and tender when pierced with a fork. Sprinkle with the salt (if using) and toss before serving.

Per serving: 59 calories, 2.6 g. total fat (36% of calories), 0.4 g. saturated fat,
0 mg. cholesterol, 6 mg. sodium

Tropical Skillet Side Dish

*T*his colorful pineapple and pepper stir-fry goes wonderfully with marinated flank steak, poultry or pork.

MAKES 4 SERVINGS

 2 tablespoons reduced-sodium soy sauce
 2 teaspoons sugar
 1 teaspoon white vinegar
 ½ teaspoon ground ginger
 1 small clove garlic, minced
 2–3 drops hot-pepper sauce
 1½ cups canned pineapple chunks (packed in juice), drained
 1 large sweet red pepper, cubed
 1 can (8 ounces) water chestnuts, drained
 ¼ cup thinly sliced scallions

Coat a large no-stick skillet with no-stick spray. Add the soy sauce, sugar, vinegar, ginger, garlic and hot-pepper sauce. Stir until combined.

Add the pineapple, red peppers, water chestnuts and scallions. Cook, stirring, over medium heat for 3 minutes, or until the sweet peppers are crisp-tender.

Per serving: 106 calories, 0.1 g. total fat (1% of calories), 0 g. saturated fat, 0 mg. cholesterol, 271 mg. sodium

---

Scalloped Apples and Raisins

Cooking the apples in the microwave first cuts down the amount of baking time needed to prepare this easy apple-raisin combination. This could double as a light dessert with frozen yogurt.

MAKES 8 SERVINGS

- 3 tablespoons granulated sugar
- 1 teaspoon ground cinnamon
- 6 cups thinly sliced tart apples, such as Granny Smith
- ½ cup raisins
- 1½ tablespoons water
- ¼ cup packed brown sugar
- 1½ tablespoons reduced-calorie tub-style margarine or butter
- 1 tablespoon dark corn syrup
- 1½ cups fresh bread crumbs

In a small bowl, combine the granulated sugar and ½ teaspoon of the cinnamon.

In a shallow 2½-quart oven-safe, microwave-safe casserole, mix the apples, raisins, water and the sugar mixture. Cover and microwave on high power for a total of 5 minutes; stop and stir after 2 minutes.

In a medium bowl, combine the brown sugar and the remaining ½ teaspoon cinnamon. Blend in the margarine or butter and corn syrup with a fork. Stir in the bread crumbs just until incorporated. Sprinkle evenly over the apples.

Bake at 400° for 15 to 20 minutes, or until the topping begins to brown and the apples are tender. Serve warm.

THINK AHEAD: Even though this dish doesn't take long to prepare, you could make it ahead and reheat individual servings in the microwave. Leftovers are also good microwaved for just a few seconds.

Per serving: 211 calories, 2.4 g. total fat (10% of calories), 0.4 g. saturated fat, 0 mg. cholesterol, 168 mg. sodium

---

Dried Fruit Compote

*U*sing ready-mixed dried fruit makes this compote really easy. If you'd like to customize your fruit mix, take your pick of pitted prunes, pears, apples, peaches and apricots. The curry powder gives this compote an unexpected savory flavor.

MAKES 8 SERVINGS

2 packages (8 ounces each) mixed dried fruit
1 cup orange juice
1 cup water
½ teaspoon curry powder
¼ teaspoon ground cinnamon
  Pinch of dried cloves

In a medium saucepan, combine the fruit, orange juice, water, curry powder, cinnamon and cloves. Bring to a boil over high heat. Cover, reduce the heat to medium-low and simmer for 20 minutes, stirring occasionally. Serve warm.

Per serving: 163 calories, 0.4 g. total fat (2% of calories), 0 g. saturated fat, 0 mg. cholesterol, 5 mg. sodium

---

Fiesta Corn and Black Beans

*U*se this piquant side dish to perk up poached or broiled chicken or fish.

MAKES 4 SERVINGS

1½ teaspoons olive oil

⅓ cup thinly sliced scallions

¼ cup chopped sweet red peppers

2 cups frozen whole kernel corn

1 can (15 ounces) black beans, rinsed and drained

2 tablespoons picante sauce

½ teaspoon chili powder

⅛ teaspoon curry powder

⅛ teaspoon ground allspice

1 medium tomato, chopped

⅛ teaspoon salt (optional)

In a large no-stick skillet, combine the oil, scallions and peppers. Cook, stirring, over medium-high heat for 3 minutes. Stir in the corn and cook until most of the liquid has evaporated from the pan and the corn is heated through.

Add the beans, picante sauce, chili powder, curry powder and allspice. Reduce heat to low and simmer gently for 5 minutes.

Stir in the tomatoes and salt (if using). Cook for 1 minute more, or until the tomatoes are heated through.

Per serving: 183 calories, 3 g. total fat (12% of calories), 0.3 g. saturated fat, 0 mg. cholesterol, 396 mg. sodium

---

Barbecued Beans

*B*arbecued beans needn't take all day to prepare. This version starts with canned beans and enlivens them with classic barbecue flavorings. We use three different types of beans here, but you can use whatever kind you prefer. A good way to use any leftovers is to heat some of the beans and spread them on a warm tortilla; sprinkle with some Monterey Jack cheese and roll up the tortilla for a quick lunch or snack.

MAKES 6 SERVINGS

- 1 medium onion, chopped
- 1 clove garlic, minced
- 1 can (15 ounces) reduced-sodium tomato sauce
- ¼ cup ketchup
- 1 tablespoon packed brown sugar
- ½ tablespoon cider vinegar
- 1 teaspoon prepared mustard
- ½ teaspoon chili powder
- ½ teaspoon dried thyme
- ⅛ teaspoon ground black pepper
- Pinch of ground cloves
- 2-3 drops hot-pepper sauce
- 1 can (15 ounces) no-salt-added kidney beans, rinsed and drained
- 1 can (19 ounces) cannellini beans, rinsed and drained
- 1 can (15 ounces) black beans, rinsed and drained

In a 1-cup glass measure, combine the onions and garlic. Cover with wax paper and microwave on high power for 1 to 2 minutes, or until the onions soften. Transfer to a large saucepan.

Add the tomato sauce, ketchup, brown sugar, vinegar, mustard, chili powder, thyme, pepper, cloves and hot-pepper sauce. Mix well. Stir in the kidney beans, cannellini beans and black beans. Bring to a boil over medium heat. Reduce the heat to low. Cover and simmer, stirring occasionally, for 20 to 25 minutes.

THINK AHEAD: This dish will keep in the refrigerator for 2 to 3 days and actually improves in flavor as it stands, so you can make it ahead.

Per serving: 244 calories, 1.7 g. total fat (5% of calories), 0 g. saturated fat, 0 mg. cholesterol, 571 mg. sodium

---

≈ Tips from the Family Chef ≈

GET A HEAD START AT THE STORE

*T*hanks to some health-conscious food producers, the start of a quick and healthy meal can begin at the supermarket, according to Ron Hook, executive chef of the Doral Saturnia International Spa in Miami.

"More and more things in the supermarket are lower in fat or salt," says Ron, who oversees the dietary requirements of the guests at the 48-suite health resort, where patrons are pampered on the inside as well as the outside.

"Everyone comes back here raving about the food," he says, noting that everything he serves is fresh. He even grows herbs for the spa's kitchen on its manicured grounds.

Yet one of Ron's favorite quick, hearty and healthy meals at home is a casserole that starts with a can of cooked beans (pinto or navy, for example), a jar of tomato sauce and some frozen vegetables. Add some bread crumbs for a topping and maybe sprinkle it with some fresh herbs. You just mix it all, put it into a casserole and bake it.

Of course, he suggests draining and rinsing the beans because the liquid they are packed in is high in sodium. And he suggests choosing one of the increasing number of low-fat tomato sauces on the market.

Texas Beans

*Y*ou can make these beans spicy by using hot chili peppers in place of mild ones.

MAKES 4 SERVINGS

- 2 teaspoons olive oil
- 1 medium onion, chopped
- 1 clove garlic, minced
- 1 can (15 ounces) reduced-sodium tomato sauce
- 2 tablespoons canned diced green chili peppers
- 2 teaspoons sugar
- 1 teaspoon chili powder
- ⅛ teaspoon ground black pepper
- 2 cans (15 ounces each) pinto beans, rinsed and drained

In a large saucepan, combine the oil and onions and garlic. Cook, stirring, over medium heat for 3 minutes. Add the tomato sauce, chili peppers, sugar, chili powder and black pepper. Mix well.

Stir in the beans. Cover and bring to a boil over medium heat. Reduce the heat to low and simmer, stirring occasionally, for 20 minutes.

Per serving: 268 calories, 3.8 g. total fat (11% of calories), 0.2 g. saturated fat, 0 mg. cholesterol, 425 mg. sodium

Spinach and Lentil Casserole

𝒯his hearty side dish could double as an entrée if accompanied by a tossed salad and crusty bread.

MAKES 6 SERVINGS

- 2½ teaspoons nondiet tub-style margarine or butter
- 1½ cups chopped mushrooms
- ¾ cup finely chopped onions
- 2⅔ cups defatted chicken broth
- ¼ cup long-grain white rice
- ¼ cup brown lentils, sorted and rinsed
- ½ teaspoon dried basil
- ¼ teaspoon dried thyme
- ¼ teaspoon ground black pepper
- 2 packages (10 ounces each) frozen chopped spinach, thawed and well-drained
- ⅔ cup 2% low-fat milk
- ¾ cup fat-free egg substitute
- 2½ tablespoons grated Parmesan cheese

Melt the margarine or butter in a large saucepan over medium heat. Add the mushrooms and onions. Cook, stirring, for 3 minutes. Stir in the broth, rice, lentils, basil, thyme and pepper. Cover and simmer for 25 minutes.

Stir in the spinach. Cover and cook for 10 minutes.

Remove the saucepan from the heat. Stir in the milk and eggs.

Coat an 11″ × 7″ baking dish with no-stick spray. Add the spinach mixture. Sprinkle with the cheese. Bake at 350° for 20 minutes, or until set in the center.

THINK AHEAD: You could assemble the casserole ahead and bake it just before serving. Increase the baking time to 25 to 35 minutes.

Per serving: 186 calories, 4.1 g. total fat (19% of calories), 1.3 g. saturated fat, 6 mg. cholesterol, 335 mg. sodium

Winter Vegetable and Chick-Pea Casserole

*Y*ou'll love the variety of textures and flavors in this easy vegetable casserole. Using the microwave for part of the cooking makes preparation a snap.

MAKES 6 SERVINGS

- 2 cups peeled and diced rutabagas
- 2 large carrots, chopped
- 2 cups chopped cabbage
- 3 teaspoons olive oil
- 1 large onion, chopped
- 2 cloves garlic, minced
- ½ cup defatted chicken broth
- 1 can (15 ounces) reduced-sodium tomato sauce
- 2 cans (15 ounces each) chick-peas, rinsed and drained
- 1¼ teaspoons dried thyme
- 1 teaspoon dried marjoram
- ¼ teaspoon salt (optional)
- ¼ teaspoon ground black pepper
- 1 cup fresh whole-wheat bread crumbs
- 2 tablespoons grated Parmesan cheese

In a 3-quart oven-safe, microwave-safe casserole, combine the rutabagas, carrots and cabbage. Cover and microwave on high power for a total of 8 minutes; stop and stir after 4 minutes.

Meanwhile, warm 2 teaspoons of the oil in a large no-stick skillet over medium heat. Add the onions, garlic and 3 tablespoons of the broth. Cook, stirring, for 5 minutes, or until the onions are tender.

Transfer the onion mixture to the casserole. Add the tomato sauce, chick-peas, thyme, marjoram, salt (if using), pepper and the remaining broth. Mix well. Stir in ½ cup of the bread crumbs.

In a small bowl, mix together the remaining ½ cup bread crumbs and the remaining 1 teaspoon oil. Sprinkle evenly over the casserole. Top with the cheese. Bake at 350° for 20 minutes.

Per serving: 266 calories, 6.1 g. total fat (20% of calories), 1.1 g. saturated fat, 2 mg. cholesterol, 714 mg. sodium

≈ Tips from the Family Chef ≈

A LIGHT, LOW-CAL SNACK

*C*lassically trained Jacques Pépin has spent a lifetime surrounded by the rich and traditional foods of France. But as one of the innovators in the culinary world, he has adapted the foods that he presents in his cookbooks and on his national television show to fit the needs of modern, healthy diets without losing any of the flavor and fun of eating.

That's why Jacques keeps an eye on the calorie and fat content of the food he serves at home as well. "We usually have fruit around the house," he says, noting that a fresh banana or crisp apple is always within reach in his Connecticut home. "And one thing we always have is soup. My wife is great at making consommé."

Jacques says chicken consommé is a favorite light, low-calorie snack he sips when he is home. With the right preparation, consommé can be low in fat. Jacques boils the bones from a Sunday-dinner chicken or holiday turkey in plenty of water with onions, leeks and herbes de Provence (a mixture of thyme, rosemary, parsley and other herbs).

Then he reduces the stock, strains it and clarifies it with beaten egg whites. This step greatly reduces the fat content.

"I just keep it in the refrigerator or in the freezer because it can be thawed quickly," Jacques says. "And if I feel like eating something, I have a cup of consommé."

Pasta with Creamy Parmesan Sauce

$\mathcal{T}$his pasta dish is so rich and creamy that you'd think it can't be low in fat. But it is. Serve it with simply prepared fish or chicken.

MAKES 6 SERVINGS

- 6 ounces fusilli
- 1 large onion, finely chopped
- 1 small clove garlic, minced
- 3 tablespoons dry sherry or nonalcoholic wine
- 1 tablespoon water
- 1 tablespoon nondiet tub-style margarine or butter
- 2 tablespoons all-purpose flour
- ½ teaspoon dry mustard
- ⅛ teaspoon ground black pepper
- 1¾ cups 1% low-fat milk
- ½ cup grated Parmesan cheese
- ⅓ cup fat-free sour cream

Cook the fusilli in a large pot of boiling water for 8 minutes, or until tender. Drain, rinse with hot water and drain again. Transfer to a large bowl and keep warm.

While the fusilli is cooking, combine the onions, garlic, sherry or wine, water and margarine or butter in a large no-stick skillet. Cook, stirring, over medium heat for 7 to 8 minutes, or until the onions are tender. If the liquid begins to evaporate, add a bit more water.

Use a wire whisk to stir in the flour, mustard and pepper. Gradually whisk in the milk. Cook, stirring, for 4 to 5 minutes, or until the sauce begins to thicken. Reduce the heat so that the sauce does not boil. Stir in the cheese and then the sour cream. Cook over low heat for 1 to 2 minutes.

Arrange the fusilli on a serving platter. Top with the sauce.

Per serving: 220 calories, 6.1 g. total fat (25% of calories), 3.3 g. saturated fat, 15 mg. cholesterol, 225 mg. sodium

---

Low-Fat Noodles Romanoff

Mushrooms embellish this noodle classic. Fat-free ricotta cheese and sour cream mimic the rich taste and creamy texture usually gotten from cream.

MAKES 6 SERVINGS

4 cups yolk-free egg noodles
2 cups sliced mushrooms
1 medium onion, minced
2 teaspoons nondiet tub-style margarine or butter
1 clove garlic, minced
1 cup fat-free ricotta cheese
1 cup fat-free sour cream
1 teaspoon Worcestershire sauce
2–3 drops hot-pepper sauce
⅛ teaspoon salt (optional)
⅛ teaspoon ground black pepper
8 tablespoons Parmesan cheese

Cook the noodles in a large pot of boiling water for 6 minutes, or until tender. Drain, rinse with hot water and drain again. Transfer to a large bowl and keep warm.

While the noodles are cooking, combine the mushrooms, onions, margarine or butter and garlic in a 2-quart microwave-safe casserole. Cover and microwave on high power for a total of 6 minutes; stop and stir after 3 minutes.

Stir in the ricotta, sour cream, Worcestershire sauce, hot-pepper sauce, salt (if using), black pepper and 6 tablespoons of the Parmesan.

Stir in the noodles and sprinkle with the remaining 2 tablespoons cheese. Cover and microwave for 5 to 6 minutes, or until heated through.

Per serving: 208 calories, 4.3 g. total fat (17% of calories), 2.4 g. saturated fat, 14 mg. cholesterol, 398 mg. sodium

---

Parmesan Fusilli with Tomatoes and Fresh Basil

*T*his is especially good with summer-fresh tomatoes.

- 6 ounces fusilli, broken
- 2 teaspoons olive oil
- 1 medium onion, finely chopped
- 1 clove garlic, minced
- 1 tablespoon finely chopped fresh basil
- 6 plum tomatoes, chopped
- ¼ cup grated Parmesan cheese

Cook the fusilli in a large pot of boiling water for 8 minutes, or until tender. Drain, rinse with hot water and drain again. Transfer to a large bowl and keep warm.

While the fusilli is cooking, warm the oil in a large no-stick skillet over medium heat. Add the onions and garlic. Cook, stirring, for 3 minutes, or until the onions are tender.

Stir in the basil, then gently stir in the tomatoes. Cook, stirring occasionally, for 3 minutes, until the tomatoes are softened. Stir in the cheese. Pour over the fusilli; toss gently to combine.

Per serving: 239 calories, 5.9 g. total fat (22% of calories), 1.7 g. saturated fat, 5 mg. cholesterol, 138 mg. sodium

---

Tropical Fruit Noodle Pudding

*Y*our kids will really like this lightly sweet side dish.

4	cups medium yolk-free egg noodles
1¼	cups fat-free ricotta cheese
1	cup fat-free sour cream
½	cup fat-free egg substitute
¼	cup light cream cheese, softened
¼	cup honey
1½	teaspoons vanilla
¼	teaspoon salt (optional)
½	cup canned crushed pineapple (packed in juice), well-drained
1	can (10½ ounces) mandarin orange sections (packed in water), well-drained
2	tablespoons sugar
⅛	teaspoon ground cinnamon

Coat a shallow 2-quart casserole dish with no-stick spray and set aside.

Cook the noodles in a large pot of boiling water for 6 minutes, or until tender. Drain, rinse with cold water and drain again. Return the noodles to the pan.

While the noodles are cooking, puree the ricotta, sour cream, eggs, cream cheese, honey, vanilla and salt (if using) in a food processor until smooth. Stir into the noodles. Then gently stir in the pineapple and oranges. Transfer to the prepared casserole and spread evenly.

In a small bowl, stir together the sugar and cinnamon. Sprinkle over the noodle mixture.

Bake at 375° for 40 to 45 minutes, until the pudding is set. Let stand for 5 minutes, then cut into squares to serve.

THINK AHEAD: This makes a lot, but that's okay. Leftovers are good for breakfast and snacks. Store the leftovers in the refrigerator for up to 4 days. Eat cold or reheat individual servings in the microwave for about 30 seconds.

Per serving: 128 calories, 0.9 g. total fat (6% of calories), 0.1 g. saturated fat, 3 mg. cholesterol, 46 mg. sodium

---

Fruited Bulgur Pilaf

Bulgur cooks quickly, making it a suitable alternative to rice for dinner. It has a pleasant, slightly nutty flavor and a chewy texture. Here it's enhanced with a fragrant array of spices, herbs, raisins and apple chunks. Ground coriander and fresh cilantro come from the same plant. The ground coriander is made from the dried seeds; the fresh cilantro is the green leaves.

MAKES 6 SERVINGS

1½	teaspoons olive oil
1	small onion, chopped
1¼	cups bulgur
2	cups defatted chicken broth
⅓	cup raisins
2	teaspoons grated fresh ginger
¾	teaspoon ground coriander
¼	teaspoon chili powder
¼	teaspoon dried thyme
¼	teaspoon ground cloves
6	tablespoons chopped fresh cilantro
⅔	cup diced tomatoes
½	cup chopped apples

In a medium saucepan, combine the oil and onions. Cook, stirring, over medium-high heat for 3 to 4 minutes, or until the onions are limp. Add the bulgur, broth, raisins, ginger, coriander, chili powder, thyme, cloves and 4 tablespoons of the cilantro. Bring to a simmer and cook for 5 minutes.

Stir in the tomatoes and apples. Cover, remove from the heat and set aside for 10 to 15 minutes, or until the liquid is absorbed. Fluff with a fork. Sprinkle with the remaining 2 tablespoons cilantro.

Per serving: 164 calories, 2.1 g. total fat (11% of calories), 0.2 g. saturated fat, 0 mg. cholesterol, 123 mg. sodium

---

Mixed-Vegetable Couscous

Couscous is a mild-flavored wheat product that's used extensively in the Middle East. Like bulgur, it cooks quickly and makes a nice change of pace from rice.

MAKES 6 SERVINGS

2	teaspoons olive oil
1	medium onion, chopped
1	large clove garlic, minced
2¼	cups defatted chicken broth
1½	cups small cauliflower florets
1	large carrot, diced
½	green pepper, chopped
¼	cup minced fresh parsley
1½	teaspoons dried thyme
1	teaspoon dried marjoram
1	bay leaf
¼	teaspoon salt (optional)
⅛	teaspoon ground black pepper
1	cup couscous

Warm the oil in a large saucepan over medium heat. Add the onions, garlic and 2 tablespoons of the broth. Cook, stirring, for 5 minutes, or until the onions are tender.

Add the cauliflower, carrots, green peppers, parsley, thyme, marjoram, bay leaf, salt (if using), black pepper and the remaining broth. Bring to a boil, then reduce the heat. Cover and simmer for 10 to 15 minutes, or until the vegetables are tender.

Stir in the couscous and return to a boil. Cover, remove from the heat and set aside for 10 minutes, or until the liquid is absorbed. Remove and discard the bay leaf. Fluff the couscous with a fork before serving.

Per serving: 163 calories, 2.3 g. total fat (13% of calories), 0.3 g. saturated fat, 0 mg. cholesterol, 157 mg. sodium

Microwave Corn and Rice Bake

Remarkably easy, delicious and colorful, this makes a great side dish for Mexican or Southwestern menus.

MAKES 6 SERVINGS

½	tablespoon olive oil
½	cup sliced scallions
1	clove garlic, minced
1½	cups defatted chicken broth
½	cup chopped pimentos
2	cups frozen whole kernel corn
1	cup chopped canned tomatoes, drained
1	cup quick-cooking rice
1	teaspoon chili powder
¼	teaspoon dried thyme
¼	teaspoon salt (optional)
⅛	teaspoon ground black pepper

In a 2-quart microwave-safe casserole, combine the oil, scallions and garlic. Cover with wax paper and microwave on high power for 1½ minutes. Add the broth, pimentos, corn and tomatoes. Cover and microwave for 5 to 6 minutes, until the liquid is almost boiling. Stir in the rice, chili powder, thyme, salt (if using) and pepper.

Cover and microwave for a total of 5 minutes; stop and stir after 3 minutes. Set aside for 10 minutes, then fluff with a fork before serving.

Per serving: 140 calories, 1.8 g. total fat (10% of calories), 0.1 g. saturated fat, 0 mg. cholesterol, 161 mg. sodium

---

Southern Vegetable and Rice Stew

*T*his makes a large pot of vegetables so you can serve it again.

1	tablespoon olive oil
1	onion, chopped
¼	cup chopped sweet red peppers
¼	cup chopped celery
3	cups defatted chicken broth
1	smoked pork hock (about 8 ounces)
1	package (10 ounces) frozen black-eyed peas
⅔	cup long-grain white rice
1¼	teaspoons dried basil
1¼	teaspoons dried marjoram
¼	teaspoon dried thyme
¼	teaspoon ground black pepper
1	package (10 ounces) frozen succotash
1	can (16 ounces) stewed tomatoes (with juice)
⅛	teaspoon salt (optional)

In a Dutch oven or large saucepan, combine the oil, onions, red peppers and celery. Cook, stirring, over medium-high heat for 5 minutes, or until the onions are limp. Add the broth, pork hock and black-eyed peas. Bring to a boil. Reduce the heat to low and simmer for 20 minutes.

Stir in the rice, basil, marjoram, thyme and black pepper. Bring the mixture to a boil again, stirring occasionally. Reduce the heat, cover and simmer, stirring occasionally, for 15 to 20 minutes, or until the rice is just tender.

Stir in the succotash and tomatoes (with juice). Cook over low heat for 10 minutes, or until the corn and beans are heated through. Discard the pork hock. Stir in the salt (if using).

Per serving: 195 calories, 3 g. total fat (13% of calories), 0.4 g. saturated fat, 1 mg. cholesterol, 283 mg. sodium

---

Rice and Broccoli Pilaf

*T*o keep the broccoli crisp, we add it halfway through the cooking period and let it steam atop the rice.

MAKES 4 SERVINGS

1	teaspoon olive oil
1	medium onion, finely chopped
1	small clove garlic, minced
2	cups defatted chicken broth
1	cup long-grain white rice
½	teaspoon dried thyme
½	teaspoon dried basil
⅛	teaspoon ground black pepper
1	bay leaf
1½	cups finely chopped broccoli florets

Warm the oil in a large saucepan over medium heat. Add the onions, garlic and 2 tablespoons of the broth. Cook, stirring, for 5 minutes, or until the onions are tender.

Add the rice, thyme, basil, pepper, bay leaf and the remaining broth. Bring to a boil, then reduce the heat. Cover and simmer for 10 minutes.

Add the broccoli. Cover and simmer for 10 minutes, or until the rice is tender and the liquid is absorbed. Remove and discard the bay leaf. Fluff with a fork to stir in the broccoli.

Per serving: 124 calories, 2.2 g. total fat (9% of calories), 0.3 g. saturated fat, 0 mg. cholesterol, 180 mg. sodium

---

Fiesta Rice

*T*his is the kind of rice that you get as a side dish in a Mexican restaurant—only it's better because it's lower in fat and sodium. Serve it with any Southwestern menu or let it add pizzazz to plain grilled chicken or seafood.

MAKES 4 SERVINGS

1	tablespoon olive oil
⅓	cup diced onions
1	cup long-grain white rice
1	clove garlic, minced
2½	cups water
2	tablespoons tomato paste
1	teaspoon chili powder
½	teaspoon salt
¼	teaspoon dried oregano
1	cup fresh or frozen peas
1	cup fresh or frozen whole kernel corn

Warm the oil in a large saucepan over medium heat. Add the onions and cook for 3 minutes. Add the rice and garlic; cook, stirring, for 2 minutes. Stir in the water, tomato paste, chili powder, salt and oregano. Mix well.

Add the peas and corn. Bring to a boil. Reduce the heat, cover and simmer for 15 minutes, or until the rice is tender and the liquid is absorbed. Let stand for 5 minutes. Fluff with a fork before serving.

Per serving: 277 calories, 3.9 g. total fat (13% of calories), 0.5 g. saturated fat, 0 mg. cholesterol, 371 mg. sodium

---

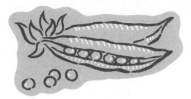

Herbed Microwave Risotto

*T*his side dish is filling enough that you can serve larger portions for a meat-less main course.

MAKES 6 SERVINGS

1 tablespoon nondiet tub-style margarine or butter
2 teaspoons olive oil
1 cup finely chopped onions
2 cloves garlic, minced
1¼ cups Arborio or long-grain white rice
3 cups hot defatted chicken broth
1 bay leaf
½ teaspoon salt (optional)
3 tablespoons minced fresh parsley
2 teaspoons minced fresh marjoram
¼ teaspoon ground black pepper

Combine the margarine or butter, oil and onions in a small no-stick skillet. Cook, stirring, over medium heat for 5 minutes, or until the onions are tender. Add the garlic and stir for 1 minute.

Transfer to a 2½-quart microwave-safe casserole. Stir in the rice. Cover and microwave on high power for a total of 1½ minutes; stop and stir after 1 minute.

Stir in the broth, bay leaf and salt (if using). Cover and microwave for a total of 15 minutes, or until the rice is thick and creamy; stop and stir every 5 minutes.

Let stand, covered, for 5 minutes. If the rice is too firm, microwave for 1 to 2 minutes more. Remove and discard the bay leaf.

Stir in the parsley, marjoram and pepper.

Per serving: 205 calories, 4.4 g.total fat (19% of calories), 1.5 g. saturated fat,
0 mg. cholesterol, 171 mg. sodium

HERBAL ESSENCES

*C*ooking, even classical French cuisine, is a science that changes with time and especially with the understanding of how food affects our health, says chef Jean-Maurice Jugé, who began his career in his father's restaurant near Chartres and went on to train in some of the best hotels and restaurants in Paris.

In keeping with today's quest for lower fat and more intense flavor, Jean-Maurice makes use of a technique he learned from his father.

"Every night before he went to bed, he would make a tea using fresh mint. I got the idea to make a tea out of other herbs to use in my cooking. So I made marjoram tea and cooked a piece of chicken in it. It was very flavorful," says Jean-Maurice, who is now the chef at the Log Cabin, near Lancaster, Pennsylvania.

"I have been doing a lot of poaching because it is both quick and healthy," he says. "And I use different herbal teas as my poaching liquid."

Making the tea is easy. Put some fresh or dried herbs in a tea ball or a piece of cheesecloth and add them to boiling water. Set aside to steep.

Jean-Maurice has also begun experimenting with other types of teas. For color and flavor, he might use things such as beets, celery or spinach.

Easy Rice Pilaf

*T*his pilaf uses quick-cooking rice and bakes in the oven, making it convenient and foolproof.

MAKES 8 SERVINGS

- ½ tablespoon nondiet tub-style margarine or butter
- ½ tablespoon olive oil
- ⅓ cup chopped onions
- 2 cups quick-cooking white rice
- 1 clove garlic, minced
- 4 cups defatted chicken broth
- ½ teaspoon salt

Melt the margarine or butter in a large ovenproof saucepan over medium heat. Add the oil and onions; sauté for 4 minutes. Add the rice and garlic; cook, stirring, for 5 minutes, or until the rice grains are milky white. (Do not allow the rice or garlic to brown; reduce the heat if necessary.)

Stir in the broth and salt; bring to a boil. Cover and place in the oven. Bake at 325° for 20 minutes, or until all the liquid has been absorbed. Fluff with a fork before serving.

Per serving: 200 calories, 2.4 g. total fat (11% of calories), 0.6 g. saturated fat,
0 mg. cholesterol, 177 mg. sodium

Golden Rice Pilaf

Serve this pilaf with poultry in place of stuffing, or as an accompaniment to pork, lamb or curried dishes.

MAKES 6 SERVINGS

- 1½ cups long-grain white rice
- 1 tablespoon olive oil
- ½ cup chopped onions
- ⅓ cup finely shredded carrots
- 1 cup defatted chicken broth
- ⅓ cup raisins
- ½ teaspoon curry powder
- 1½ teaspoons dried marjoram
- ¼ teaspoon dried oregano
- ¼ teaspoon dried thyme
- ¼ teaspoon dried basil
- ¼ teaspoon ground coriander
- 1 can (11 ounces) mandarin oranges (packed in light syrup), drained
- ⅛ teaspoon salt (optional)

Cook the rice according to the package directions.

While the rice is cooking, combine the oil, onions and carrots in a large nostick skillet. Cook, stirring, over medium-high heat for 5 minutes, or until the onions are tender. Stir in the broth, raisins, curry powder, marjoram, oregano, thyme, basil and coriander. Bring to a simmer and cook, stirring frequently, for 5 minutes or until the raisins are plumped and the liquid is reduced by half. Set aside until the rice is ready.

Fluff the rice with a fork and stir into the skillet. Add the oranges and salt (if using). Cook for 2 minutes to heat the oranges.

THINK AHEAD: You can cook the white rice ahead. To reheat it before adding to the other ingredients, place it in a large microwave-safe bowl, sprinkle with a little water, cover and microwave for about 4 minutes.

Per serving: 194 calories, 2.8 g. total fat (13% of calories), 0.3 g. saturated fat, 0 mg. cholesterol, 63 mg. sodium

Wild Rice with Leeks and Mushrooms

*T*his hearty dish is a perfect complement for all types of game, meat or fowl. Be sure to clean the leeks well, because they often have dirt between the layers. Trim off the green tops and tough outer leaves. Halve them lengthwise, slice and place in a strainer. Rinse well with cold water to remove any dirt. When purchasing wild rice, look for whole grains rather than broken pieces. Wild rice is often gritty, so it needs to be rinsed well with cold water.

MAKES 8 SERVINGS

3	cups water
1½	cups wild rice
3¼	cups defatted chicken broth
1	tablespoon olive oil
3	leeks, chopped
1½	cups sliced mushrooms
¼	teaspoon ground black pepper

In a large saucepan, combine the water and rice. Bring to a boil over high heat. Cover, remove from the heat and let stand for 20 minutes. Drain well and return to the pan.

Add 3 cups of the broth. Bring to a boil over medium-high heat. Stir, cover, reduce the heat and simmer for 25 minutes, or until the rice is just tender and the liquid has been absorbed.

While the rice is cooking, warm the oil in a large no-stick skillet over medium heat. Add the leeks and sauté for 3 minutes. Add the mushrooms; sauté for 3 minutes. Add the pepper and remaining ¼ cup broth. Cover and simmer for 5 minutes. Set aside until the rice is ready.

Add the rice to the pan and mix well.

Per serving: 164 calories, 2.7 g. total fat (14% of calories), 0.3 g. saturated fat, 0 mg. cholesterol, 159 mg. sodium

---

Green Rice

a lively blend of parsley, cilantro and scallions gives this side dish a pleasant green color as well as great flavor. If you have leftover cooked rice, use about 3 cups of it instead of cooking rice from scratch.

MAKES 6 SERVINGS

- 1½ cups long-grain white rice
- 1 tablespoon olive oil
- ¾ cup chopped scallions
- ¾ cup minced fresh parsley
- ⅔ cup chopped fresh cilantro
- 1 cup defatted chicken broth
- ¼ teaspoon ground black pepper
- ⅛ teaspoon salt (optional)

Cook the rice according to the package directions.

While the rice is cooking, combine the oil, scallions, parsley and cilantro in a large no-stick skillet. Cook, stirring, over medium-high heat for 5 minutes. Stir in the broth and let it come to a simmer. Simmer, stirring frequently, until the liquid reduces to half. Stir in the pepper and salt (if using). Set aside off the heat until the rice is ready.

Fluff the rice with a fork and add to the skillet. Stir to mix well.

Per serving: 133 calories, 2.8 g. total fat (19% of calories), 0.4 g. saturated fat, 0 mg. cholesterol, 62 mg. sodium

---

Quick Breads & Muffins

Apple-Oat Muffins

*T*hese flavorful muffins will keep for several days at room temperature in a tightly closed container.

MAKES 12

¼ cup quick-cooking rolled oats
¼ cup water
1½ cups all-purpose flour
¼ cup cornstarch
1½ teaspoons baking powder
½ teaspoon baking soda
1 teaspoon ground cinnamon
¼ teaspoon ground cloves
½ cup applesauce
¾ cup fat-free plain yogurt
¼ cup sugar
1 egg white
2 tablespoons honey
1 tablespoon canola oil
1 teaspoon vanilla
½ cup raisins

Coat 12 (2½") muffin cups with no-stick spray and set aside.

In a cup, stir together the oats and water. Set aside.

In a medium bowl, stir together the flour, cornstarch, baking powder, baking soda, cinnamon and cloves.

In a large bowl, whisk together the applesauce, yogurt, sugar, egg white, honey, oil and vanilla. Stir in the oat mixture. Add the flour mixture and raisins. Stir just until moistened; do not overmix (the batter will be lumpy).

Spoon the batter evenly into the prepared muffin cups. Bake at 425° for 11 to 15 minutes, or until the muffins are lightly browned and a toothpick inserted in the center comes out clean.

Per muffin: 144 calories, 1.5 g. total fat (9% of calories), 0.1 g. saturated fat, 0 mg. cholesterol, 111 mg. sodium

Pineapple Muffins

a distinctive pineapple flavor gives these muffins a taste of Hawaii.

MAKES 12

- 1 can (8 ounces) crushed pineapple (packed in juice)
- 1 egg white
- ½ cup skim milk
- ⅓ cup packed brown sugar
- 3 tablespoons canola oil
- 1¾ cups all-purpose flour
- 1½ teaspoons baking powder
- ½ teaspoon baking soda
- ½ teaspoon ground cinnamon
- ⅛ teaspoon salt (optional)

Coat 12 (2½″) muffin cups with no-stick spray and set aside.

Place the pineapple in a sieve over a 1-cup measure and press with the back of a spoon to remove the excess liquid. Reserve ¼ cup of the juice and set aside with the pineapple.

In a small bowl, whisk together the egg white, milk, brown sugar, oil and reserved pineapple juice. Stir in the pineapple.

In a medium bowl, stir together the flour, baking powder, baking soda, cinnamon and salt (if using). Add the pineapple mixture. Stir just until moistened (the batter will be lumpy).

Spoon the batter evenly into the prepared muffin cups. Bake at 400° for 13 to 15 minutes, or until the muffins are lightly browned and a toothpick inserted in the center comes out clean.

Per muffin: 137 calories, 3.6 g. total fat (24% of calories), 0.3 g. saturated fat,
0 mg. cholesterol, 106 mg. sodium

Better Muffins

To ensure success when preparing muffins, follow these tips.

- Be sure to preheat the oven. Muffins need a hot oven to rise properly. Position the rack so the muffin tin will be in the center of the oven.
- Grease the cups well with no-stick spray.
- Thoroughly mix all the dry ingredients in one bowl and the wet ones in another.
- Combine the ingredients from the two bowls and mix them using a wide rubber spatula or a wooden spoon. Mix only until the dry ingredients are well-moistened. The batter should be a little lumpy. Overmixing makes muffins tough.
- Use the batter immediately. Spoon it into the pan. A general rule is to fill the cups two-thirds full, but individual recipes can vary. Don't worry about making the tops even.
- If any muffin cups remain unfilled, add some water to them to keep them from scorching.
- Bake the muffins immediately. Test by inserting a toothpick into the center of a muffin; it should come out clean.
- Allow the muffins to stand in their pan on a wire rack for 5 minutes.
- Loosen the muffins from the pan by running a knife around the edges. Unmold them onto a rack covered with a tea towel to avoid getting indentations from the rack on them.
- Most muffins are best served hot. Store leftovers in a tightly sealed plastic bag or freeze them.
- To reheat leftovers, wrap them loosely in foil and bake at 325° for about 10 minutes, or until heated through. Or wrap one muffin at a time in a barely damp paper towel and microwave on high power for 20 to 30 seconds.
- To have freshly baked muffins first thing in the morning, separately mix the dry and wet ingredients the night before. Cover the bowl containing the dry ingredients and let it stand at room temperature overnight. Cover and refrigerate the wet ingredients. In the morning, preheat the oven, grease the pans and quickly combine the ingredients. The muffins can bake while you shower or get dressed.

Banana and Honey Bran Muffins

*H*earty, moist and delicious, these are good for breakfast or a snack. The flavor will be fullest if you use a very ripe or even slightly overripe banana. The muffins are best fresh but may be stored in an airtight container for a day or two.

MAKES 12

- 1⅔ cups raisin bran cereal
- 1 cup skim milk
- ⅓ cup honey
- 1 egg white
- 3 tablespoons canola oil
- 1¼ cups all-purpose flour
- 1½ teaspoons baking powder
- ½ teaspoon baking soda
- ½ teaspoon ground cinnamon
- ¼ teaspoon salt
- 1 ripe banana, diced

Coat 12 (2½") muffin cups with no-stick spray and set aside.

In a medium bowl, stir together the cereal, milk, honey, egg white and oil.

In a large bowl, stir together the flour, baking powder, baking soda, cinnamon and salt.

Stir the milk mixture into the flour mixture. Add the bananas and mix just until moistened; do not overmix (the batter will be lumpy).

Spoon the batter evenly into the prepared cups. Bake at 425° for 13 to 16 minutes, or until the muffins are nicely browned and spring back when lightly pressed.

Per muffin: 146 calories, 3.7 g. total fat (22% of calories), 0.3 g. saturated fat, 0 mg. cholesterol, 192 mg. sodium

---

Blueberry and Banana Muffins

*F*or the very best banana flavor, use a banana that's overly ripe. If you don't have fresh blueberries, use unsweetened frozen ones that are loose enough to pour when still frozen. These muffins are best served warm. To reheat leftovers, wrap them in foil and bake them for a few minutes.

MAKES 12

- 1 large ripe banana, chopped
- 6 tablespoons sugar
- 3½ tablespoons honey
- 1 egg white
- 3 tablespoons canola oil
- ¼ teaspoon grated orange peel
  About ½ cup skim milk
- 2 cups all-purpose flour
- 2¼ teaspoons baking powder
- ¼ teaspoon baking soda
- ¼ teaspoon salt
- ¾ cup blueberries

Coat 12 (2½") muffin cups with no-stick spray and set aside.

In a food processor process the bananas, sugar, honey, egg white, oil and orange peel for 30 seconds, or until well-combined. Transfer the mixture to a 2-cup measure. Stir in enough of the milk to make 1¾ cups.

In a large bowl, stir together the flour, baking powder, baking soda and salt. Add the banana mixture. Stir just until moistened; do not overmix (the batter will be lumpy). Fold in the blueberries.

Spoon the batter evenly into the prepared muffin cups. Bake at 425° for 13 to 16 minutes, or until a toothpick inserted near the center comes out clean. (Do not overbake.)

Per muffin: 167 calories, 3.7 g. total fat (20% of calories), 0.3 g. saturated fat,
0 mg. cholesterol, 134 mg. sodium

Cinnamon Blueberry Muffins

*T*hese moist, tender, cakelike muffins get a little extra tang from the buttermilk. Leftovers heated in the toaster oven are good the next morning.

MAKES 12

1	cup fresh blueberries
2	cups all-purpose flour
1½	cups fat-free buttermilk
1	egg
3	tablespoons canola oil
1	teaspoon vanilla
½	cup sugar
1	teaspoon baking powder
½	teaspoon baking soda
½	teaspoon salt
½	teaspoon ground cinnamon
¼	teaspoon ground mace

Coat 12 (2½″) muffin cups with no-stick spray and set aside.

In a small bowl, toss the blueberries with 2 teaspoons of the flour.

In another small bowl, whisk together the buttermilk, egg, oil and vanilla.

In a large bowl, mix the remaining flour with the sugar, baking powder, baking soda, salt, cinnamon and mace. Add the buttermilk mixture. Stir just until moistened; do not overmix (the batter will be lumpy). Fold in the blueberries.

Spoon the batter evenly into the prepared muffin cups. Bake at 400° for 20 minutes, or until the muffins are golden brown.

Per muffin: 163 calories, 4 g. total fat (23% of calories), 0.4 g. saturated fat, 18 mg. cholesterol, 210 mg. sodium

---

Carrot Muffins

Substantial but not too heavy, these muffins are lightly sweet and full of flavor from a mixture of spices. To turn them into wholesome cupcakes for the kids, increase the sugar to ⅔ cup and frost with a low-fat cream cheese icing.

MAKES 12

2	egg whites
1	cup fat-free buttermilk
2	tablespoons canola oil
1	teaspoon vanilla
1¼	cups finely shredded carrots
2	cups all-purpose flour
½	cup sugar
1½	teaspoons baking soda
½	teaspoon cinnamon
¼	teaspoon ground mace
¼	teaspoon ground cloves
¼	teaspoon salt
¼	cup chopped toasted walnuts

Coat 12 (2½″) muffin cups with no-stick spray and dust lightly with flour. Set aside.

In a small bowl, whisk together the egg whites, buttermilk, oil and vanilla. Stir in the carrots.

In a large bowl, stir together the flour, sugar, baking soda, cinnamon, mace, cloves and salt. Add the walnuts and mix well. Add the carrot mixture. Stir just until moistened; do not overmix (the batter will be lumpy).

Spoon the batter evenly into the prepared muffin cups. Bake at 375° for 20 minutes, or until the muffins turn golden brown and a toothpick inserted in the center comes out clean.

Per muffin: 160 calories, 4 g. total fat (22% of calories), 0.3 g. saturated fat, 0 mg. cholesterol, 236 mg. sodium

---

Savory Corn Muffins

*J*f your family likes chili peppers, they'll adore these Tex-Mex muffins.

MAKES 12

> 1½   cups 1% low-fat milk
> 1   egg
> 1   tablespoon canola oil
> 1½   cups cornmeal
> ½   cup all-purpose flour
> 1½   teaspoons baking powder
> ½   teaspoon baking soda
> 1   tablespoon sugar
> 1   cup whole kernel corn
> ⅓   cup diced onions
> 1   can (4 ounces) chopped green chili peppers, drained

Coat 12 (2½") muffin cups with no-stick spray and set aside.

In a small bowl, whisk together the milk, egg and oil.

In a large bowl, stir together the cornmeal, flour, baking powder, baking soda and sugar. Add the corn, onions and chili peppers. Add the milk mixture. Stir just until moistened; do not overmix (the batter will be lumpy).

Spoon the batter evenly into the prepared muffin cups. Bake at 400° for 18 to 20 minutes, or until a toothpick inserted in the center comes out clean.

Per serving: 123 calories, 2.5 g. total fat (18% of calories), 0.5 g. saturated fat, 19 mg. cholesterol, 231 mg. sodium

---

Sour Cream Cranberry Muffins

*T*he cinnamon topping nicely balances the tartness of the cranberries. Fresh cranberries are at their peak in October and November. During the rest of the year, they are sold frozen. If you use the frozen berries, thaw them before chopping them.

MAKES 12

Muffins

¾ cup skim milk
½ cup fat-free sour cream
3 tablespoons canola oil
1 egg white
1 teaspoon vanilla
2 cups all-purpose flour
½ cup sugar
1½ teaspoons baking powder
1 teaspoon ground cinnamon
½ teaspoon baking soda
¼ teaspoon salt
1 cup coarsely chopped cranberries

Cinnamon Topping

2½ tablespoons sugar
1 teaspoon light corn syrup
¼ teaspoon ground cinnamon
¼ teaspoon water

To make the muffins: Coat 12 (2½″) muffin cups with no-stick spray and set aside.

In a medium bowl, whisk together the milk, sour cream, oil, egg white and vanilla.

In a large bowl, stir together the flour, sugar, baking powder, cinnamon, baking soda and salt. Add the sour cream mixture. Stir just until moistened; do not overmix (the batter will be lumpy). Fold in the cranberries.

Spoon the batter evenly into the prepared muffin cups. Bake at 400° for 12 to 15 minutes, or until a toothpick inserted near the center comes out clean. (Do not overbake.)

To make the cinnamon topping: While the muffins are baking, stir together the sugar, corn syrup, cinnamon and water in a small bowl.

Remove the muffins from the oven. Spoon the topping evenly over the hot muffins, spreading it to the edges. Return the muffins to the oven and bake about 2 minutes more, or until the topping is bubbly.

Per muffin: 176 calories, 3.7 g. total fat (19% of calories), 0.3 g. saturated fat, 0 mg. cholesterol, 134 mg. sodium

---

≫ Tips from the Family Chef ≪

EQUIPMENT KNOW-HOW

*O*ne way to save time in the kitchen is to get ready to cook even before you know what you're going to make, says Jonathan Zearfoss, one of the course developers at the Culinary Institute of America in Hyde Park, New York.

"If there's a chance you're going to use the oven, turn it on as soon as you get into the kitchen. Then start rummaging around for ingredients and ideas. It helps cut down on time waiting for the oven to preheat."

Get the jump on cleanup by investing in no-stick pans. You'll use less oil in cooking—and less elbow grease when washing the dishes.

Soup is another timesaver. "You can make a big batch at your leisure and heat it up as you need it," he says.

Lemon-Lime Ginger Muffins

$\mathcal{T}$hese low-fat citrus muffins have a secret ingredient—zucchini—that adds fiber and also keeps the muffins moist and tender for up to 3 days.

MAKES 12

Muffins
- 1 large lime
- 1 small lemon
- ½ cup sugar
- 1 slice (½" thick) fresh ginger
- 1 small zucchini, coarsely chopped
- ½ cup skim milk
- ¼ cup fat-free plain yogurt
- 1 egg white
- 3 tablespoons canola oil
- 1 teaspoon vanilla
- 2 cups all-purpose flour
- 2 teaspoons baking powder
- ½ teaspoon baking soda
- ¼ teaspoon salt

Glaze
- 2½ tablespoons sugar
- 1¼ teaspoons skim milk
- ⅛ teaspoon vanilla

To make the muffins: Coat 12 (2½") muffin cups with no-stick spray and set aside.

Using a vegetable peeler, cut strips of peel from the lime and lemon. Be careful to remove only the colored portion of the peels and not the bitter white portion underneath. Place the peels in a food processor. Reserve the lime and lemon for another use.

Add the sugar and ginger. Process for 2 minutes, or until the peels and ginger are very finely chopped. Add the zucchini; process with a few on/off turns. Add the milk, yogurt, egg white, oil and vanilla. Process with on/off turns until the zucchini is finely chopped (stop and scrape down the sides of the container as necessary).

In a large bowl, stir together the flour, baking powder, baking soda and salt. Add the zucchini mixture. Stir just until moistened; do not overmix (the batter will be lumpy).

Spoon the batter evenly into the prepared muffin cups (the cups will be very full). Bake at 400° for 13 to 15 minutes, or until a toothpick inserted near the center comes out clean. (Do not overbake.)

To make the glaze: While the muffins are baking, stir together the sugar, milk and vanilla in a small cup.

Remove the muffins from the oven. Using a pastry brush, generously brush the glaze on the muffin tops. Return the muffins to the oven and bake for 1 minute, or until the glaze just begins to bubble.

Per muffin: 161 calories, 3.6 g. total fat (21% of calories), 0.3 g. saturated fat, 0 mg. cholesterol, 167 mg. sodium

---

Pumpkin Muffins

*T*hese muffins have the nutritional punch of beta-carotene and the spicy flavor of gingerbread.

MAKES 12

- 1 egg white
- ⅔ cup canned pumpkin
- ⅓ cup skim milk
- ¼ cup light molasses
- 3 tablespoons canola oil
- 3 tablespoons sugar
- 1½ cups all-purpose flour
- 1 teaspoon baking powder
- ¾ teaspoon ground ginger
- ½ teaspoon baking soda
- ¼ teaspoon ground cloves
- ¼ teaspoon ground cinnamon
- ⅛ teaspoon salt (optional)
- ¾ cup raisins

Preheat the oven to 400°. Coat 12 (2½″) muffin cups with no-stick spray and set aside.

In a small bowl, whisk together the egg white, pumpkin, milk, molasses, oil and sugar.

In a medium bowl, stir together the flour, baking powder, ginger, baking soda, cloves, cinnamon and salt (if using). Add the pumpkin mixture. Stir just until moistened; do not overmix (the batter will be lumpy). Then stir in the raisins.

Spoon the batter evenly into the prepared muffin cups. Bake at 400° for 14 to 16 minutes, or until the muffins are lightly browned or until a toothpick inserted in the center comes out clean.

Per serving: 152 calories, 3.7 g. total fat (21% of calories), 0.3 g. saturated fat, 0 mg. cholesterol, 91 mg. sodium

---

Rosemary-Raisin Muffins

*M*ake every effort to use fresh rosemary in these aromatic muffins. If you don't have fresh, you may substitute about half as much dried rosemary. But since the dried herb tends to be tough, be sure to chop or crush it until very fine before adding it to the batter.

MAKES 12

¾ cup raisins
2½ teaspoons finely chopped fresh rosemary
¼ cup hot water
¾ cup skim milk
½ cup sugar
3 tablespoons canola oil
¼ cup fat-free plain yogurt
1 egg white
1¾ cups all-purpose flour
¼ cup cornstarch
2¼ teaspoons baking powder
¼ teaspoon baking soda
¼ teaspoon salt

Coat 12 (2½") muffin cups with no-stick spray and set aside.

In a medium bowl combine the raisins, rosemary and water. Set aside for 10 minutes.

Add the milk, sugar, oil, yogurt and egg white. Mix well.

In a large bowl, stir together the flour, cornstarch, baking powder, baking soda and salt. Add the raisin mixture. Stir just until moistened; do not overmix (the batter will be lumpy).

Spoon the batter evenly into the prepared cups. Bake at 425° for 12 to 16 minutes, or until the muffins are lightly browned and spring back when touched.

Per muffin: 180 calories, 3.7 g. total fat (18% of calories), 0.3 g. saturated fat, 0 mg. cholesterol, 150 mg. sodium

---

Whole-Grain Honey Muffins

*A*lthough these muffins contain cornmeal, wheat germ and whole-wheat flour, they're surprisingly light, with the texture of cake.

MAKES 12

1⅓	cups skim milk
1	egg
⅓	cup honey
3	tablespoons canola oil
¾	cup cornmeal
¾	cup whole-wheat flour
½	cup all-purpose flour
2	tablespoons wheat germ
2½	teaspoons baking powder
½	teaspoon salt

Coat 12 (2½″) muffin cups with no-stick spray and set aside.

In a small bowl, whisk together the milk, egg, honey and oil.

In a large bowl, stir together the cornmeal, whole-wheat flour, all-purpose flour, wheat germ, baking powder and salt. Add the milk mixture. Stir just until moistened; do not overmix (the batter will be lumpy).

Spoon the batter evenly into the prepared muffin cups. Bake at 400° for 18 minutes, or until the muffins turn golden brown.

Per muffin: 151 calories, 4.4 g. total fat (26% of calories), 0.4 g. saturated fat, 18 mg. cholesterol, 180 mg. sodium

Spiced Orange-Marmalade Muffins

*D*ates, honey, cinnamon, cloves and orange marmalade give these muffins full-bodied flavor.

MAKES 12

 1 egg white
 ¾ cup orange marmalade
 3 tablespoons canola oil
 2 tablespoons honey
 ½ teaspoon grated orange peel
 ¼ teaspoon lemon extract
 ¾ cup skim milk
 ½ cup pitted and finely chopped dates
 2 cups all-purpose flour
 2 teaspoons baking powder
 1 teaspoon ground cinnamon
 ¾ teaspoon ground cloves
 ½ teaspoon baking soda
 ¼ teaspoon salt

Coat 12 (2½″) muffin cups with no-stick spray and set aside.

In a medium bowl, whisk together the egg white, marmalade, oil, honey, orange peel and lemon extract. Add the milk and dates; mix well.

In a large bowl, stir together the flour, baking powder, cinnamon, cloves, baking soda and salt. Add the marmalade mixture. Stir just until moistened; do not overmix (the batter will be lumpy).

Spoon the batter evenly into the prepared muffin cups. Bake at 425° for 13 to 16 minutes, or until a toothpick inserted near the center comes out clean. (Do not overbake.)

Per muffin: 197 calories, 3.8 g. total fat (16% calories), 0.3 g. saturated fat,
0 mg. cholesterol, 149 mg. sodium

Buttermilk Cornbread

*S*erve this no-fuss bread with soup, chili or a main-dish salad for a satisfying, simple dinner.

MAKES 9 SQUARES

      1   cup fat-free buttermilk
      ⅓   cup water
      1   egg white
      3   tablespoons canola oil
    1¼   cups cornmeal
      1   cup all-purpose flour
      3   tablespoons sugar
    1¾   teaspoons baking powder
      ½   teaspoon baking soda
      ½   teaspoon salt

Coat an 8″ × 8″ baking pan with no-stick spray and set aside.

In a medium bowl, whisk together the buttermilk, water, egg white and oil.
Stir in the cornmeal and mix well.

In a large bowl, stir together the flour, sugar, baking powder, baking soda
and salt. Add the cornmeal mixture. Stir just until moistened; do not overmix
(the batter will be lumpy).

Evenly spread the batter in the prepared pan. Bake at 425° for 13 to 16
minutes, or until a toothpick inserted near the center comes out clean. (Do not
overbake.) Cut into squares.

Per square: 180 calories, 5.2 g. total fat (26% of calories), 0.5 g. saturated fat,
0 mg. cholesterol, 293 mg. sodium

Pumpkin Bread

*T*his recipe makes two large loaves. If you'd like smaller ones, use 4 mini pans (6″ × 3″). Bake them for 30 minutes.

MAKES 36 SLICES

2   eggs
2   egg whites
¾   cup sugar
½   cup packed brown sugar
2   cups canned pumpkin
¾   cup fat-free buttermilk
3   tablespoons canola oil
1   teaspoon vanilla
3   cups all-purpose flour
¼   cup cornstarch
1½ teaspoons baking powder
¾   teaspoon baking soda
½   teaspoon salt (optional)
¼   teaspoon ground allspice
¼   teaspoon ground cloves
½   teaspoon ground cinnamon
½   teaspoon ground nutmeg

Coat 2 (9″ × 5″) loaf pans with no-stick spray and set aside.

In food processor, blend the eggs, egg whites, sugar and brown sugar until smooth. Add the pumpkin, buttermilk, oil and vanilla; process until blended.

In a large bowl, combine the flour, cornstarch, baking powder, baking soda, salt (if using), allspice, cloves, cinnamon and nutmeg. Add the pumpkin mixture. Stir just until moistened; do not overmix (the batter will be lumpy).

Pour the batter evenly into the prepared pans. Bake at 350° for 50 minutes, or until the bread turns golden brown. Cool the loaves in the pans for 10 minutes. Then remove the bread from the pans and cool on a wire rack.

Per slice: 91 calories, 1.6 g. total fat (16% of calories), 0.2 g. saturated fat,
12 mg. cholesterol, 37 mg. sodium

Holiday Fruit Bread

a colorful assortment of candied and dried fruit makes this fragrant bread very festive. A small amount of diced yellow summer squash adds moistness.

MAKES 12 SLICES

- ⅓ cup orange juice
- ½ cup mixed candied fruit, diced
- ⅓ cup raisins
- ¼ cup finely chopped dried apricots
- ⅓ cup finely chopped yellow summer squash
- ¼ cup honey
- ¼ cup packed brown sugar
- ⅔ cup fat-free buttermilk
- ¼ cup fat-free egg substitute
- ¼ cup canola oil
- 1 teaspoon vanilla
- ½ teaspoon almond extract
- ⅛ teaspoon grated lemon peel
- 2 cups all-purpose flour
- ¼ cup cornstarch
- 2½ teaspoons baking powder
- ¾ teaspoon baking soda
- ¼ teaspoon salt

Coat an 8″ × 4″ loaf pan with no-stick spray and set aside.

In a 4-cup glass measure, combine the orange juice, candied fruit, raisins and apricots. Cover loosely with plastic wrap and microwave on high power for a total of 5 minutes, or until the mixture is almost boiling; stop and stir every 2 minutes. Add the squash, honey and brown sugar. Stir until the brown sugar dissolves.

Add the buttermilk, eggs, oil, vanilla, almond extract and lemon peel. Mix well.

In a large bowl, stir together the flour, cornstarch, baking powder, baking soda and salt. Add the orange juice mixture. Gently stir just until moistened; do not overmix (the batter will be lumpy).

Spoon the batter into the prepared pan. Bake at 350° for 40 to 50 minutes, or until golden brown on top and a toothpick inserted in the center comes out clean. (If the top browns too rapidly, cover it with foil during the last 10 to 15 minutes of baking.)

Cool the loaf in the pan for 10 minutes. Then remove the bread from the pan and cool on a wire rack.

Per slice: 220 calories, 4.8 g. total fat (20% of calories), 0.4 g. saturated fat, 0 mg. cholesterol, 216 mg. sodium

---

≫ Tips from the Family Chef ≪

SECRETS OF LOW-FAT BAKING

I always loved desserts, and I still do," says Susan G. Purdy, author of *Have Your Cake and Eat It, Too*. "But baking just doesn't work without some fat. It's a question of chemistry."

The trick, she says, is to intensify flavors while you cut back on fat. Here are some of her suggestions.

If you have a baking recipe that calls for nuts, use fewer of them but toast them first to bring out their flavor. "And sprinkle them on the tops of baked goods. That way you bite into them first and you know they are there."

Sometimes Susan does omit the nuts entirely and replaces them with a small amount of a very flavorful nut oil—usually walnut or hazelnut. "The oil gives extra flavor to such things as crumb crusts and streusel toppings," she says.

She also cuts fat by reducing the number of whole eggs called for in recipes. "If a recipe calls for three eggs, I use one whole egg and the whites from two eggs."

Zucchini Bread

Zucchini helps keep this bread exceptionally moist. The recipe makes two loaves; for convenience you may want to freeze one for later use.

MAKES 20 SLICES

3	cups shredded zucchini
1⅓	cups sugar
½	cup skim milk
½	cup fat-free egg substitute
¼	cup canola oil
¼	cup honey
2	teaspoons ground cinnamon
2	teaspoons vanilla
¾	teaspoon ground cloves
2⅔	cups all-purpose flour
1½	teaspoons baking powder
1	teaspoon baking soda
¼	teaspoon salt

Coat 2 (8″ × 4″) loaf pans with no-stick spray and set aside.

Place the zucchini on a triple layer of paper towels and pat dry.

In a medium bowl, whisk together the sugar, milk, eggs, oil, honey, cinnamon, vanilla and cloves.

In a large bowl, stir together the flour, baking powder, baking soda and salt. Add the zucchini and the milk mixture. Using a large wooden spoon, stir just until the ingredients are thoroughly combined (do not overmix).

Divide the batter between the prepared pans. Bake at 350° for 35 to 45 minutes, or until a toothpick inserted in the center comes out clean.

Cool the loaves in the pans for 10 minutes. Then remove the bread from the pans and cool on a wire rack.

Per slice: 156 calories, 2.9 g. total fat (17% of calories), 0.2 g. saturated fat, 0 mg. cholesterol, 105 mg. sodium

---

Irish Soda Bread

*T*here are many recipes for soda bread; the most basic is simply flour, baking soda and buttermilk. Traditionally, soda bread is made with a whole-grain flour, which makes the bread fairly dense and chewy. We've lightened it up a bit and embellished it with raisins and caraway. This recipe is quick to make and is best eaten warm or just-cooled.

MAKES 12 WEDGES

2¾ cups all-purpose flour
¼ cup whole-wheat flour
⅓ cup sugar
1 teaspoon baking soda
½ teaspoon baking powder
½ teaspoon salt
¾ cup raisins
1 tablespoon caraway seeds, lightly crushed
1½ cups fat-free buttermilk

Coat an 8″ round cake pan with no-stick spray and dust it lightly with flour. Set aside.

In a large bowl, stir together the all-purpose flour, whole-wheat flour, sugar, baking soda, baking powder and salt. Stir in the raisins and caraway seeds.

Add the buttermilk and stir vigorously with a wooden spoon until all the flour is moistened. The dough will be a bit sticky.

Flour your hands and form the dough into a round. Place it in the prepared pan. Slash the top with a sharp knife in the shape of a cross.

Bake at 350° for 45 to 50 minutes, or until the bread turns a deep golden brown. Remove the bread from the pan and let cool for a few minutes. Cut into wedges.

Per wedge: 174 calories, 0.4 g. total fat (2% of calories), 0.1 g. saturated fat, 0 mg. cholesterol, 241 mg. sodium

---

Savory Buttermilk Scones

Scones are generally a bit sweet and served with jam. These, however, are not sweet at all and are more like a biscuit. They are perfect for afternoon tea as well as with soup or a hearty salad for lunch or dinner. Feel free to substitute other herbs for the rosemary. Sage, savory and thyme are all especially good.

MAKES 24

- 1 cup fat-free buttermilk
- 2 teaspoons finely chopped fresh rosemary
- 2 cups all-purpose flour
- 2 teaspoons baking powder
- 1 teaspoon sugar
- ½ teaspoon baking soda
- ½ teaspoon salt
- 3 tablespoons nondiet tub-style margarine or butter

In a small bowl, combine the buttermilk and rosemary.

In a large bowl, stir together the flour, baking powder, sugar, baking soda and salt. Using a pastry blender, cut the margarine or butter into the flour mixture until coarse crumbs form.

Add the buttermilk mixture and stir to form a soft dough. Transfer the dough to a floured surface. Knead gently to form a ball. Roll out to ½" thickness. Cut into 2" rounds, squares or diamonds. Gather the scraps, roll and cut to use all the dough. Place on an ungreased baking sheet.

Bake at 425° for 10 to 12 minutes, or until light golden brown.

Per scone: 56 calories, 1.6 g. total fat (26% of calories), 1 g. saturated fat, 1 mg. cholesterol, 109 mg. sodium

---

Scones with Dried Cranberries

*T*he proper way to eat a scone is to split it in half. Spread each half with a little marmalade or jam. If desired, add a dollop of nonfat vanilla yogurt to each piece.

MAKES 24

- ¾ cup fat-free vanilla yogurt
- ⅓ cup 1% low-fat milk
- 1 teaspoon grated lemon or orange peel
- ½ teaspoon vanilla
- ⅓ cup dried cranberries
- 2¼ cups all-purpose flour
- 2 teaspoons baking powder
- 1 tablespoon sugar
- ½ teaspoon salt
- ½ teaspoon baking soda
- 2½ tablespoons nondiet tub-style margarine or butter

In a small bowl, whisk together the yogurt, milk, lemon or orange peel and vanilla. Stir in the cranberries.

In a large bowl, combine the flour, baking powder, sugar, salt and baking soda. Using a pastry blender, cut the margarine or butter into the flour mixture until coarse crumbs form.

Add the yogurt mixture and stir to form a soft dough. Transfer the dough to a floured surface. Knead gently to form a ball. Roll out to ½" thickness. Cut into 2" rounds, squares or diamonds. Gather the scraps, roll and cut to use all the dough. Place on an ungreased baking sheet.

Bake at 425° for 10 to 12 minutes, or until light golden brown.

Per scone: 65 calories, 1.4 g. total fat (20% of calories), 0.8 g. saturated fat, 1 mg. cholesterol, 104 mg. sodium

---

MAKE GOOD FOOD FUN

*F*or younger children, the way food looks can be more important than how it tastes. So why not make food fun, says chef Katharina Trask, who is the director of consumer education for Tops supermarkets in Buffalo.

"I try to make food an adventure, especially in our cooking schools," says Katie, who has created special nutrition-oriented classes for children. "Our nature series is a favorite, focusing on themes like the rain forest and dinosaurs. Kids have a lot of fun while they learn about good nutrition."

Does it work? Sure, Katie says.

"For sandwiches, I use a cookie cutter to cut shapes that appeal to the children," she says, relating how she fashioned a dinosaur cutter. The kids loved them—even though the sandwiches contained tofu and were on whole-wheat bread.

"Try creating a little excitement about the food without preaching about nutrition," she says.

Another trick: Get kids to eat that hearty bowl of oatmeal on frosty winter mornings by letting them decorate it. Make a face with raisins, nuts and seeds. The children will love the touch of whimsy.

And oatmeal doesn't have to be hot to be nutritious and delicious, she says. "My kids don't like hot oatmeal. So I make it cold by soaking it overnight with juices and fruits," she says, noting that orange juice and apple juice are her family's favorites. You can add diced apples, nuts or seeds to the oatmeal.

Katie also suggests letting kids make their own granola mixtures for breakfast cereals and snacks. Parents can exert some control over the ingredients while still allowing children to use their imaginations in assembling the granola.

Biscuits with Garlic and Sage

*Y*ou can whip up these biscuits very quickly. In fact, they're so easy the kids can help make them. Use other herbs to vary the flavor.

MAKES 12

2¼ cups all-purpose flour
¼ cup whole-wheat flour
1 teaspoon sugar
1 teaspoon dried sage
½ teaspoon baking soda
½ teaspoon baking powder
¼ teaspoon salt
1 clove garlic, minced
3 tablespoons nondiet tub-style margarine or butter
¾ cup + 2 tablespoons fat-free buttermilk

Coat a baking sheet with no-stick spray and set aside.

In a large bowl, stir together the all-purpose flour, whole-wheat flour, sugar, sage, baking soda, baking powder, salt and garlic. Using a pastry blender, cut the margarine or butter into the flour mixture until coarse crumbs form.

Add the buttermilk and stir to form a soft dough. Transfer the dough to a floured surface. Knead gently to form a ball. Roll out into a square ¾" thick. Cut into 12 squares or rectangles. Place on the prepared baking sheet.

Bake at 400° for 18 to 20 minutes, or until the biscuits are just beginning to turn golden brown.

Per biscuit: 126 calories, 3.1 g. total fat (22% of calories), 1.8 g. saturated fat, 0 mg. cholesterol, 160 mg. sodium

---

Homey Desserts

Chocolate Mocha Pudding Cake

*T*his moist, fluffy, chocolate cake bakes up in its own succulent sauce. It is best served still warm from the oven but will keep, refrigerated, for a day or two. Reheat a single portion for a short time in the microwave.

MAKES 15 SERVINGS

1¼ cups all-purpose flour
1 teaspoon baking powder
¼ teaspoon baking soda
¼ teaspoon salt
⅓ cup + 3 tablespoons unsweetened cocoa powder
¼ cup fat-free plain yogurt
1½ tablespoons canola oil
1 egg white
2 teaspoons vanilla
2¼ cups hot coffee
¾ cup + ⅓ cup sugar
¾ cup mini chocolate chips
2½ teaspoons cornstarch

Coat a 13″ × 9″ baking pan with no-stick spray and set aside.

In a large bowl, mix the flour, baking powder, baking soda, salt and ⅓ cup of the cocoa.

In a blender, combine the yogurt, oil, egg white and vanilla. Add ¼ cup of the coffee, ¾ cup of the sugar and ¼ cup of the chocolate chips. Blend well. Pour over the flour mixture and stir just until blended. Transfer to the prepared pan.

In the blender, combine the cornstarch with the remaining ⅓ cup sugar, the remaining 3 tablespoons cocoa and the remaining ½ cup chocolate chips. With the motor running, slowly add the remaining 2 cups coffee and blend until smooth. Pour the mixture over the batter; do not stir.

Bake at 350° for 20 to 25 minutes, or until a toothpick inserted in the center comes out clean. Cool on a wire rack for 5 to 10 minutes.

Per serving: 172 calories, 4.2 g. total fat (21% of calories), 0.2 g. saturated fat, 0 mg. cholesterol, 96 mg. sodium

---

Old-Fashioned Angel Food Cake

*a*n easy way to adorn a plain angel food cake is to bake crystal sprinkles right into the batter. Look for the sprinkles in the cake decorating area of the supermarket. Add red ones for Valentine's Day, green for St. Patrick's Day, a rainbow assortment for birthday parties and pink or blue for a baby shower. You can also serve the cake without the sprinkles. In either case, you can top it with fresh berries and regular or frozen yogurt.

MAKES 12 SERVINGS

1	cup + 2 tablespoons sifted cake flour
1¼	cups + 2 tablespoons sugar
12	egg whites, at room temperature
1¼	teaspoons cream of tartar
¼	teaspoon salt
1½	teaspoons vanilla
½	teaspoon almond extract
3–4	tablespoons colored crystal sprinkles (optional)

Sift the flour with ½ cup of the sugar two times.

Place the egg whites in a large bowl and sprinkle the cream of tartar and salt over top. Beat with an electric mixer until the egg whites form soft peaks. Slowly beat in the remaining sugar. Add the vanilla and almond extract; beat until glossy.

Fold the flour mixture into the egg white mixture in 3 parts, folding just enough to blend. Fold in the sprinkles (if using) with the last addition of flour. Gently pour the batter into an ungreased 9″ or 10″ straight-sided tube pan. Smooth the top with a spatula.

Bake at 350° for 40 to 45 minutes, or until the cake turns golden brown. Invert the pan over the top of a soda or wine bottle and let cool for 1½ to 2 hours. Gently remove the cake from the pan and place it on a serving platter.

Per serving: 146 calories, 0.1 g. total fat (1% of calories), 0 mg. saturated fat, 0 mg. cholesterol, 100 mg. sodium

---

Sugar and Spice Cake

Here's an easy coffee cake you can whip up in a jiffy. The cake will keep for 2 or 3 days at room temperature if well-wrapped.

MAKES 9 SERVINGS

Cake

- 1¾ cups all-purpose flour
- 1 teaspoon baking powder
- ½ teaspoon baking soda
- 1 teaspoon ground cinnamon
- 1 teaspoon ground ginger
- ¼ teaspoon ground cloves
- ¾ cup fat-free buttermilk
- ⅔ cup sugar
- 1 egg white
- 3 tablespoons canola oil
- 1 teaspoon vanilla

Glaze

- ¾ cup powdered sugar
- ½ teaspoon ground ginger
- ¼ teaspoon ground cinnamon
- 1 tablespoon honey
- 2 teaspoons water
- ½ teaspoon vanilla

To make the cake: Coat an 8″ × 8″ baking pan with no-stick spray and set aside.

In a medium bowl, combine the flour, baking powder, baking soda, cinnamon, ginger and cloves.

In a large bowl, mix the buttermilk, sugar, egg white, oil and vanilla. Add the flour mixture and stir until just combined. Pour the batter into the prepared pan and spread evenly with the back of a large spoon.

Bake at 350° for 30 to 35 minutes, or until a toothpick inserted in the center comes out clean. Cool on a wire rack for 10 to 15 minutes.

To make the glaze: Sift the powdered sugar into a medium bowl. Stir in the ginger and cinnamon. Add the honey, water and vanilla; stir until smooth. Drizzle the glaze over the top of the cake and spread it out with the back of a large spoon.

Per serving: 245 calories, 4.8 g. total fat (18% of calories), 0.4 g. saturated fat, 0 mg. cholesterol, 134 mg. sodium

---

It's So Easy ... It's Kid Stuff

A CHILD'S CAKE

*I*f Jean-Louis Palladin, the chef at Jean-Louis at the Watergate in Washington, D.C., is looking over his shoulder these days, it is because he is being challenged by some intense competition—from his nine-year-old daughter, Verveine.

"I can't keep her out of the kitchen," he laughs. "Her only dream is to come into the restaurant and cook."

One day Jean-Louis gave her a challenge—to make a cake. The result was a fruit-filled cake that was so tasty he shared the recipe with his friend and colleague Chef Michel Richard in Los Angeles.

"Yet the recipe is so simple that any child could make it using a store-bought cake. It is like the kind of cake that is common in southwest France," Jean-Louis beams with fatherly pride.

Verveine made her cake from scratch, but kids can also use a pack-aged white cake mix. Once the batter is prepared, stir in some fruit, such as peaches, apples or berries. Pour the batter into a pan and bake according to the package instructions. "Let the baked cake cool, unmold it and enjoy," he says.

Carrot Cake

*M*oist and flavorful, this carrot cake has hardly any fat. And there's none in the icing either, since it's made with fat-free cream cheese. Some brands of cream cheese taste better than others, so experiment to find one you like.

MAKES 9 SERVINGS

Cake

1¼	cups all-purpose flour
1½	teaspoons baking powder
½	teaspoon baking soda
1	teaspoon ground cinnamon
¼	teaspoon ground nutmeg
⅛	teaspoon salt
⅔	cup sugar
2	tablespoons nondiet tub-style margarine or butter, softened
2	egg whites
¼	cup applesauce
⅓	cup canned crushed pineapple (packed in juice), well-drained
1½	cups grated carrots
¼	cup raisins

Icing

½	cup powdered sugar
3	tablespoons soft-style fat-free cream cheese
½	teaspoon skim milk
½	teaspoon vanilla

To make the cake: Coat an 8″ × 8″ baking pan with no-stick spray and set aside.

In a medium bowl, combine the flour, baking powder, baking soda, cinnamon, nutmeg and salt.

In a large bowl, use an electric mixer to blend the sugar and margarine or butter. Beat in the egg whites, applesauce and pineapple until well-combined. Add the flour mixture and beat, stopping to scrape down the sides of the bowl once, until just combined. Stir in the carrots and raisins.

Pour the batter evenly into the prepared pan. Bake at 350° for 32 to 38 minutes, or until the top is nicely browned and a toothpick inserted in the center comes out clean. Cool thoroughly in the pan.

To make the icing: Sift the powdered sugar into a medium bowl. Add the cream cheese, milk and vanilla. Blend until smooth. Spread evenly on top of the cooled cake.

Per serving: 207 calories, 2.8 g. total fat (12% of calories), 1.7 g. saturated fat, 0 mg. cholesterol, 216 mg. sodium

---

Gingerbread

*E*verybody's favorite when warm from the oven, this spicy gingerbread is moist yet light.

MAKES 9 SERVINGS

1	egg
1	egg white
½	cup packed brown sugar
⅔	cup molasses
¼	cup canola oil
½	cup fat-free buttermilk
1	teaspoon vanilla
1¾	cups unbleached flour
½	teaspoon baking soda
½	teaspoon baking powder
1	tablespoon ground ginger
½	teaspoon ground cinnamon
½	teaspoon ground mace
⅛	teaspoon ground allspice
⅛	teaspoon ground cloves
¼	teaspoon salt

Coat an 8″ × 8″ baking pan with no-stick spray and set aside.

In a medium bowl, whisk the egg and egg white together. Whisk in the brown sugar and then the molasses. Add the oil, buttermilk and vanilla and blend well.

In a large bowl, mix the flour, baking soda, baking powder, ginger, cinnamon, mace, allspice, cloves and salt. Add the egg mixture and stir until just blended. Pour the batter into the prepared pan.

Bake at 350° for 25 minutes, or until a toothpick inserted in the center comes out clean. Cool in the pan.

Per serving: 260 calories, 6.9 g. total fat (24% of calories), 0.7 g. saturated fat, 23 mg. cholesterol, 206 mg. sodium

Orange Pecan Streusel Cake

This is very good for breakfast, brunch and teatime as well as a not-too-sweet dessert. The cake is best still warm from the oven.

MAKES 12 SERVINGS

Cake

1	cup fat-free plain yogurt
¾	cup sugar
¼	cup skim milk
3½	tablespoons canola oil
2	egg whites
2	teaspoons vanilla
2	teaspoons grated orange peel
½	teaspoon ground cinnamon
⅓	cup raisins
2	cups all-purpose flour
1½	teaspoons baking powder
¾	teaspoon baking soda
¼	teaspoon salt

Streusel

- ¼ cup all-purpose flour
- ⅓ cup packed brown sugar
- ½ teaspoon ground cinnamon
- 1 tablespoon nondiet tub-style margarine or butter, cut into small pieces
- 1 tablespoon canola oil
- 1 teaspoon light corn syrup
- 3 tablespoons chopped pecans

To make the cake: Coat an 11″ × 7″ baking pan with no-stick spray and set aside.

In a medium bowl, whisk together the yogurt, sugar, milk, oil, egg whites, vanilla, orange peel and cinnamon. Stir in the raisins.

In a large bowl, combine the flour, baking powder, baking soda and salt. Add the yogurt mixture and stir with a wooden spoon just until thoroughly blended (do not overmix).

Pour the batter into the prepared pan.

To make the streusel: In a medium bowl, combine the flour, brown sugar and cinnamon. Using a pastry blender, cut in the margarine or butter and oil until the mixture is crumbly. Stir in the corn syrup.

Sprinkle evenly over the batter. Sprinkle the pecans over top.

Bake at 350° for 30 to 35 minutes, or until a toothpick inserted in the center comes out clean. Transfer to a cooling rack and let stand at least 10 minutes before serving.

Per serving: 254 calories, 7.5 g. total fat (27% of calories), 1.2 g. saturated fat, 0 mg. cholesterol, 194 mg. sodium

---

Peach Skillet Cake

*T*his moist, rather dense cake is baked like an upside-down cake in an iron skillet. Fresh peaches are preferable for this recipe, but you can substitute 16 ounces of canned sliced peaches; drain well before using. For variety, replace the peaches with an even layer of blueberries or raspberries.

MAKES 8 SERVINGS

- 3 ripe peaches, peeled and sliced
- 1 tablespoon lemon juice
- ½ cup packed brown sugar
- 1 egg
- 2 egg whites
- 1 cup fat-free vanilla yogurt
- 1 cup sugar
- 2 tablespoons canola oil
- 1½ teaspoons grated lemon rind
- 1 teaspoon vanilla
- 1¾ cups all-purpose flour
- 1 teaspoon baking powder
- ½ teaspoon baking soda
- ½ teaspoon salt
- ¼ teaspoon ground mace

In a small bowl combine the peaches and lemon juice.

Coat a large cast-iron skillet with no-stick spray. Add the brown sugar; cook, stirring, over medium-low heat until melted. Remove from the heat and arrange the peaches in the pan.

In a medium bowl, whisk together the egg, egg whites, yogurt, sugar, oil, lemon rind and vanilla.

In a large bowl, mix the flour, baking powder, baking soda, salt and mace. Add the egg mixture and mix well.

Pour the batter over the peaches.

Bake at 350° for 30 minutes, or until a toothpick inserted in the center comes out clean. Let the skillet stand for 5 minutes. Run a metal spatula around the sides to loosen the cake. Place a serving platter on top of the skillet and carefully flip the skillet over onto the platter. The cake should turn out easily. If a few of the peaches stick to the skillet, remove them with a knife and put them in their places. Let the cake cool slightly.

Per serving: 332 calories, 4.4 g. total fat (12% of calories), 0.4 g. saturated fat, 28 mg. cholesterol, 298 mg. sodium

---

It's So Easy... It's Kid Stuff

60-SECOND ICE CREAM

*I*f kids are old enough to use a food processor, they can whip up a quick soft dessert that's low in fat and tastes very good," says Jean Anderson, coauthor of *The New German Cookbook*.

This 60-second, fruit-flavored "ice cream" is such a favorite with Jean that she serves it to company. "I've served this to people with persnickety palates, and they love it," she says. "And you can play around with different flavors."

The soul of the dessert is a package of frozen unsweetened berries. Jean favors raspberries but says that strawberries, peaches or other frozen fruit is good too.

"Put the frozen berries in a food processor, add some honey, some frozen orange juice concentrate, limeade concentrate and a cup of evaporated skim milk or nonfat yogurt," she says. "Then blend it until you get a soft ice–cream consistency."

Pineapple Upside-Down Cake

$\mathcal{T}$his updated version of an American favorite has all the flavor of the original but less than half the fat.

MAKES 8 SERVINGS

Topping

- 1 can (20 ounces) pineapple rings (packed in juice)
- 6 tablespoons packed brown sugar
- 2 teaspoons nondiet tub-style margarine or butter

Cake

- 1½ cups all-purpose flour
- 1¼ teaspoons baking powder
- ½ teaspoon baking soda
- ¼ teaspoon salt
- ¼ teaspoon ground ginger
- ¼ teaspoon ground cinnamon
- 6 tablespoons sugar
- 1½ tablespoons nondiet tub-style margarine or butter, softened
- 1½ tablespoons canola oil
- ¼ cup fat-free egg substitute
- ¾ teaspoon grated lemon peel
- 2 teaspoons vanilla
- ⅔ cup fat-free plain yogurt

To make the topping: Drain the pineapple, reserving ¾ cup of the juice.

Combine the brown sugar, margarine or butter and the reserved juice in a large cast-iron skillet. Bring the mixture to a boil over medium heat. Cook, stirring frequently, for 3 to 4 minutes, or until reduced by half. Add the pineapple. Bring to a boil again and cook for 3 to 4 minutes, turning the pineapple occasionally, until the syrup is slightly thickened and the pineapple is slightly browned. Remove from the heat.

To make the cake: In a medium bowl, combine the flour, baking powder, baking soda, salt, ginger and cinnamon.

In a large bowl, beat the sugar, margarine or butter and oil with an electric mixer until smooth. Beat in the eggs, lemon peel and vanilla until well-blended. Stir in the yogurt.

Add the flour mixture and stir just until evenly incorporated (do not overmix). Immediately spoon the batter evenly over the pineapple.

Bake at 375° for 20 to 24 minutes, or until a toothpick inserted in the center comes out clean. Let the skillet stand for 5 minutes. Run a metal spatula around the sides to loosen the cake. Place a serving platter on top of the skillet and carefully flip the skillet over onto the platter. The cake should turn out easily. If any pineapple rings stick to the skillet, remove them with a knife and put them in their places. Let the cake cool slightly.

Per serving: 267 calories, 5.8 g. total fat (19% of calories), 0.8 g. saturated fat, 0 mg. cholesterol, 238 mg. sodium

Poppy Seed Orange Cake

a light cake, this could be served for dessert or tea. To make it fancy, dust the top with sifted powdered sugar.

MAKES 12 SERVINGS

- 2 cups all-purpose flour
- ½ teaspoon salt
- ½ teaspoon baking powder
- 2 eggs
- 1¼ cups sugar
- 4 egg whites
- ¾ cup orange juice
- ¼ cup canola oil
- 1 tablespoon grated orange peel
- 1 teaspoon vanilla
- ½ cup poppy seeds

Coat a 9″ or 10″ tube pan with a removable bottom with no-stick spray and dust lightly with flour. Set aside.

In a medium bowl, mix the flour, salt and baking powder.

In a large bowl, beat the eggs and sugar with an electric mixer until pale yellow and fluffy.

In a third bowl, use clean beaters to beat the egg whites until soft peaks form.

Fold a third of the orange juice into the egg mixture. Then add a third of the flour mixture. Repeat twice, ending with the flour. Fold in the oil, orange peel, vanilla and poppy seeds.

Fold a third of the egg whites into the batter, then fold in the rest. Pour the batter into the prepared pan.

Bake at 350° for 40 minutes, or until a toothpick inserted in the center comes out clean. The cake will rise and crack on top, then deflate a bit as it cools. Let the cake cool in the pan. Carefully loosen the cake around the edges of the pan and around the center with a metal spatula. Unmold.

Per serving: 253 calories, 8 g. total fat (29% of calories), 0.8 g. saturated fat, 35 mg. cholesterol, 135 mg. sodium

---

Cherry-Filled Cake

*H*ere's a quick and easy dessert that gives you cherries in every bite. The cake is best served the day it's made.

MAKES 12 SERVINGS

1¾ cups all-purpose flour
1 teaspoon baking powder
½ teaspoon baking soda
1 cup fat-free plain yogurt
⅔ cup sugar
1 egg white
3 tablespoons canola oil
1 teaspoon vanilla
½ teaspoon almond extract
1½ cups light canned cherry pie filling

Coat an 11″ × 7″ baking pan with no-stick spray and set aside.

In a medium bowl, mix the flour, baking powder and baking soda.

In a large bowl, mix the yogurt, sugar, egg white, oil, vanilla and almond extract. Add the flour mixture and stir until just combined.

Pour half of the batter into the prepared pan and smooth with the back of a large spoon so that it covers the bottom of the pan. Spoon dollops of the filling over the batter and spread them out with the back of the spoon. Spoon dollops of the remaining batter over the filling. Smooth them out, leaving some of the filling showing through.

Bake at 325° for 36 to 42 minutes, or until a toothpick inserted in the center comes out clean. Cool on a wire rack for 10 to 15 minutes.

Per serving: 210 calories, 3.8 g. total fat (16% of calories), 0.3 g. saturated fat, 0 mg. cholesterol, 104 mg. sodium

Brownies

*T*hese dark-chocolate brownies contain a smidgen of applesauce, which helps keep them moist. The amount required is so tiny that no one will ever detect your secret ingredient.

Makes 24

1	cup all-purpose flour
¼	cup unsweetened cocoa powder
½	teaspoon baking soda
⅛	teaspoon salt
5½	ounces semisweet chocolate, chopped
2	tablespoons canola oil
3	tablespoons unsweetened applesauce
1	cup packed brown sugar
1½	tablespoons light corn syrup
3	egg whites
2	teaspoons vanilla

Coat a 13″ × 9″ baking pan with no-stick spray and set aside.

Sift the flour, cocoa, baking soda and salt into a medium bowl.

In a large heavy saucepan, combine the chocolate and oil. Stir over heat until the chocolate is just melted and smooth (be careful not to scorch it). Remove from the heat and stir in the applesauce, brown sugar and corn syrup.

Vigorously stir in the egg whites and vanilla. Continue to stir until all the sugar dissolves. Gently stir in the flour mixture and blend well. Pour the batter into the prepared pan.

Bake at 350° for 18 to 22 minutes, or until the center top is almost firm when lightly tapped. Transfer to a wire rack and let cool.

Per brownie: 106 calories, 3.4 g. total fat (28% of calories), 1.3 g. saturated fat, 0 mg. cholesterol, 50 mg. sodium

---

Oatmeal Bars

*T*hese bars have a hard crunchy crust and a chewy center. They're sure to please cookie lovers who have an undeniable sweet tooth. If you like, replace all or part of the raisins with chocolate chips.

MAKES 24

- 1 egg
- 1 egg white
- ¾ cup sugar
- ½ cup packed brown sugar
- 3 tablespoons canola oil
- 1 teaspoon vanilla
- 1½ cups all-purpose flour
- 1 teaspoon baking soda
- ½ teaspoon salt
- 1½ cups rolled oats
- ½ cup raisins

Coat a 13″ × 9″ baking pan with no-stick spray and set aside.

In a food processor, mix the egg, egg white, sugar and brown sugar until smooth. Add the oil and vanilla; process for 10 to 15 seconds. Add the flour, baking soda and salt. Process until the mixture is just blended. Add the oats and incorporate with on/off turns.

Sprinkle with the raisins and use a fork to lightly mix them in. Transfer the dough to the prepared pan. Wet your fingers with water and press the dough evenly into the pan.

Bake at 350° for 25 to 30 minutes, or until a toothpick inserted in the center comes out clean. Cool in the pan.

Per bar: 117 calories, 2.3 g. total fat (17% of calories), 0.3 g. saturated fat, 9 mg. cholesterol, 104 mg. sodium

---

Fig Bars

*O*at bran adds richness and texture to the crust of these easy fig bars. If stored tightly wrapped, the bars will keep for 4 or 5 days at room temperature.

MAKES 24

- 1 pound dried figs, stems removed
- 1½ cups water
- ¼ cup honey
- ⅛ teaspoon ground cinnamon
- ¾ cup all-purpose flour
- ½ cup oat bran
- ¼ cup packed brown sugar
- ⅛ teaspoon salt (optional)
- 1 tablespoon oil
- 1 tablespoon nondiet tub-style margarine or butter, cut into small pieces

Coat a 13″ × 9″ baking pan with no-stick spray and set aside.

Chop the figs and place in a food processor. Puree with on/off turns. Transfer to a medium saucepan. Add the water, honey and cinnamon. Bring to a boil over medium-high heat. Reduce the heat to medium and cook, stirring occasionally, for 8 minutes, or until the mixture thickens. Remove from the heat.

Place the flour, oat bran, brown sugar and salt (if using) in a food processor. Mix with on/off turns. Drizzle with the oil and dot with the margarine or butter. Mix well with on/off turns.

Press half the mixture into the prepared pan. Spoon dollops of the fig mixture evenly over the crust; use the back of a spoon to spread it out evenly. Sprinkle the remaining crust mixture evenly over the top and spread it out with the back of a spoon. Press it lightly into place.

Bake at 400° for 22 to 26 minutes, or until lightly browned. Cut while still warm.

Per bar: 96 calories, 1.4 g. total fat (12% of calories), 0.2 g. saturated fat, 0 mg. cholesterol, 10 mg. sodium

Spicy Molasses Drop Cookies

*H*omey and easy to make, these chewy drop cookies are great for lunch boxes or after-school snacks. Store in an airtight container for up to a week.

2½ cups all-purpose flour
1¼ teaspoons baking powder
 ½ teaspoon baking soda
 ⅛ teaspoon salt
  1 tablespoon ground ginger
 ½ teaspoon ground cinnamon
 ¼ teaspoon ground cloves
 ½ cup packed brown sugar
  6 tablespoons dark corn syrup
 ¼ cup canola oil
 ¼ cup molasses
  1 egg white
2½ teaspoons vanilla

Coat several baking sheets with no-stick spray and set aside.

In a medium bowl, mix the flour, baking powder, baking soda, salt, ginger, cinnamon and cloves.

In a large bowl, combine the brown sugar, corn syrup, oil, molasses, egg white and vanilla. Beat with an electric mixer until smooth. Beat in half the flour mixture, just until blended. Stir in the remaining flour mixture until evenly incorporated.

Drop heaping teaspoons of the dough about 2½″ apart on the prepared baking sheets.

Bake at 375° for 5 to 8 minutes, or until the cookies are just slightly darker at the edges than at the center. Transfer the baking sheet to a wire rack. Let stand for 2 minutes. Remove the cookies and arrange on wire racks to cool thoroughly.

Per cookie: 76 calories, 1.7 g. total fat (20% of calories), 0.1 g. saturated fat, 0 mg. cholesterol, 45 mg. sodium

---

Lemon Pudding Cake

*T*his dessert features a moist, fragrant cake and a fairly tart lemon sauce. Note that the sauce will be thin when the cake comes out of the oven but thickens somewhat as it cools. If you desire a sweeter sauce, simply add an extra tablespoon or two of sugar. The cake will keep, covered and refrigerated, for up to 2 days. Serve slightly warm or at room temperature.

MAKES 12 SERVINGS

Sauce

- ¾ cup sugar
- ¼ cup cornstarch
- 2 egg yolks
- 1 cup hot water
- 1 tablespoon nondiet tub-style margarine or butter
- ⅔ cup orange juice
- ⅓ cup lemon juice
- 2½ teaspoons grated lemon peel
- 1½ teaspoons vanilla
- ⅛ teaspoon salt

Cake

- ½ cup sugar
- 2 tablespoons canola oil
- 2 egg whites
- 2 teaspoons grated lemon peel
- 2 teaspoons vanilla
- ⅓ cup fat-free plain yogurt
- ⅔ cup orange juice
- 1¼ cups all-purpose flour
- 1 teaspoon baking powder
- ½ teaspoon baking soda
- ¼ teaspoon salt

To make the sauce: In a medium bowl, mix the sugar and cornstarch. Stir in the egg yolks, water and margarine or butter until smoothly incorporated. Stir in the orange juice, lemon juice, lemon peel, vanilla and salt until smoothly incorporated.

To make the cake: Coat an 11″ × 7″ baking pan with no-stick spray.

In a medium bowl, whisk together the sugar, oil, egg whites, lemon peel and vanilla. Beat in the yogurt, then the orange juice.

In a large bowl, mix the flour, baking powder, baking soda and salt. Add the yogurt mixture and stir just until evenly incorporated (do not overmix). Pour the batter evenly into the prepared pan. Pour the sauce over the batter; do not stir.

Bake at 350° for 30 to 40 minutes, or until a toothpick inserted in the center comes out clean. Cool on a wire rack for 10 minutes. Serve in bowls.

Per serving: 200 calories, 5.6 g. total fat (19% of calories), 0.6 g. saturated fat, 35 mg. cholesterol, 175 mg. sodium

---

Stovetop Rice Pudding

*T*his simple low-fat rice pudding is simmered on the stove rather than baked, as so many are. It is surprising how creamy this is even though it is made with skim milk. You can use leftover cooked rice or prepare rice from scratch.

MAKES 6 SERVINGS

- 3 cups cooked white rice
- 3 cups skim milk
- ⅓ cup sugar
- Pinch of salt
- ¼ teaspoon ground nutmeg
- ¼ teaspoon ground cinnamon
- 2 teaspoons grated lemon peel
- ½ teaspoon vanilla

In a large saucepan, combine the rice, milk, sugar and salt. Bring to a simmer over medium heat. Reduce the heat. Add the nutmeg and cinnamon. Simmer, stirring occasionally, for 20 minutes.

(continued)

Add the lemon peel and cook for 5 minutes, or until the mixture is thick and bubbling.

Remove from the heat and stir in the vanilla. Spoon into individual custard cups. Serve at room temperature or chilled.

Per serving: 190 calories, 0.5 g. total fat (2% of calories), 0.2 g. saturated fat, 2 mg. cholesterol, 64 mg. sodium

---

Raisin Spice Bread Pudding

*H*ere's an updated version of an old-fashioned favorite. It's particularly good made with oat bread.

MAKES 6 SERVINGS

Topping
- 1 tablespoon sugar
- ½ teaspoon ground cinnamon
- ¼ teaspoon ground nutmeg
- ⅛ teaspoon ground cloves

Bread Pudding
- ⅓ cup raisins
- 3 tablespoons apple juice
- ¼ cup sugar
- ¼ cup packed brown sugar
- 2 tablespoons all-purpose flour
- ⅛ teaspoon salt
- Pinch of ground cinnamon
- Pinch of ground nutmeg
- 1 egg
- 2 egg whites
- 2⅔ cups 2% low-fat milk
- 1½ teaspoons vanilla
- 3⅓ cups bread cubes

To make the topping: In a cup, mix the sugar, cinnamon, nutmeg and cloves.

To make the bread pudding: Coat an 8″ × 8″ baking pan with no-stick spray and set aside.

Combine the raisins and apple juice in a small microwave-safe bowl. Microwave on high power for 1 minute.

In a 4-cup glass measure, mix the sugar, brown sugar, flour, salt, cinnamon and nutmeg. Using a fork, beat in the egg and egg whites until smoothly incorporated. Stir in the milk. Microwave for a total of 3 minutes; stop and stir after every minute.

Microwave for an additional 1 to 2 minutes, until the mixture is hot but not boiling; stop and stir every 30 seconds. Stir in the vanilla.

Spread the bread cubes in the prepared pan. Sprinkle with the raisins and any unabsorbed juice. Pour the milk mixture over the bread, taking care to moisten all the cubes.

Bake at 350° for 15 minutes. Remove from the oven and sprinkle with the topping mixture. Continue baking for 15 to 20 minutes, or until the pudding is puffy and set in the center when the pan is jiggled. Transfer the dish to a wire rack and let stand at least 10 minutes before serving.

Per serving: 244 calories, 3.7 g. total fat (14% of calories), 1.7 g. saturated fat, 44 mg. cholesterol, 227 mg. sodium

---

Chocolate Pudding with Bananas and Graham Crackers

Older children can prepare this by themselves with adult supervision; younger children love to mash and distribute the graham cracker crumbs and arrange the banana slices.

MAKES 6 SERVINGS

- 3 whole graham crackers, crushed
- 1 ripe banana, thinly sliced
- ½ cup sugar
- ¼ cup unsweetened cocoa powder
- 3 tablespoons cornstarch
  Pinch of salt
- 3 cups 2% low-fat milk
- ½ teaspoon vanilla

Evenly divide the graham cracker crumbs among 6 custard cups or ramekins. Press them into the bottom. Top with banana slices.

In a large saucepan, mix the sugar, cocoa, cornstarch and salt. Stir in the milk. Whisk over medium heat until the pudding comes to a boil and thickens. Cook for 1 minute longer. Remove from the heat and stir in the vanilla. Pour into the prepared custard cups. Chill.

Per serving: 181 calories, 3.1 g. total fat (15% of calories), 1.7 g. saturated fat, 9 mg. cholesterol, 129 mg. sodium

---

Old-Fashioned Apple Betty

We speeded up preparation of this classic dessert by using the microwave to soften the apples. Serve the apple betty plain or with nonfat frozen yogurt. If you don't have dry bread cubes on hand, slightly toast bread slices by putting them on the oven racks while the oven is preheating, then cut them into cubes.

MAKES 6 SERVINGS

Topping

- ½ cup packed brown sugar
- 2 tablespoons dark corn syrup
- 1½ tablespoons nondiet tub-style margarine or butter, melted
- 1 tablespoon canola oil
- ½ teaspoon ground cinnamon
- 3 cups dry bread cubes

Filling

- 6 cups sliced cooking apples
- 2 tablespoons sugar
- ¼ teaspoon ground cinnamon

To make the topping: In a large bowl, stir together the brown sugar, corn syrup, margarine or butter, oil and cinnamon. Add the bread cubes and stir until coated.

To make the filling: Place the apples in a 2½-quart oven-safe, microwave-safe casserole.

In a cup, stir together the sugar and cinnamon. Add to the apples and toss until coated. Cover and microwave on high power for a total of 3 to 4 minutes, or until the apples are tender; stop and stir after 2 minutes.

Transfer half of the apples to a medium bowl. Spread the remaining apples evenly in the bottom of the casserole. Add half of the topping mixture in an even layer. Top with the remaining apples, then the remaining topping.

Cover and bake at 375° for 20 minutes. Uncover and bake for 12 to 15 minutes, or until the bread is crisp on top.

Per serving: 246 calories, 5.2 g. total fat (18% of calories), 0.7 g. saturated fat, 0 mg. cholesterol, 131 mg. sodium

---

Apple Cranberry Crisp

*W*e've given this pleasing old-fashioned dessert a modern twist by adding cranberries—and removing most of the fat. Cooking the apples first in the microwave speeds the preparation.

MAKES 6 SERVINGS

Filling

- 7½ cups thinly sliced tart apples
- ¼ cup dried cranberries
- 2 tablespoons water
- 3 tablespoons sugar
- ½ teaspoon ground cinnamon

Topping

- ½ cup rolled oats
- ½ cup all-purpose flour
- ¼ cup packed brown sugar
- ½ teaspoon ground cinnamon
- 1 tablespoon dark corn syrup
- 1 tablespoon canola oil
- 2 teaspoons nondiet tub-style margarine or butter, softened

To make the filling: Place the apples, cranberries and water in a 2½-quart oven-safe, microwave-safe casserole.

In a cup, stir together the sugar and cinnamon. Add to the apple mixture and toss until coated. Cover and microwave on high power for a total of 5 to 6 minutes; stop and stir after 3 minutes. Stir well.

To make the topping: In a medium bowl, mix the oats, flour, brown sugar and cinnamon. Add the corn syrup, oil and margarine or butter. Mix with a fork until crumbly. Sprinkle evenly over the apples.

Bake at 400° for 25 to 30 minutes, or until the topping begins to brown and the apples are tender.

Per serving: 256 calories, 5.3 g. total fat (18% of calories), 0.5 g. saturated fat, 0 mg. cholesterol, 32 mg. sodium

---

Blueberry Crunch

*T*his baked dessert uses frozen blueberries, so you can enjoy it year-round. If desired, serve it with frozen yogurt.

MAKES 6 SERVINGS

Blueberries

⅓ cup sugar

1 tablespoon all-purpose flour

1 package (16 ounces) frozen unsweetened blueberries, rinsed and well-drained

¼ teaspoon grated lemon peel

Topping

½ cup all-purpose flour

½ cup packed brown sugar

¼ teaspoon ground cinnamon

2 tablespoons nondiet tub-style margarine or butter, cut into small pieces

1½ cups quick-cooking rolled oats

1½ teaspoons light corn syrup

1 tablespoon canola oil

To make the blueberries: Coat a shallow 2-quart casserole with no-stick spray. Add the sugar and flour; mix. Stir in the blueberries and lemon peel.

To make the topping: In a medium bowl, mix the flour, brown sugar and cinnamon. Using a pastry blender, cut in the margarine or butter until coarse crumbs form. Stir in the oats, corn syrup and oil; mix well. Sprinkle evenly over the berries.

Bake at 400° for 20 to 25 minutes, or until bubbly and nicely browned on top. Cool for 10 minutes before serving.

Per serving: 332 calories, 8.2 g. total fat (22% of calories), 2.9 g. saturated fat,
0 mg. cholesterol, 11 mg. sodium

Raspberry-Rhubarb Slump

a slump is a fruit cobbler crowned with dumplings. In early American recipes, the entire dish was prepared on top of the stove or in a Dutch oven in a fireplace. This modern version calls for starting the cooking on the stove, then finishing the job in the oven.

MAKES 6 SERVINGS

Filling
- ⅔ cup sugar
- 2½ tablespoons cornstarch
- ⅛ teaspoon ground cinnamon
- 1 package (10 ounces) frozen red raspberries (packed in syrup), thawed
- 1 bag (16 ounces) frozen cut rhubarb, partially thawed

Dumplings
- 1¼ cups all-purpose flour
- 2 tablespoons sugar
- 1 teaspoon baking powder
- ¼ teaspoon baking soda
- ⅛ teaspoon ground cinnamon
- ¼ teaspoon salt
- 1½ tablespoons nondiet tub-style margarine or butter, cut into small pieces
- 1½ tablespoons canola oil
- ½ cup fat-free buttermilk

To make the filling: In a Dutch oven, mix the sugar, cornstarch and cinnamon. Drain the juice from the raspberries into a small bowl; set the raspberries aside. Add the juice to the sugar mixture, stirring until smooth.

Stir in the rhubarb. Bring the mixture to a boil over medium-high heat. Boil for 2 minutes, or until the mixture thickens and clears. Stir in the raspberries. Remove from the heat.

To make the dumplings: In a food processor, combine the flour, sugar, baking powder, baking soda, cinnamon and salt. Add the margarine or butter and oil. Process with on/off turns until the flour mixture is smooth.

Add the buttermilk and incorporate it with on/off turns (do not overmix or the dumplings may be tough).

Drop large spoonfuls of the dough over the fruit mixture; try to keep the dumplings from touching each other. Cover with a lid or foil. Simmer over medium heat for 10 minutes.

Remove the cover and transfer the pot to the oven. Bake at 375° for 15 to 20 minutes, or until a toothpick inserted in a center dumpling comes out clean. Let cool at least 10 minutes before serving.

Per serving: 337 calories, 6.9 g. total fat (18% of calories), 2.3 g. saturated fat, 8 mg. cholesterol, 252 mg. sodium

---

Winter Fruit Bowl with Orange-Custard Dressing

*T*his almost fat-free custard sauce is a snap to make, and it adds a wonderfully rich touch to a simple fruit combination.

MAKES 8 SERVINGS

- 2 cups orange juice
- ½ cup fat-free egg substitute
- ⅓ cup sugar
- ¼ cup cornstarch
- ½ cup fat-free sour cream
- 1½ teaspoons vanilla
- 3 tart apples, cubed
- 3 large oranges, sectioned
- 2 bananas, sliced
- 1 package (10 ounces) frozen red raspberries (packed in juice), thawed and drained
- 1½ cups canned pineapple chunks (packed in juice)

In a 4-cup glass measure, whisk together the orange juice and eggs. Cover with wax paper. Microwave on high power for a total of 2 minutes; stop and stir after 1 minute. If the mixture seems lumpy, transfer it to a blender and process for 20 seconds.

In a medium saucepan, stir together the sugar and cornstarch. Whisk in the juice mixture until smooth. Cook, stirring constantly, over medium heat for 4 to 5 minutes, or until thickened.

Remove from the heat and whisk in the sour cream and vanilla. Cover and refrigerate for at least 1 hour.

In a large bowl, combine the apples, oranges, bananas and raspberries. Drain the pineapple, reserving ¼ cup of the juice. Add the pineapple and the reserved juice to the bowl. Cover and refrigerate for at least 1 hour.

To serve, spoon the fruit with juices into individual bowls. Top each serving with the custard.

THINK AHEAD: You may prepare the custard up to 24 hours ahead. You may also section the oranges and mix them with the pineapple ahead. Since apples and bananas discolor if cut too far ahead, prepare them closer to serving time. Also, frozen berries are at their best soon after being thawed, so don't prepare them too far ahead.

Per serving: 235 calories, 0.7 g. total fat (3% of calories), 1.1 g. saturated fat, 0 mg. cholesterol, 33 mg. sodium

---

Cherry Cobbler

*T*his recipe uses a combination of sweet and sour cherries.

MAKES 6 SERVINGS

Cherries

- 2 **cups pitted sweet cherries**
- 2 **cups pitted sour cherries**
- ⅔ **cup sugar**
- 2 **tablespoons cornstarch**
- 1 **tablespoon lemon juice**

Topping

- 1 **cup flour**
- 1½ **tablespoons sugar**
- ¼ **teaspoon salt (optional)**
- 1 **teaspoon baking soda**
- ½ **teaspoon baking powder**
- 2 **tablespoons nondiet tub-style margarine or butter, cut into small pieces**
- ¾ **cup fat-free buttermilk**
- ½ **teaspoon vanilla**

To make the cherries: Coat a pie plate with no-stick spray and set aside.

In a medium saucepan, combine the cherries, sugar, cornstarch and lemon juice. Bring to a boil over high heat. Reduce the heat to low. Stir and simmer for 2 to 3 minutes, or until the mixture begins to thicken. Pour into the pie plate.

To make the topping: In a medium bowl, mix the flour, sugar, salt (if using), baking soda and baking powder. Add the margarine or butter; cut in with a pastry blender until coarse crumbs form.

Add the buttermilk and vanilla; mix until just blended.

Spoon heaping tablespoons of the batter evenly over the cherries.

Bake at 350° for 20 to 25 minutes, or until the cherries are bubbling and the topping is a deep golden brown.

Per serving: 281 calories, 4.3 g. total fat (14% of calories), 2.5 g. saturated fat, 1 mg. cholesterol, 315 mg. sodium

---

Plum Cobbler

*T*he microwave is a wonderful tool for speeding the preparation of crisps and cobblers. In this recipe, the plums are microwaved first. Then the topping is added, and the dish is baked in a conventional oven.

Makes 6 servings

Filling
7	cups sliced red or black plums
¾	cup sugar
2	tablespoons all-purpose flour
⅛	teaspoon ground cinnamon

Topping
1¼	cups all-purpose flour
¼	cup sugar
1½	teaspoons baking powder
3	tablespoons canola oil
⅔	cup fat-free buttermilk

To make the filling: Place the plums in a shallow 2½-quart oven-safe, microwave-safe casserole.

In a small bowl, stir together the sugar, flour and cinnamon. Stir into the plums.

Cover and microwave on high power for a total of 5 minutes; stop and stir after 2 minutes. Stir well.

To make the topping: In a medium bowl, mix the flour, sugar and baking powder. Using a pastry blender, cut in the oil until the mixture resembles coarse crumbs. Stir in the buttermilk until just combined; do not overmix.

Drop large spoonfuls of the topping over the plums and spread it out evenly with the back of a spoon.

Bake at 375° for 35 to 50 minutes, or until the topping is cooked through and lightly browned. Let cool for 10 minutes before serving.

Per serving: 401 calories, 7.5 g. total fat (17% of calories), 0.6 g. saturated fat,
0 mg. cholesterol, 133 mg. sodium

Strawberry and Rhubarb Cobbler

When strawberries and rhubarb are in season, they make an ideal combination for desserts. This home-style cobbler is both tart and sweet.

MAKES 8 SERVINGS

Filling

- 4 cups diced rhubarb
- 4 cups fresh strawberries, halved
- 1 cup sugar
- 3 tablespoons all-purpose flour

Topping

- 1⅔ cups all-purpose flour
- 2½ tablespoons sugar
- 2 teaspoons baking powder
- ½ teaspoon salt
- ¼ teaspoon baking soda
- 2 tablespoons nondiet tub-style margarine or butter, cut into small pieces
- ½ cup 1% low-fat milk
- ½ cup fat-free buttermilk

To make the filling: Coat a 2½-quart casserole with no-stick spray.

In a medium saucepan, combine the rhubarb, strawberries and sugar. Bring to a simmer over medium-high heat. Reduce the heat to medium-low and cook, stirring occasionally, for 3 to 5 minutes.

Set aside for 5 minutes. Stir in the flour. Transfer to the prepared casserole.

To make the topping: In a medium bowl, combine the flour, sugar, baking powder, salt and baking soda. Cut in the margarine or butter until coarse crumbs form. Add the milk and buttermilk; mix with a fork until just blended. Spoon over the fruit. Bake at 425° for 15 minutes. Reduce the heat to 350° and bake for 15 to 20 minutes, or until the topping is golden brown.

Per serving: 292 calories, 3.9 g. total fat (12% of calories), 2 g. saturated fat, 1 mg. cholesterol, 283 mg. sodium

---

Cherry Trifle

*T*his elegant, colorful dessert is so easy that you'll want to make it often. Evaporated skim milk adds extra richness to the custard without contributing the fat that heavy cream usually does.

MAKES 10 SERVINGS

- 2 cups 1% low-fat milk
- ⅓ cup evaporated skim milk
- ½ cup fat-free egg substitute
- ½ cup sugar
- ¼ cup cornstarch
- ⅛ teaspoon salt (optional)
- 1 tablespoon nondiet tub-style margarine or butter
- 1½ teaspoons vanilla
- 1 angel food cake
- 2 tablespoons kirsch (optional)
- 2 cans (20 ounces each) light cherry pie filling

In a 4-cup glass measure, whisk together the low-fat milk, skim milk and eggs. Cover with wax paper and microwave on high power for 2½ to 3 minutes, or until the mixture is hot.

In a medium saucepan, mix together the sugar, cornstarch, and salt (if using). Whisk in the milk mixture, stirring vigorously and scraping the bottom of the pan until smooth. Cook over medium-low heat, stirring continuously, for 5 minutes, or until the custard thickens.

Remove the custard from the heat. Stir in the margarine or butter and vanilla. Cover and refrigerate for at least 30 minutes.

To assemble the trifle, use a serrated knife to cut the cake into bite-size pieces. Place the cake in a medium bowl and mix with the kirsch (if using).

Transfer a third of the cake pieces to a large, straight-sided glass bowl. Spoon a third of the custard over the cake, followed by a third of the pie filling. Repeat twice to use all the cake, custard and pie filling. Cover and refrigerate for at least 1 hour.

Per serving: 298 calories, 2.1 g. total fat (6% of calories), 1.1 g. saturated fat,
2 mg. cholesterol, 285 mg. sodium

Cantaloupe Sorbet with Raspberries

𝒯his light and refreshing sorbet is just the thing for a summer evening.

MAKES 8 SERVINGS

1¾ cups water
⅔ cup sugar
1 medium cantaloupe, cut into chunks
1 cup raspberries

Bring the water and sugar to a boil in a small saucepan over high heat.
Reduce the heat to medium and let simmer for 2 minutes to dissolve the sugar.
Let cool to room temperature.

Working in batches if necessary, puree the cantaloupe with the syrup in a
blender. Transfer to the canister of an ice cream maker. Stir in the raspberries.
Freeze according to the manufacturer's instructions.

Remove the sorbet from the freezer about 10 minutes before serving. It
should be served firm but just slightly slushy.

Per serving: 121 calories, 0.3 g. total fat (2% of calories), 0 g. saturated fat,
0 mg. cholesterol, 31 mg. sodium

Poached Pears

*F*or a more grown-up dessert, you could replace the juice with red wine and slightly increase the amount of sugar. For the best results, use pears that are ripe but still a bit firm.

MAKES 6 SERVINGS

- 6 **pears**
- 2 **cups cider or apple juice**
- 2 **cups water**
- ⅓ **cup sugar**
- 3 **strips lemon peel**

Peel the pears, leaving the stems in place.

In a saucepan large enough to hold the pears, combine the cider or apple juice, water, sugar and lemon peel. (The pan should be deep enough so that the liquid covers about two-thirds of the pears when they are standing.)

Place the pears in the pan to test the amount of liquid required, then add more water if necessary. Remove the pears from the pan and set aside.

Bring the liquid to a boil over high heat. Reduce the heat to low, so the liquid simmers. Add the pears and poach for 25 minutes, or until they are tender but still firm. Turn the pears occasionally so that they cook evenly.

Remove the pears from the liquid and cool on a platter. Boil the liquid until the amount remaining is reduced by half. Cool to room temperature.

To serve, stand the pears on individual dessert plates or in bowls and drizzle them with the reduced poaching liquid.

Per serving: 182 calories, 0.6 g. total fat (3% of calories), 0 g. saturated fat,
0 mg. cholesterol, 52 mg. sodium

PERFECT PEARS

*F*resh fruit is an all-time favorite with kids because it is as sweet as candy. And because it has no fat and is easy to serve up on short notice, fruit also gets high marks from parents.

One perennial favorite is the pear. It is, however, one of the few fruits picked before it is ripe, so it may need some help to reach that firm-but-juicy stage that children particularly like. The best approach is to put the fruit in a paper bag. Natural gases produced by the pear will speed the ripening process.

To test for ripeness, press the pear at the neck. If it gives to the pressure of your thumb, it is ready to eat. Be aware that different varieties ripen at different speeds. Anjou pears, for instance, ripen faster than Boscs.

For a healthful after-school treat or dessert, your kids can cut the pears lengthwise into eight equal segments and serve the pieces with a yogurt dip.

For another easy snack, cut a pear in half, scoop out the seed section with a melon baller or spoon and fill the indentation with reduced-fat peanut butter, cream cheese or a combination of raisins and nuts.

Citrus Ambrosia

*T*his makes a refreshing conclusion to a hearty meal. It's also good as part of a brunch or luncheon menu. High in vitamin C, this is a good dish to serve in the winter months when oranges, tangerines and grapefruit are plentiful. If mangoes are available, add some peeled cubes—they'll make the ambrosia sweeter and more dessertlike.

MAKES 10 SERVINGS

- 1 pineapple, peeled, cored and cut into bite-size chunks
- 2 naval oranges, sectioned and chopped
- 2 tangerines, sectioned and chopped
- 1 ruby red grapefruit, sectioned and chopped
- ⅓ cup unsweetened shredded coconut
- 1 teaspoon grated orange peel

In a large bowl, combine the pineapple, oranges, tangerines and grapefruit. Toss lightly. Add the coconut and orange peel. Mix well.

Cover and refrigerate for at least 30 minutes.

Per serving: 97 calories, 1.5 g. total fat (13% of calories), 0.8 g. saturated fat, 0 mg. cholesterol, 2 mg. sodium

---

Pineapple Coconut Granita

Granita is an Italian ice that's similar to a sorbet but a bit more granular. It is a refreshing, light dessert that you can assemble quickly and place in the freezer until needed. For a smoother texture, use an ice cream maker and follow the manufacturer's instructions for preparing sherbet.

MAKES 8 SERVINGS

¾ cup boiling water
½ cup sugar
¼ cup cream of coconut
1 tablespoon lime juice
 Pinch of ground nutmeg
1 can (16 ounces) pineapple chunks (packed in juice)

In a small bowl, mix the water, sugar and cream of coconut. Stir until the sugar is dissolved. Cool to room temperature. Stir in the lime juice and nutmeg.

Process the pineapple (with juice) in a blender until smooth. Add the coconut mixture and blend well.

Transfer to a large, shallow plastic container with a tight-fitting lid. Place in the freezer until the granita is frozen solid.

THINK AHEAD: The granita keeps well in the freezer for a few days so you can make it well ahead. Allow it to stand at room temperature for a few minutes before scooping it out and serving it.

Per serving: 90 calories, 2.6 g. total fat (25% of calories), 2.3 g. saturated fat,
0 mg. cholesterol, 1 mg. sodium

4 Weeks of Great Menus

$\mathcal{I}$f you're the family's chief cook and bottle-washer, you know what a challenge it is to get an evening meal on the table fast—and at the same time please the finicky eaters in your household. Children are, by definition, finicky. But they're not the only ones who have a few favorite foods and turn up their noses at anything new or different.

Even with an entire cookbook of quick and delicious ideas, you might have difficulty coming up with new menus night after night that make everyone happy. To help you out, we've created four weeks' worth of weekday dinners and targeted each to a special audience. So you'll find a week of kid-pleaser meals, another of meatless menus, a third targeted toward waist watchers and a fourth for the really time-pressed that showcases make-ahead foods.

So that we can provide you with nutrient information about each meal, we've given the meals in the form of single servings. (Figures given for the Kid Pleasers reflect adult-size servings.)

Kid Pleasers

If burgers, fries and hot dogs are the only meals your kids want to eat, try these surefire hits. They're foods that kids would serve if they were in charge. All are super-delicious, healthy *and* kid tested.

Monday

1 serving Turkey Pot Roast Dinner (page 158)

1 serving Creamy Cucumber Salad (page 87)

2 brown-and-serve rolls

2 teaspoons reduced-calorie tub-style margarine

1 cup skim milk

½ cup vanilla ice cream

Per serving: 841 calories, 25.7 g. total fat (28% of calories), 8.5 g. saturated fat, 87 mg. cholesterol, 796 mg. sodium

Tuesday

1 (3-ounce) hamburger with ketchup on a bun

½ cup oven-fried potatoes

1 serving Scalloped Apples and Raisins (page 303)

1 cup skim milk

1 Chocolate Frozen Yogurt Pop (page 31)

Per serving: 803 calories, 24.9 g. total fat (28% of calories), 8.7 g. saturated fat, 77 mg. cholesterol, 1,012 mg. sodium

Wednesday

1 serving Taco Casserole (page 180)

3 celery sticks stuffed with peanut butter

½ cup cooked peas

1 cup skim milk

1 serving Chocolate Pudding with Bananas and Graham Crackers (page 380)

Per serving: 780 calories, 21.5 g. total fat (25% of calories), 6 g. saturated fat, 43 mg. cholesterol, 1,080 mg. sodium

Thursday

1 serving Barbecued Turkey Sandwich (page 152)

½ cup Italian green beans

1 serving Molded Berry and Fruit Salad (page 99)

1 cup skim milk

2 sugar wafer cookies

Per serving: 692 calories, 9.4 g. total fat (12% of calories), 2 g. saturated fat, 54 mg. cholesterol, 1,088 mg. sodium

Friday

1 serving Beef and Noodle Casserole (page 176)

½ cup cucumber slices

2 slices Italian bread with 2 teaspoons reduced-calorie tub-style margarine

1 cup skim milk

2 Oatmeal Bars (page 373)

Per serving: 815 calories, 20.4 g. total fat (23% of calories), 5.3 g. saturated fat, 62 mg. cholesterol, 942 mg. sodium

Meatless Meals

When you want to cut back on the amount of meat your family eats, rely on no-meat meals such as these. They're high in nutrients and easy on the pocketbook.

Monday

1 serving Lentil Stew (page 237)

2 brown-and-serve rolls with 2 teaspoons reduced-calorie tub-style margarine

¼ cup 1% fat cottage cheese with sliced tomatoes

1 cup 2% low-fat milk

1 cup grapes

Per serving: 820 calories, 18.1 g. total fat (20% of calories), 5.2 g. saturated fat, 20 mg. cholesterol, 823 mg. sodium

Tuesday

1 serving Southwestern Frittata (page 243)

1 cup low-fat frozen hash brown potatoes

2 Pineapple Muffins (page 331) with 2 teaspoons reduced-calorie tub-style margarine

1 cup tomato juice

¼ cantaloupe

Per serving: 783 calories, 21 g. total fat (24% of calories), 3.6 g. saturated fat, 216 mg. cholesterol, 781 mg. sodium

Wednesday

1 serving Crustless Onion-Mushroom Quiche (page 246)

1 serving Cheese, Zucchini and Carrot Casserole (page 238)

2 slices French bread with 2 teaspoons reduced-calorie tub-style margarine

1 cup orange juice

½ cup vanilla ice cream

Per serving: 902 calories, 30.4 g. total fat (30% of calories), 11 g. saturated fat, 102 mg. cholesterol, 1,473 mg. sodium

Thursday

1 serving Vegetarian Chili (page 254)

1 tossed salad (lettuce, 1 ounce shredded reduced-fat Cheddar cheese and 2 tablespoons reduced-calorie French dressing)

6 whole-wheat crackers

1 cup 2% low-fat milk

1 Brownie (page 372)

Per serving: 799 calories, 24.7 g. total fat (28% of calories), 7.8 g. saturated fat, 35 mg. cholesterol, 1,114 mg. sodium

Friday

1 serving Tomato Macaroni and Cheese (page 252)

½ cup cooked broccoli florets

2 Whole-Grain Honey Muffins (page 344) with 2 teaspoons reduced-calorie tub-style margarine

1 cup 2% low-fat milk

½ cup canned pears

Per serving: 915 calories, 27.8 g. total fat (27% of calories), 8.4 g. saturated fat, 76 mg. cholesterol, 1,197 mg. sodium

Lean and Light Cuisine

These are the meals to serve when you're watching your weight, but the rest of the family doesn't want to go on a diet with you. All the dinners are reasonably low in calories—in the neighborhood of 500 each. Those with heartier appetites can help themselves to larger portions.

Monday

1 serving Salmon Loaf (page 214)

1 serving Creamy Cabbage Slaw with Dill (page 81)

1 brown-and-serve roll

1 cup skim milk

1 fresh plum

Per serving: 486 calories, 11.4 g. total fat (21% of calories), 2.8 g. saturated fat, 46 mg. cholesterol, 1,087 mg. sodium

Tuesday

1 serving Pork and Sauerkraut Dinner (page 189)

½ cup green beans

1 Biscuit with Garlic and Sage (page 355)

1 cup skim milk

½ cup fresh peach slices

Per serving: 505 calories, 9 g. total fat (16% of calories), 3.9 g. saturated fat, 46 mg. cholesterol, 840 mg. sodium

Wednesday

1 serving Easy Chicken and Stuffing (page 112)

1 small baked potato with 2 tablespoons fat-free sour cream

1 serving Waldorf Salad (page 107)

1 serving Citrus Ambrosia (page 394)

Per serving: 485 calories, 10.8 g. total fat (20% of calories), 3.6 g. saturated fat, 54 mg. cholesterol, 409 mg. sodium

Thursday

1 serving Quick Spaghetti Sauce with Pasta (page 178) with 1 tablespoon grated Parmesan cheese

1 serving Marinated Italian Salad (page 88)

½ cup strawberries

Per serving: 481 calories, 13.1 g. total fat (25% of calories), 3.7 g. saturated fat, 28 mg. cholesterol, 417 mg. sodium

Friday

1 serving Layered Fish Stew (page 220) with 15 oyster crackers

Carrot and celery sticks

1 Savory Corn Muffin (page 337)

1 serving Pineapple Coconut Granita (page 395)

Per serving: 540 calories, 12.3 g. total fat (21% of calories), 3.6 g. saturated fat, 74 mg. cholesterol, 626 mg. sodium

Heat-and-Eat Meals

When your family has so many extracurricular activities that you barely have time to eat—let alone cook—rely on dinners like these. You can prepare make-ahead dishes on the weekend or during a free evening and have home-cooked meals on the table in a snap. You'll notice that we repeat the desserts. The recipes make enough for a couple of nights, so you'll want to take advantage of that.

Monday

1 serving Black Bean and Rice
Soup (page 65)
6 saltine crackers
½ cup apple slices
1 cup skim milk
1 serving Carrot Cake (page 362)

Per serving: 582 calories, 7.6 g. total fat
(12% of calories), 2.7 g. saturated fat,
4 mg. cholesterol, 585 mg. sodium

Tuesday

1 chef's salad (lettuce, shredded
carrots, sliced cucumbers, sliced
mushrooms, chopped sweet red
peppers, 2 ounces julienned turkey
breast and 2 tablespoons
reduced-calorie French dressing)
1 Banana and Honey Bran Muffin
(page 333) with 2 teaspoons
reduced-calorie tub-style
margarine
1 serving Carrot Cake (page 362)

Per serving: 722 calories, 19.4 g. total fat
(24% of calories), 3.2 g. saturated fat,
49 mg. cholesterol, 982 mg. sodium

Wednesday

1 serving Slow-Simmered
Tex-Mex Chili (page 171)
6 saltine crackers
½ cup tossed salad with
1 tablespoon reduced-calorie

French dressing
1 cup iced tea
2 Spicy Molasses Drop Cookies
(page 375)

Per serving: 682 calories, 16.7 g. total fat
(22% of calories), 3.8 g. saturated fat,
41 mg. cholesterol, 732 mg. sodium

Thursday

1 serving Turkey Tortilla Roll-Ups
(page 159)
1 ear corn with 2 teaspoons
reduced-calorie tub-style
margarine
½ cup tomato wedges
1 cup skim milk
1 Fig Bar (page 374)

Per serving: 784 calories, 18.4 g. total fat
(21% of calories), 4.2 g. saturated fat,
66 mg. cholesterol, 843 mg. sodium

Friday

1 serving Ricotta-Stuffed Shells
(page 253)
½ cup cooked peas
1 cup strawberry and banana slices
2 Spicy Molasses Drop Cookies
(page 375)

Per serving: 757 calories, 9.8 g. total fat
(12% of calories), 0.9 g. saturated fat,
20 mg. cholesterol, 1,247 mg. sodium

Index

e